A

2ND EDITION

BEGINNER'S GUIDE TO

short-term trading

MAXIMIZE
YOUR PROFITS
IN 3 DAYS
TO 3 WEEKS

TONI TURNER

T0089210

Adams Media
New York   London   Toronto   Sydney   New Delhi

Adams Media
An Imprint of Simon & Schuster, Inc.
100 Technology Center Drive
Stoughton, MA 02072

For information about special discounts for bulk purchases, please contact Simon &
Schuster Special Sales at 1-866-506-1949 or business@simonandschuster.com.

The Simon & Schuster Speakers Bureau can bring authors to your live event. For
more information or to book an event contact the Simon & Schuster Speakers Bureau
at 1-866-248-3049 or visit our website at www.simonspeakers.com.

Manufactured in the United States of America

21 2024

Library of Congress Cataloging-in-Publication Data has been applied for.

ISBN 978-1-59869-580-9

Contents

How the Romance Began; My Relationship with the Stock Market; Why I Wrote This Book; Strategy Overview; Short-Term Trading: The Good News; The Journey . . . ; It's Showtime!

Where It All Started; Out of Chaos Comes Order: The Crash Of 1929; The New York Stock Exchange: How It Works; The NASDAQ Stock Market: How It Works; The American Stock Exchange: How It Works; Let's Dissect the Indexes; Wall Street as "The Animal House": The Bulls and the Bears, the Sheep and the Hogs; Two Emotions That Rule the Markets (And the Rest of the World); Check Your Understanding; What Are "Center Points"?; Center Point: You . . . A Golden Buddha

Map Your Business Plan; Selecting/Updating Your Office Equipment; Choosing a Broker; The Commission Maze; Slippage: What It Means; Margin Accounts: How They Work; Establish Realistic Goals; Check Your Understanding; Center Point: Commit: Convert Your Dreams into Goals

The Market as an Unstructured Entity; The Stock Market Is Always Right; Meet Your Emotions—Up Close and Personal; The End Result: What It Looks Like; R &

CHAPTER 9—Additional Chart Indicators: Techniques for Using Them Successfully 147

Oscillators: What They Are; The RSI: What It Is, How to Use It; Stochastic Oscillator: What It Is, How to Use It; The MACD: What It Is, How It Works; On-Balance Volume: What It Is, How to Read It; Bollinger Bands: What They Are, How to Read Them; Fibonacci Retracements: What They Are, How to Read Them; Price Gaps: Play Them Wisely; Quiz; Center Point: You Are Perfect Right Now

CHAPTER 10—It's Showtime! 173

Continuation and Reversal Patterns: What They Are; Trading Reversal Patterns in Non-Trending Markets; Let's Take It from the Top; Quiz; Center Point: Forgiveness: Key to Success

CHAPTER 11—Where the Rubber Meets the Road: Money-Management Techniques 201

Plan Your Trade and Trade Your Plan; Piece of the Pie; Risk/Reward Ratio: What It Means, How to Calculate It; Where to Place Your Stop Orders; Now That You've Got It, What Do You Do with It?; Intraday Reversal Periods: What They Are, What They Mean to You; Order Types: Market Orders, Limit Orders, and More; In Times of Crises; Quiz; Center Point: The Circle of Giving

CHAPTER 12—Winning Strategies for Selling Short. 221

Overcoming Mental and Emotional Roadblocks to Selling Short; Fundamentals: What to Look For; Chart Patterns and Setups: What to Look For; Shorting Indicators: Ugly Is Good!; How to Place Your Order; Shorting Strategy: The Overextended Stock; Shorting Strategy: The Overextended Double Top; Shorting Strategy: The 18 / 40 Moving Average Crossover; Quiz; Center Point: Let Go of Fear and Let Your Light Shine

Acknowledgments

This book, as all the books I've written, was created out of patience and love.

I consider myself blessed to have been surrounded by so many people who gave of their encouragement and support while I revised the original edition of *A Beginner's Guide to Short-Term Trading* into this second edition.

My thanks and gratitude go to . . .

My ever-patient and positive husband, Mike, who endured vague answers, lukewarm dinners, and "bachelor" weekends.

My daughter, Adrienne, who lights my path with laughter, inspiration, and wisdom.

The rest of my wonderful family: Gail, Chuck and Tammy, Missy and Steve, Jenny and Darick, John and Sonia, Mishelle and Matt, and "junior traders" Julian, Leah, Justin, Jacob, Julia, Ava, Lexi, Nate, Chance, and Dottie.

My agent, Deidre Knight, the best ally an author could have, along with being a business partner, friend, and mother of two more beautiful souls, Tyler and Riley.

Meredith O'Hayre and the other folks at Adams Media who helped mold this book into its final form.

ToniTurner.com's director of operations, Tina Hoesli, who gave unending support and more than a few gentle, but much-needed prods.

Chris Tyler, who did a wonderful research job, and Frank Mallinder, a fountain of inspiration and guidance.

My friends Jacqueline Middleton, Joyce Smith, and Reni LaVoie, who were always ready with a glass of wine and a sympathetic ear.

Professor David England and the members of his finance classes at John A. Logan College in Carterville, Illinois, who use this book as a textbook and are an inspiration to traders, everywhere . . .

Again, thank you all, and God bless!

FOREWORD

by Steve Nison

I had the pleasure of first meeting Toni when she introduced herself to me after I gave an online trading seminar. Toni told me how important candle charts are to her. Immediately, I knew she was intelligent, perceptive, generous, and had excellent taste. But then again, I might be biased.

All kidding aside, I have to be honest and say that when I first met her, I was outside of the public speaking circuit (all my seminars previously had only been for financial institutions). I did not recognize her name, nor did I know how popular she was.

Her name, though, did sound familiar for some reason. I soon realized why. I had purchased her online trading book, *A Beginner's Guide to Day Trading Online*, a few months previously. Toni flattered me by asking for a foreword to this book. I can think of no better testimonial than saying that before I knew who she was, I had gone to many bookstores to find just the right online trading book, and ultimately chose hers above all the others.

The reason I selected that book is the same reason I recommend this one: It has the perfect blend of the tools and psychological components needed to win your daily trading battles.

Toni has a sentence in this book: "I traveled a challenging road to learn this business, and now you can profit from my mistakes." This brings to mind a Japanese proverb: "If you wish to know the road, inquire of those who have traveled it." I can recommend no better guide than Toni to lead you down the road to successful online trading.

—Steve Nison, CMT
President of Candlecharts.com
Author of *Japanese Candlestick Charting Techniques*

INTRODUCTION

America's Love Affair

America's having a love affair with the stock market—a big, juicy love affair! Oh, to be sure, this affair has its ups and downs, and our emotions run the gamut from rosy to rocky, but it's a love affair, pure and simple!

And what a wild and fickle lover our temptress is. She's gentle and considerate one minute, then witchy and irritable the next. She's apt to treat good news like poison, and wave off bad news as though it's no news at all. A mere word (read: inflation) sends her to the moaning depths of despair, while the rumor of war may turn her giddy with delight. She's rude and bossy, genteel and loving. Her moods ricochet between selfish and generous, hostile and benign, pessimistic and euphoric.

Did she give you a present? Or take away more than you wanted to give? Your gratitude or groans are equally ignored. She laughs when you cry, and smirks at your happiness.

When at last you stalk off in anger, she waits for the right moment, then lures you back into her arms, whispering sweet promises you can't refuse.

HOW THE ROMANCE BEGAN

America's infatuation with the stock market started with the inception of the "great bull market" that began in the early 1990s and rocketed to nosebleed highs in early 2000. While the bear market that followed—from early 2000 to October 2002—discouraged some folks from playing in this fickle temptress's backyard, her subsequent rise from 2003 to blazing new highs has attracted even more interest.

As we catapult into the twenty-first century, those who have learned how to capitalize on the market's price swings are pocketing hefty profits. With many stocks rising multiple points a day, and then plummeting as quickly, nimble players have learned to capitalize on both upward and downward movements by buying during the dips and selling during the rallies.

The Internet Played Cupid

The mighty Web has transformed global communications, and in doing so, has liberated us to think and act for ourselves with regard to our financial affairs. All the financial data we can ever hope to digest resides right at our fingertips. Stock research reports, news, institutional holdings, company fundamentals, and price charts are only a mouse click away.

As early as the 1960s, only about one-fifth of the U.S. population owned stocks, and the mysterious world of the stock market remained a province of financial institutions. Fast-forward to May of 1975, when the Securities and Exchange Commission (SEC) lifted the standardized broker commissions.

The earliest electronic trading technology was introduced in 1983, when discount broker Quick & Reilly introduced DOS-based software for private traders. Then, 1984 ushered in the NASDAQ's electronic SOES (Small Order Execution System), offering individual traders—some of whom banded together to be known as the "SOES bandits"—the ability to electronically execute small orders against the best quotations from institutions. Finally, in 1985, Charles Schwab & Company unveiled the Equalizer, linking PCs directly to the discounter.

In 1993, the World Wide Web, an electronic cyberspace known only to intrepid tech explorers, became more accessible to the public, via a new browser called Mosaic. Traffic on the Web increased that year by 289,000 percent.

In 1997, discount broker Ameritrade launched an online price war, and lowered its commission to $8 per trade. Except for those traders/investors who are still willing to pay for the luxury of a full-service broker, three-digit commission schedules have dissolved. Today's commissions average $12 per transaction, down from $48 in 1996.

MY RELATIONSHIP WITH THE STOCK MARKET

I started investing more than seventeen years ago, and quickly decided that if I were going to support myself from my investments, I would have to know as much as my stockbroker. Most brokers haven't the time to dote on our portfolios the way we do—or rather, should.

In the mid-1990s, I became an active trader. When I started, I made tons of mistakes. The market slapped me around—hard.

Although I kept losing money, I refused to give up. I watched CNBC until my eyes crossed. At night, I studied charts until I fell asleep in my chair. I read every book about trading I could get my hands on. I traveled to New York, studied under top traders who became my mentors, and asked so many questions I drove those around me bananas. Finally, I crawled out of the learning curve as somewhat of a victor. I knew how to take consistent profits out of the market.

My friends, relieved that I survived the fiery trial, suggested that I could help others who wanted to learn how to trade. I agreed, and combining my writing background (I had been a professional writer for fourteen years) with my trading skills, I wrote *A Beginner's Guide to Day Trading Online*. Published by Adams Media in March 2000, the book became a bestseller in the day trading field. (The second edition of this book was published in February 2007.)

Now, when I teach trading seminars and workshops, I tell audiences that I hold stocks from "two minutes to two years," which I do. My favorite time frames, however, are those that target swing trading and position trading, the subjects of this book. When properly executed, these two styles of trading put you in the market when the "gettin's good," and keep you on the sidelines when the market corrects.

WHY I WROTE THIS BOOK

I believe that once you learn the principles of short-term trading, defined in this book as swing and position trading, you can make the consistent profits with the least amount of time and risk.

➤ If you day trade, you can make quick profits; however, during market hours, you have to stay glued to your computer screen. You must cultivate the concentration level of a fighter pilot, and the bladder of a camel.

➤ The traditional investing stance of "buy-and-hold" has lost much of its sanctity. With a few exceptions, gone are the days when you could buy a national icon of American industry and rest secure in the knowledge that it would pay for your children's college education, or your retirement condo in Hawaii. Global politics and events have imbued our markets with an edginess that dictates we remain financially nimble.

➤ When executed properly, the styles known as swing trading (intended hold: two to five days) and position trading (intended hold: four to eight weeks or longer) can deliver the juiciest gains with the least amount of risk.

STRATEGY OVERVIEW

Here's the strategy: Just like everything else on this planet, stock prices move in cycles. You'll learn about these in detail later, but for now, know that four stages make up a cycle.

In your mind, picture a valley, then a hill that rises and falls down into another valley. Now, overlay a stock price pattern onto the topography. The stock bases in the valley, and then breaks into an uptrend (side of the hill) that may last from weeks to months. After the uptrend exhausts itself, the price action moves sideways, usually for a shorter time period (top of the hill). When buyers refuse to purchase the stock at higher prices, the stock price "rolls over" into a downtrend (the other side of the hill). At last, sellers grow exhausted and the downtrend slows to a halt, usually near the previous valley price. Now, the cycle is complete. In time, a new cycle begins.

As relatively short-term traders, our moneymaking goal will be to grab the middle—or "sweet spot"—of a stock's uptrend (or downtrend). We'll know when to enter a stock, when to exit, and when to stand on the sidelines. Since you can apply these principles to any style of trading, that's priceless knowledge no matter what time frame you play!

SHORT-TERM TRADING: THE GOOD NEWS

Maybe you're a professional in your field, an entrepreneur, a retiree, a student, or a homemaker. You've probably observed the stock market and realized that tidy profits can be made from the market's current volatility. Whether you plan to trade on a full-time or part-time basis, the benefits of trading are fantastic.

If you make trading your full-time occupation, you can choose when, where, and if you choose to work. You can trade from any location, as long as your computer has a reliable connection to the Internet. Office politics? *There are none.* A persnickety boss? *You're the boss.* Want to wear your crocodile slippers to work? *Put 'em on.* Catch the flu? *Pull the covers over your head and stay in bed.* Got the time and money to take a week off? *Have fun!*

If you'd rather trade part-time, harmonize it with your regular job and add "luxury" money to your wallet.

When you learn how to trade cautiously and wisely, your earnings may transform dreams into real rewards, such as the sailboat you always wanted, the vacation cottage in the mountains, or a college education for your children.

Here's a benefit some folks don't think of: When executed properly, short-term trading can involve lower risk than does long-term investing. Many traditional buy-and-holders ride out bear markets fully invested, gritting their teeth while they watch their capital shrivel in value.

Now you'll know when to go "flat," or close all of your positions. You'll calmly put your holdings in cash during corrections and/or bear markets (if you don't like to sell short). Then you'll have plenty of capital to shop with when the bulls again take control.

The Flip Side

The stock market is the most challenging arena on earth. It takes no prisoners. It's a dog-eat-dog world, and only the fittest survive. Those who jump in without adequate knowledge or discipline get their heads handed to them.

To compete in this field, you have to be willing to persist and study hard. You have to cultivate the nerves of a bomb detonator and develop the discipline of a Marine Corps drill sergeant.

Short-term trading is riskier than socking your money into fixed-income returns, such as Treasury bonds or money market funds. And the truth is, you will—especially at the beginning of the learning curve—experience losses. (The size of those losses is within your control.) Are you highly risk-averse? Does the thought of losing money send you running for the Maalox bottle? If so, you may want to choose a different investing avenue.

Are you naturally a disciplined person? Can you control your emotions, or do you let your impulses run away with you? Market players who rake in the big bucks trade like steely-eyed robots, sans emotions. Can you develop that attitude?

When you first step into trading, remember the adage "Speed kills." Are you willing to enter the market at a turtle's pace and take small profits while you learn how the game is played? As a wise trader, are you primed to observe the markets, apply your knowledge, plan your next step, and then take that step while adhering strictly to your plan? That's how the pros fatten their wallets, and if you follow in their footsteps, you can join them.

Short-term trading isn't for everyone. So, ask yourself the preceding questions before you plunk your money into the pot. Self-examination isn't always the most enjoyable project to undergo, but it rewards us by keeping us on a path that best suits our personal lifestyle and goals.

THE JOURNEY . . .

In the pages that follow, I'll give you an overview of the most exciting street on earth—Wall Street. Then, we'll talk about setting up your trading business, delve into winning market psychology, and discuss fundamental and technical analyses. You'll learn how to read chart patterns, how to choose stocks, and how to play them. You'll also master money-management techniques. (It's easy to buy a stock position—the profits arrive in knowing when to sell it.) We'll also discuss news and recurring market events, and how to interpret them.

Most important, we're going to have fun along the way. I'm going to talk to you as though we're friends conversing over a cup of coffee.

I promise you this: Every sentence in this book comes from my heart. I traveled a challenging road to learn this business, and now you can profit from my mistakes. In the following pages, you'll learn how to dodge market potholes and seize gains by using wisdom and common sense. Believe me, if I can do it—you can do it.

IT'S SHOWTIME!

Here's where the rubber meets the road. It's time for you to decide whether or not short-term trading is for you. Only you can make this decision.

Again, you're going to need a firm commitment—from yourself, to yourself—of your time and money. If you decide to join me on this journey, let's get going. Hang on tight, 'cause it's going to be the most exciting ride of your life.

Good luck and good trading!

MEET

Jesse Livermore . . .

If ever a book has been recognized as the "bible" of this industry, it's *Reminiscences of a Stock Operator*. Originally published in 1923, it is the classic story of Jesse Livermore, a legendary, turn-of-the-twentieth-century trader.

The author, Edwin Lefevre, interviewed Livermore for several weeks. Then, giving Livermore the pseudonym of Larry Livingston, Lefevre did a masterful job of capturing Livermore's thoughts and recollections of his trading career.

Now, more than seventy years after Livermore made and lost fortunes trading commodities and stocks in rowdy bucket shops, his observations ring true and accurate. You'll find his comments at the beginning of each chapter. Please enjoy them, reflect upon them, and integrate them into your trading career.

CHAPTER 1

Wall Street: The Greatest Game on Earth

"The game taught me the game."—Jesse Livermore

W all Street and the financial markets represent a global tournament played with heart-stopping stakes, where people from the world over come together to trade money for dreams. Will humans ever stop trading? Doubtful. No matter whether the assets involved are tangible or intangible, the act of trading seems inherent to our very souls.

WHERE IT ALL STARTED

Mankind's love of trading—or swapping items of equal value—started with our earliest ancestors, who swapped meat for fish and furs. As human thought processes evolved into more complex frames of reference, trading systems reached higher levels of sophistication. Now we, as contemporary men and women, have transformed the exchange of goods of perceived equal value into a refined (well, mostly) art form that involves all sorts of maneuvering.

The first stock exchange opened its doors in 1602 in Amsterdam, Holland. It was called the Dutch Bourse (*bourse* means "moneybag") and it was backed by the Dutch East India Company.

The U.S. financial center, Wall Street, originated from an earthen embankment, which was erected in 1644 to keep the cows from wandering around the southern tip of the farmland. The farmland is now known as Manhattan.

In 1663, Governor Peter Stuyvesant of New York (then called New Amsterdam) ordered that the embankment be raised and fortified with logs to protect colonists from the British, whom he suspected would attack New York by land. The British, however, arrived in 1664 by sea. They captured the settlement without firing a shot. In 1699, the makeshift wall was torn down. The street that ran alongside survived, though, and retained its name: Wall Street.

The securities markets in the United States began with speculative trading in the debts of the new colonies and government. When the first Congress met in New York's Federal Hall in 1789, it issued roughly $80 million in government notes, creating an exciting new market in securities. These securities, along with additional stocks, bonds, orders for commodities, and warehouse receipts, were offered to the public for purchase.

To participate in these markets, investors funded American companies by buying shares of ownership. In this way, common citizens had "equity" and could prove so by the "certificates of stock" issued by the company in exchange for capital given by the investor. The stock proved the investor's participation, and secured the debt. That's why shares of stock are alternately called stocks, equities, and securities.

In 1790, the first U.S. stock exchange was established in Philadelphia. At the same time, New York City's exchange was more informal; traders gathered each day under the buttonwood tree at 68 Wall Street to buy and sell securities.

The New York Exchange began trading formally in 1792, when two dozen brokers formed a club. Competition was fierce. The brokers focused on padding their own profits and commissions, rather than on their customers. When the public rebelled, the brokers regrouped and instituted brokerage houses that offered stocks to the public at fair prices.

In 1827, the new Merchants Exchange building, erected at Wall and Hanover streets, housed the New York Stock and Exchange Board. By 1842, the American Stock Exchange opened its doors, and the New York Stock Exchange (NYSE) adopted its present name. Both exchanges enforced strict rules governing the sale of stocks.

In the early 1900s, leading up to the Crash of 1929, "bucket shops" flourished. These independent businesses provided opportunities for individual traders and investors to speculate on the price of securities by tossing money into a bucket carried around by a clerk.

The action in these shops—most of which were unlicensed and illegal—ran fast and furious. The speculators bought and sold the stocks as clerks called out prices from a nonstop telegram called the "ticker." One clerk read the ticker tape while another jotted prices on a chalkboard.

The honesty of the bucket shop operators determined how much money the traders won or lost, and honesty was a rare commodity. As "Larry Livingston," the character who represents the turn-of-the-twentieth-century trader Jesse

Livermore in Edwin Lefevre's *Reminiscences of a Stock Operator*, lamented, "There are no bucket shops here [in New York] that a fellow could trust."

In the early 1930s the exchanges became strictly regulated, and they evolved into premier financial centers: the New York Stock Exchange (NYSE, or the Big Board), the NASDAQ Stock Market, and the American Stock Exchange. Regional exchanges include the Boston Stock Exchange (BOS), the Philadelphia Stock Exchange (PHLX), Chicago Mercantile Exchange (CME, which trades commodities), and Chicago Board Options Exchange (CBOE, which trades options).

As previously mentioned, the floors of the New York Stock Exchange and the American Stock Exchange are located in New York City, in the financial district, at the lower tip of Manhattan. The NASDAQ Stock Market is an electronic market, and doesn't have an actual trading "floor." If you watch the financial television networks, though, you've probably seen the NASDAQ MarketSite Tower on television, which is located in New York City's Times Square.

OUT OF CHAOS COMES ORDER: THE CRASH OF 1929

The Crash of 1929, and the Great Depression that followed it, transformed America's way of transacting business. In 1934, Congress established the U.S. regulatory commission now known as the Securities and Exchange Commission (SEC).

To ensure that another market crash would not take place, the newly formed SEC instituted sweeping regulations to restore investor confidence by ending misleading sales practices and stock manipulations.

Once in gear, the SEC established regulations that prohibited purchasing equities without having adequate funds to cover the transaction. Next, it provided for the registration and supervision of all U.S. securities markets and stockbrokers, wrote rules for solicitation of proxies, and prevented unfair use of nonpublic information in stock trading. The organization stipulated that a company offering securities make full public disclosure of all relevant data. Finally, the commission decided to act as adviser to the court in corporate bankruptcy cases.

In 1971, the National Association of Securities Dealers (NASD) created a fully integrated, computerized trading system called the NASDAQ, or National Association of Securities Dealers Automated Quotron. Its purpose was to automate and trade over-the-counter securities, and it linked the terminals of more than 500 market makers to its automated system in Connecticut. By the 1990s, the NASDAQ grew into the second-largest securities market in the United States, and the third-largest in the world.

The Crash of 1987: More Chaos and the Resulting Order

During the 1970s and 1980s, the exchanges fluctuated between bull and bear markets until the collapse of October 19, 1987. The "crash" caused America's investing public to panic. Frightened customers overwhelmed their stockbrokers with sell orders, yelling "Get me OUT." Frantic stockbrokers flooded specialists and market makers with orders. As the day wore on, some market makers stopped answering their phones—which caused frustrated stockbrokers to stop answering their phones. This forced many unhappy investors to ride out the fall.

After the panic subsided, the SEC executed new regulations to protect the individual investor. The organization ruled that when individual investors wanted to sell their securities, NASDAQ market makers were obliged to buy a specified amount of stock from them.

Later, additional regulations allowed investors to participate in the market by connecting them directly to the market via their computers and the Internet, and market makers were required to handle the transactions. Just like specialists on the NYSE, market makers were held responsible for conducting "fair and orderly" markets.

THE NEW YORK STOCK EXCHANGE: HOW IT WORKS

In terms of market capitalization, the New York Stock Exchange (*www .nyse.com*) is the largest stock market in the world. That's why it's also termed "the Big Board." It's located at 11 Wall Street. CNBC and other financial television networks televise the busy floor of the exchange each morning.

The first stock listed on the NYSE in 1792 was the Bank of New York. Presently the NYSE lists more than 3,000 companies, and averages trading volume of 1.5 billion shares per day. These equities are referred to as "listed stocks," and most have large market capitalizations.

"Market cap" is measured by an equity's number of shares outstanding (shares available to the public not held by corporate insiders) multiplied by the price of a single share of stock.

For example, as of this writing, industry titan General Electric (GE) has 10.3 billion shares outstanding. The price per share is approximately $38. So GE's market cap is a whopping $387.3 billion.

You may have heard GE referred to as "the bluest of the blue chips." The term "blue chip," a moniker applied to the thirty stocks that make up the Dow Jones Industrial Average, comes from the game of poker. Of the chips used to represent dollar valuations in that game, the blue chip has the highest value of all: $500.

In 2006, the NYSE merged with the Archipelago Exchange, a fully electronic exchange known as "ArcaEx." In 2007, the NYSE bought pan-European market operator Euronext, forming the first intercontinental stock market. The NYSE Euronext stock trades under the symbol NYX. For our purposes, we will still refer to the exchange as "NYSE."

The NYSE operates on an integrated, or hybrid, system that combines the NYSE's original centralized auction system with Archipelago's electronic system.

On the floor of the NYSE, "posts" (small booths), each representing a different stock, pepper the floor of the exchange. At each post, a specialist (read "auctioneer") conducts a two-way auction between buyers and sellers and provides a market for that stock. Only one specialist represents each stock; for example, GE has only one specialist. Specialists, however, can represent more than one stock.

NYSE-listed stocks typically are assigned symbols with one, two, or three letters. For example, AT&T Inc. trades under the symbol T. The Coca-Cola Company trades under the symbol KO, and JPMorgan Chase & Co. trades under the symbol JPM.

Where You Come In

Say you want to buy 200 shares of Citigroup, Inc. (C), a listed stock. Basically, your order can be filled one of three ways:

1. You call your full-service broker and place your order over the telephone. Your broker shoots your order to the floor of the NYSE via his computer. There it is filled by the specialist, or the NYSE's Direct + automatic system. Your broker is notified of the "fill" (price per share at which your order was filled), and then your broker notifies you by telephone. Please know that unless you need the advice of a registered stockbroker, calling in your buy and sell orders entails high costs in both time and money.
2. You go onto the Internet, open your online trading account, and send your buy order for 200 shares of Citigroup to your online broker. Your order is actually an ultra-fast email. If your broker has Citigroup shares in its inventory, the broker may sell it to you directly. Otherwise, your order is sent to the floor of the NYSE, where it is filled by the specialist, or electronically by NYSE's Direct + system.

3. You enter your buy order for your Citigroup shares through your direct-access order-entry system, furnished by your direct-access broker. This enables you to send your order directly to the floor of the NYSE (thus the name "direct-access"). Professional day traders use this order entry method, because it assures the highest likelihood of receiving the desired entry and exit price in the quickest possible manner. Direct-access broker commissions are comparable to those of online brokers.

If you were to physically walk onto the floor of the NYSE, hand your order to the Citigroup specialist, and ask him for the "market" in Citigroup, he would announce it. When we say the specialist announces the "market" in Citigroup, he might say, "Fifty-two, thirty-eight by fifty-two, thirty-seven, size 5,000 by 10,000." Translation: A buyer, or buyers, is waiting to buy a total of 5,000 shares of Citigroup and is willing to pay $52.38 per share. A seller, or sellers, currently offers (wants to sell) a total of 10,000 shares at $52.37 per share.

The price difference between the best (lowest) price you can purchase the stock for and the best (highest) price you will receive if you sell it is called the "spread." In the previous example, the spread is one penny per share.

If stocks were people, most NYSE stocks would bear the reputation of acting like statesmen and dignitaries. Because their specialists are charged with keeping "a fair and orderly market," most listed stocks tend to step up and down their price ranges in a mannerly fashion.

If you're new to the stock market, I recommend you target NYSE issues for your first trades. You'll be less prone to the eye-bugging, stomach-clutching attacks that can be brought on by NASDAQ high-flyers.

THE NASDAQ STOCK MARKET: HOW IT WORKS

The NASDAQ Stock Market (*www.NASDAQ.com*) is a shareholder-owned, for-profit company and trades under the symbol NDAQ. The exchange currently lists more than 3,200 companies. It is the largest fully electronic stock market in the United States, with average volume running at about 2.5 billion shares per day.

While there is no "floor" of the NASDAQ (it's electronic), you've surely seen the NASDAQ MarketSite in New York City's Times Square, with the brightly lit, electronic billboard that wraps around the seven-story cylindrical NASDAQ building. CNBC and other financial networks televise the Market Site each trading day.

By now, you've undoubtedly heard the NASDAQ referred to as "the tech-heavy NASDAQ." Although NASDAQ companies cover the entire spectrum of the U.S. economy—from financial services to biotechnology to transportation—its main theme targets technology. Technology-focused industry groups include wireless telecom, software, computers, semiconductors, Internet, networking, and broadband companies. You'll surely recognize some of the NASDAQ tech icons—Cisco Systems (CSCO), Microsoft (MSFT), Google, Inc. (GOOG), and Intel Corp. (INTC).

NASDAQ stocks, which typically trade under stock symbols with four letters, are the NYSE's rowdy cousins. As I said earlier, most NYSE stocks tend to be purchased and sold in a somewhat genteel and dignified manner. Rambunctious NASDAQ stocks, however, can trade like a raucous free-for-all. No doubt it's due to the way shares change hands. In comparison to having a single specialist orchestrating the trades, a NASDAQ stock may have as many as fifty or sixty market makers (think middlemen) and ten ECNs (electronic communications networks, or trader "stock swaps") bidding on and offering it at any given moment. Prices can soar and tumble at mind-numbing speed.

Trades processed through the NASDAQ are executed on the exchange's Market Center—a high-capacity, fast, and fully redundant platform.

Where You Come In

As with stocks listed on the NYSE, you can enter your order for a NASDAQ-listed stock by calling your broker, accessing your Internet account with your online broker, or accessing your direct-access brokerage account.

If you want a current quote for Dell (DELL), your answer might be "26.81 by 26.82." This means that $26.81 is the "inside bid" or the highest price you can demand if you want to sell Dell as a market order.

Twenty-six dollars and eighty-two cents is the "inside offer" or the "ask." ("Offer" and "ask" are interchangeable terms.) This represents the lowest price for which you can buy Dell if you want to buy at the market price. (Remember, when you get a quote from any exchange, whether verbal or written, the bid is always announced first; the offer, second.)

If you're new at this game, please avoid trading explosive NASDAQ stocks until you've got some experience under your belt. These roller-coaster stocks can expose your account—and your heart—to unnecessary risks.

THE AMERICAN STOCK EXCHANGE: HOW IT WORKS

As the nation's second-largest floor-based exchange and third most active exchange, the American Stock Exchange (*www.amex.com*) lists common stocks, options, and exchange traded funds (ETFs). From the exchange's regal building at 86 Trinity Place (adjacent to Wall Street), buyers and sellers compete in a centralized auction market that includes electronic functionality.

The Amex is well known for its broad listing of securities derivatives, such as options and ETFs. Stocks listed on the Amex may represent younger companies, and their prices are many times less volatile than their NYSE and NASDAQ counterparts.

LET'S DISSECT THE INDEXES

As a savvy market participant, from now on you'll focus much of your time on the indexes that the financial markets use as benchmarks.

Dow Jones Industrial Average

The Dow Jones Industrial Average (DJIA) is a price-weighted index of thirty giants of American industry. Price-weighted means that higher-priced stocks receive more weighting than do their lower-priced companions. Often called "blue chips," DJIA companies include Microsoft, Intel, IBM, General Electric, and General Motors, among others.

Maintained and published by Dow Jones & Co., "the Dow," as we call it, is the oldest and most quoted of all market indexes. The average is calculated by adding the closing prices of the component stocks and using a divisor adjusted for splits and dividends equal to 10 percent or more of the market value of an issue. Just as with all of the averages discussed here, it's quoted in points (not dollars).

The Dow's most-traded tracking fund, or ETF, is the Dow Diamonds, and trades under the symbol DIA.

NYSE Composite Index

The NYSE Composite Index is a market-value-weighted index made up of all NYSE issues. (Market-value-weighted means price-weighted.) As with the Dow, each company's security affects the index in proportion to its market value, or price per share.

Standard & Poor's 500 Index

Standard & Poor's 500 Index (SPX), commonly called the "S&P 500," and "the broader market," is a market-capitalization-weighted index (shares outstanding multiplied by stock price per share). Companies listed must have a market capitalization in excess of $4 billion.

Currently, financial companies make up the largest percentage of the index, at 22.3 percent. Fifteen percent of the index is represented by information technology companies; 10 percent of the index represents the industrials. The remaining S&P sectors are represented in varying percentages.

Because this comprehensive index tracks 500 stocks from all ten of the S&P sectors, which represent a wide variety of companies listed on the NYSE, Amex, and NASDAQ, the S&P 500 is considered to be *the* benchmark of the American economy. Standard and Poor's Corporation, a division of McGraw-Hill, maintains this index.

The most widely traded index tracking fund for this index (an ETF) trades under the symbol SPY.

NASDAQ 100 Index

The NASDAQ 100 Index, which was launched in January 1985, includes 100 of the largest domestic and international non-financial companies listed on the NASDAQ Stock Market.

Each security in the index is represented by its market capitalization in relation to the total market value of the index. The index reflects the NASDAQ's largest growth companies across major industry groups, including Technology, Consumer Services, Health Care, Industrials, Consumer Goods, Telecom, Basic Materials, and Oil & Gas.

The most widely known index fund, or ETF, that represents the NASDAQ 100 is called the "QQQ," and trades under the symbol QQQQ.

NASDAQ Composite Index

The NASDAQ Composite Index is a statistical measure that indicates changes in the NASDAQ Stock Market by measuring all NASDAQ common stocks. The index is market-value-weighted; higher-priced equities are assigned more weight than are lower-priced issues.

Russell 2000 Index

The Russell 2000 represents the small-capitalization (small-cap) stock index. Some gurus insist that the small caps lead us into—and out of—bear markets.

So, it's worth keeping an eye on this index. You can also compare your small-cap holdings, if any, to its trending action.

The most widely traded index fund, or ETF, tracking the Russell 2000 is the iShares Russell 2000 Index Fund, which trades under the symbol IWM.

WALL STREET AS "THE ANIMAL HOUSE": THE BULLS AND THE BEARS, THE SHEEP AND THE HOGS

Perhaps because the island of Manhattan previously served as farmland, Wall Street's prominent players are still referred to by animal names. These "party animals" have clear-cut characteristics.

Bulls fight by striking upward with their horns. Therefore, stock market "bulls" make money from advancing prices. During soaring markets, they profit from the uptrend. When the market corrects or drops, bulls are the optimists who insist it will soon head back to the upside.

Bears fight by striking downward with their claws. Market "bears" rake in the profits when the market falls. Many bears are short-sellers who profit from ugly downtrends by selling falling stocks and buying them back at an even lower price (we'll discuss techniques for selling short in Chapter 12).

Whenever the market surges skyward, the pessimistic bears crawl out of their caves to growl that the good times will be over soon.

Sheep follow anybody with a tambourine. Too lazy to learn for themselves, they rush in and out of stock positions on the advice given by the guru du jour. Listen to them bleat as their portfolios take a beating!

One of the oldest sayings on Wall Street goes, "The bulls make money, and the bears make money, but the hogs get slaughtered." Count on it. Hogs always get sliced into bacon. When piggies go to market, they load up on high-flying issues that many times flop faster than they fly. Greedy gluttons also "bet the ranch" on risky issues, or hold on when they could take reasonable gains.

TWO EMOTIONS THAT RULE THE MARKETS (AND THE REST OF THE WORLD)

Two polar opposites reign side by side over the world's financial markets: greed and fear. This ruling duo passes the scepter back and forth at lightning speed, inciting the volatility we witness—and participate in—each day.

To be sure, greed operates up and down the scale from mild optimism to euphoria. Fear varies from apprehension to outright panic. The degree to which these two emotions exert power propels stock prices upward or downward.

Further, these emotions are never spent, never exhausted. As timeless as the markets they rule, they reign supreme, fueled by their own energy.

Want to see them in action? You can watch them command stock prices any time during the trading day. For example, on a volatile morning, check the price of a liquid (high-volume) stock from one hour to the next. Let's say we're watching Research in Motion (RIMM), the communications equipment giant. When the market opens, RIMM is priced at $136.50 per share. By midday, the price has risen to $139.68. The tech stock closes at $141.32.

Now, did RIMM's fundamentals (quarterly earnings, new product offering, or market share) change significantly during that time period? Probably not. Greed pushed the price up—greed and the resulting demand created by buyers who decided to "pay up" for the stock. When the price falls—and it will at some point—fear will be the culprit. Much of the time, these two emotions rule according to perception, not logic or fundamental value.

What's this got to do with you? *Everything.*

Are you greedy? *Sure.* Are you fearful? *I'd bet my duck slippers on it.*

"Yeah?" you reply, crossing your arms over your chest and squinting at me through narrowed eyes. "What about you? Haven't you ever been greedy or scared?"

Absolutely. Although experience has tempered these two emotions in me, there was a time very early in my trading career when I'd happily stuff my account with high-flying stocks. If (when) they tanked, I'd get scared and sell, usually at big losses.

When you first venture into the stock market, greed and fear will be your constant companions. Those two emotions are part of human nature. The trouble is, in large doses they color your perception of the market and urge you to make choices you wouldn't make in more rational moments. Some of those choices can be harmful to your wealth.

Greed causes us to "chase" stocks, or to buy into the momentary euphoria by paying higher and higher prices for a rocketing stock. By the time our order is filled, the buying frenzy has nearly dissipated. Soon, the stock begins to stagger south, taking our money with it.

When everyone around us screams that a stock is going to the moon, greed also urges us to "load the truck." As our good sense dissolves, we max out our accounts with this dream baby that will surely send our kids to college and us on a round-the-world vacation. Unfortunately, the dream stock's overblown price will suddenly dissolve into the mist, along with all of its supporters and our would-be profits.

Greed convinces us to hold oversized positions in rocky markets. It spurs us to grab IPOs (initial public offerings) on the first day they trade. It drives us to gobble up market laggards and losers "because they're cheap."

Greed's ruling partner, fear, on the other hand, motivates us to action even more quickly. The fear of losing money reigns uppermost in our minds. Fear causes us to sell a winning position too quickly. Interestingly enough, it also causes us to hang on to a losing position too long. When the market slaps us hard, fear stops us from capitalizing on the next good opportunity, because we're afraid to get burned again.

How do you eliminate these unsavory feelings from your trading and investing decisions? By learning how to replace them with positive ones. Read this book and others on the subject. Learn how to read market actions and reactions. Move slowly, study hard, and apply what you've learned in a disciplined, cool-headed fashion. If you can accomplish that, you'll have the edge over 99 percent of all market players.

Supply and Demand

Fear and greed act as trailblazers for those age-old economic factors of supply and demand. These two factors move world markets—from rocket ships to jelly beans—around the clock.

Many market advisors talk about fear/greed and supply/demand as if they are separate entities. They are not. They are intertwined and perpetuate one another into action.

The concept is simple: *We want what we can't have.*

Pretend it's your birthday. Over the last six months you've been saving your money for the biggest, most expensive present you've ever given to yourself. Heck, you've worked hard. You deserve it.

Now, you're on the way to the showroom floor to plunk down your money on one of the sleekest, fanciest sports cars ever to spin off of an assembly line. Your heart starts to race. An afternoon spent on the telephone and researching the Internet affirmed this was the only model in your area. It's the perfect color—a deep, brilliant red—with buttery, camel-colored leather seats.

Once you reach the dealership, you park and start walking toward the showroom. What if it's not there? What if someone else feels the same way you do? No, it couldn't be. That glorious hunk of precision has got your name on it.

You enter the showroom and the car fills your vision. Sparkling in the lights, feverish and ruby red, it seems to whisper your name.

You approach the car, then reach out and touch its cool, gleaming metal. This baby is yours.

You open the door and slip into the driver's side. Sinking into the seat, you breathe in the scent of polished leather. The satinlike wooden steering wheel nestles into the palm of your left hand. Your right foot touches the gas pedal, a perfect fit. Your fingers wrap around the gearshift knob, ready to take control of the gutsiest hunk of machinery this side of heaven.

"Here again?" The salesman's voice jolts you out of your reverie.

You take a deep breath. "What's the best bottom line you can give me on this baby?"

"The bottom line is gone." The salesman smirks and slaps the windshield. "I just sold it."

"What? No!" You jerk your body out of the seat and jam your feet onto the showroom floor. Your stomach flips upside down. "You couldn't have."

"Sorry, buddy."

"Wait. Hold it." You put your hand on the salesman's arm as he tucks a "Sold" sticker under the windshield wiper. "I'll pay you more for it. I'll pay the sticker price—maybe more."

The salesman's eyes glitter behind his glasses. "No can do. Got me a signed contract. A deal's a deal."

Frantically, you clutch your checkbook. "When is the next one coming in?"

The salesman sighs and rolls his eyes. "We're not getting any more in, probably not for months."

You turn to walk away.

"Hey," he calls. "This isn't the only car in the showroom. Couldn't I interest you in another model? Why, I've got a sweet—"

"No. No, thank you." With your heart tightening in your chest, you turn and trudge out of the showroom.

A few days later, you're driving through the other side of town. Suddenly, you spot a large automobile dealership and your gaze travels down the line of cars at the front of the lot. You blink in disbelief. Are you seeing things? Four cars identical to the model you want sit idle in the sunlight, flags waving on their antennas. You slow and park.

Before you can get out of your car, a salesman approaches. "Wanna take one of these babies home? Just park it in your driveway and watch your neighbors drool."

You stand and squint at the lot, shading your eyes from the sun. "How many of that model do you have?"

He chuckles. "I've got four of these creampuffs on the front lot and five more out back. That's why I can give you such a terrific deal."

You eye him warily. "What's your lowest price?"

He spews out the same sticker price displayed by the other dealer.

You shrug, waving him off. "You gotta do better than that. I'll check back with you later."

As you drive away, you think, *That salesman must be nuts if he thinks I'm paying sticker price. Why, he's got a lot crammed with that model. I love that car, but I'm not going to get suckered.*

Get the picture?

When only a limited amount of a quality item exists at a certain price—remember the Harley-Davidson craze?—we are willing to pay retail prices, and sometimes higher, to own it (demand). But if a huge quantity (supply) of that same item floods the market, the owner typically has to lower his price to sell it.

Prices in the commodities markets reflect supply and demand in a big way. If severe winter weather causes the orange trees in Florida to freeze, the reduced orange crop causes the cost of orange juice to rise in the grocery stores (demand).

Likewise, say you're monitoring your target stock, Bossy Banks, Inc., and it soars to a new 52-week high of $50 per share. You quickly buy 200 shares at that price. The next day Bossy rolls over and slides to the mid-$40s. "That stupid stock," you mutter, watching in dismay. "If it ever gets back to $50, I'm going to sell and get out even!"

During the following week, Bossy sinks to $38. After moving sideways in the mid-$30s for a few days, Bossy perks up and climbs to $40 (demand—buyers are willing to pay a higher price). Within another two weeks, fueled by more demand, the stock struggles back to $50.

You breathe a sigh of relief, then shoot your "limit sell" order to the market: Sell 200 Bossy at $50. Bossy falls to $48.75. *Huh?* There were too many shares (supply) to be absorbed at $50—by too few buyers. Your order is left hanging. You cancel and lower your price to $48.75. *Too late.* The stock sinks to $48.65.

Frantically, you cancel your order again, and throw in a market order (sell at current inside bid). A moment later, your order is filled at $48.60. By the way, this is called "chasing a stock down."

Here's where fear and greed, the motivating factors, come in. When you originally purchased Bossy Banks at $50 and it immediately sold off, the fear shown by other buyers that they would pay no more than $50 per share drove the price down. That created supply. The continued supply drove the price down even lower, down to the mid-$30s.

When supply dried up as new buyers came in, the stock moved sideways (indecision). As buyers committed to higher prices (demand created by greed) at each level, the price rose higher.

At the point it reached the previous high of $50, fear of getting burned again caused you to throw in your sell order. Others felt the same way, and together you flooded the market with supply, once again forcing the stock down. Lowered prices, sustained by fear, pushed the stock back down to $48.60. Eventually, greed will step back in and create demand . . . and the cycle will repeat itself.

Remember, greed and fear act as the fuel for demand and supply. Later, we're going to add *support* and *resistance* to the equation.

CHECK YOUR UNDERSTANDING

Now that we've covered market basics, here's a quick review:

1. The securities markets in the United States began with speculative trading in the debts of the new colonies and government. When the first Congress met in New York's Federal Hall in 1789, it issued about $80 million in government notes, creating a market in securities.
2. Congress established the U.S. regulatory commission, the Securities and Exchange Commission (SEC), in 1934.
3. The NYSE lists more than 3,000 companies and trades about 1.5 billion shares per day. These equities are referred to as "listed stocks," and most have large market capitalizations.
4. "Market cap" equals number of shares outstanding (shares available to the public not held by corporate insiders) multiplied by the price of a single share of stock.
5. On the NYSE, shares are traded via a centralized auction and electronic hybrid system. Each stock has a "specialist," who facilitates the trades and is charged with conducting "a fair and orderly market" in that stock.
6. The price difference between the best (lowest) price you can purchase the stock for, and the best (highest) price you will receive if you sell it, is called the "spread."
7. The NASDAQ Stock Market lists more than 3,200 companies and trades an average of 2.5 billion shares per day. Although NASDAQ companies cover the entire spectrum of the U.S. economy, its staples are technology stocks.
8. Shares on the NASDAQ trade hands via broker/dealers represented by market makers, who act as middlemen. Many market makers may participate in a stock at one time. Traders and institutions can also place orders with electronic communications networks (ECNs).
9. "Bulls" make money from the rising stock prices. "Bears" profit from falling stock prices.

10. Fear and greed and fear rule the financial markets. They are the precursors to supply and demand.
11. Limited quantities of a high-quality item create demand. Sellers can raise their prices as long as greed goads buyers to continue to "pay up."
12. Large quantities of an item flooding the market creates supply. As fearful buyers flee, sellers must lower their prices to unload the product.

WHAT ARE "CENTER POINTS"?

Many of us who live and breathe the financial markets get caught up in the dizzying pace of this ever-changing arena. We fall prey to this linear world of numbers, charts, and technical rhetoric, and many times we're too busy calculating and analyzing to look up and take notice of the non-financial world around us. Inadvertently, we forget that we are "whole people" who need balance in our lives to thrive and achieve happiness.

The market moves fast, and it takes no prisoners. Fortunes are won and lost in a heartbeat, and only the fittest survive.

When I was new to this field, I spent many a day feeling battered and beaten. I often wondered if I would ever escape in one piece, mentally and monetarily. Only my stubborn resolve to emerge victorious, coupled with my strong belief system, kept me in the game.

In my previous book, *A Beginner's Guide to Day Trading Online, 2nd Edition,* I shared balancing concepts at the completion of each chapter, in brief, one-page discussions called "Center Points." The positive feedback I received on these Center Points encouraged me to continue them in this book.

Through the years, these concept s have encouraged me to keep reaching for my dreams, both financial and non-financial.

I trust they will also inspire you to move forward on your pathway to success.

CENTER POINT

You . . . A Golden Buddha

> *"Come to the edge, he said. They said: We are afraid. Come to the edge, he said. They came. He pushed them and they flew."*

> —Guillaume Apollinaire

It was 1957 in Thailand. In the process of relocating a Buddhist monastery, a group of monks were appointed to move the giant clay Buddha that resided within.

The monks started to push the huge statue, but soon noticed a crack down one side. They decided to wait until the next day to continue with the job. By then, maybe they could think of a way to move the precious cargo without damaging it.

That night, however, a curious monk returned to examine the clay Buddha. He shined a light close to the crack. To his astonishment, he saw something glitter.

Quickly, the monk grabbed a hammer and chisel, and chipped away at the clay. Hours later, he finished his chipping and stood back in awe. He could hardly believe his eyes. Standing before him was a huge, solid gold Buddha!

It was later discovered that several centuries before, while the Burmese army was advancing on the area, Thai monks had concealed the Buddha in clay to keep it from being stolen. During the attack, however, all the monks were killed, so the true nature of the treasure lay in secret until 1957.

You and I resemble the golden Buddha. We often conceal our true brilliance with protective clay shells. We use social masks, boisterous masks, impatient masks, tough masks, insensitive masks, even masks of false humor and enthusiasm, to hide who we really are. Disguising our feelings of inadequacy, these masks also shield us from the outside world—a world we may perceive as overwhelming, uncomfortable, or simply tiresome.

Once we become aware of these masks, we can chip away at the clay and toss the pieces behind us. Only then can we reveal who we really are: caring and successful beings on the road to achieving our dreams!

CHAPTER 2

Off to a Running Start:
Setting Up Your Business

"A man must believe in himself and his judgment if he expects to make a living at this game."

—Jesse Livermore

Short-term trading is a business like any other. You'll want to formulate a plan and set goals so that you have a clear-cut sense of direction.

First, you need to establish how much time and money you can realistically dedicate to your trading business. Then, you can choose your equipment or update existing equipment. Finally, you have to decide which kind of trading account best suits your needs and goals, and establish that account with a broker.

MAP YOUR BUSINESS PLAN

When you set out to drive somewhere you've never been before, you check a map and ask for directions from someone who's been there. Otherwise, odds are you'll get lost and have a much longer trip than you anticipated—if you get there at all.

Your journey into the financial markets as a trader is much the same. Unless you've traveled this road before, you'll succeed far more quickly and easily if you have a map or plan.

The optimal plan is a *written* one. It's a fact: People who write down their plans on paper achieve their goals a high percentage of the time. People who merely hold their plans in mind as vague generalities achieve a lot less. If you'd like to meet your objectives more quickly and efficiently, create your trading business plan as we outline the basic concepts in the next few pages.

What's Your Time Commitment?

First, do you intend to be a full-time or part-time trader? If you intend to tackle the market full-time, you may have a large portfolio. Possibly you've been trading part-time and want to become fully involved. Or, maybe you want to study hard and fast. You realize that by watching market action as much as possible, you'll absorb the most knowledge at the fastest possible rate.

A benefit of swing and position trading (holding positions from two to five days, or four to eight weeks or duration of a stock's trend, respectively), the two styles of trading we discuss in this book, is that the longer-term time frames (as opposed to day trading) lend themselves to part-time participation.

Most part-time traders fall into one of three categories:

1. Closet traders. These are people such as dentists, physicians, attorneys, office managers, and assistants who keep an eye on their stock positions between drilling teeth, removing appendixes, taking phone calls, and attending meetings.
2. First-and-last-hour traders. They pinpoint the stock(s) that they want to enter the night before, and then depending on market conditions at the open the next morning, they make their move. Before the market closes, they check out their positions again for exit or entry and money-management decisions.
3. Laid-back traders. They enter one or two positions a week, max. Once in, they set automatic stop-loss orders with their brokers. They keep an ear to overall market action, and every few days peruse their portfolio for possible profit-taking opportunities.

Do you fit in any of the previous examples? All of the options are valid and have high potential for success. Please remember that in the beginning, though, whether you commit to being a full-time or part-time trader, besides the time commitment for actual trading, you'll need to allocate extra time for study and research.

While we're on the subject, keep in mind that you'll *never* know everything there is to know about this business. If you're still trading years from now, you'll still be studying years from now. Trading is a journey, not a destination.

Your Most Important Commitment: Money

Next, let's look at the capital you've earmarked for your trading account. First, size does matter! You're better off knowing the truth up front: You *must* start with a large enough balance to get you through the learning curve.

Unfortunately, an account funded with a few hundred dollars won't make the cut. You'll also find that most online brokers and all direct-access brokers require minimum amounts for opening accounts.

Next, the money you've targeted for your trading account is now labeled "high risk." This capital has to be money you can afford to lose. This point is not negotiable—for many reasons.

When you enter the stock market as a newcomer and make your initial trades, you're going to make mistakes. Result? You're going to lose money. Count on it.

If you follow the money-management techniques discussed in this book, you'll minimize your drawdown (paper loss). Even so, you will probably incur losses. That's why I stress so firmly that when you open your trading account, you do not fund it with money intended for your children's college education or the down payment on a new house. Simply put, don't fund your trading account with money that, if lost, will alter your lifestyle in any way!

If you trade with money that isn't disposable, it will be "scared money." Trading with scared money colors your perception of the market. Your common sense flees under these conditions. Greed and fear mushroom out of control. Controlled losses are no longer a cost of doing business—they balloon into catastrophes. At the least, your fear of losing money will stop you from entering proper setups that have a great chance of profitability.

Finally, if you've thought of borrowing the money to fund your trading account, please don't. That's considered instant scared money. Instead, sock away a percentage of your income over time until you have enough to start with.

The flip side of all of these cautionary notes: If you have a clear mind because you're trading with money you've set aside for just this purpose, you will approach the market with a calm and confident mindset that is conducive to reaping profits.

Quick Asset Allocation Plan

For those who have large portfolios, consider this method of asset allocation: Subtract your age from 100. If you're fifty-one, that leaves forty-nine. Fifty-one percent of your portfolio should be in relatively low-risk investments, such as bonds, annuities, and money market funds. Forty-nine percent may be invested in higher-risk instruments, such as large-cap stocks. Finally, allocate 5 percent of the 49 percent for your trading account.

SELECTING/UPDATING YOUR OFFICE EQUIPMENT

One of the great perks of trading is that setting it up requires far fewer expenditures than those normally associated with a traditional start-up business.

Identify your office space first—whether it's a grand, mahogany-paneled suite, a corner in a spare bedroom, or somewhere in between. Of mega-importance, no matter where you set up to trade, is that your environment supports your ability to focus. Make sure you have a quiet, private place from which you can study, research, and place your trades.

Got zero equipment with which to start? For starters, set up a television. Tune it to CNBC or another financial network.

Next, you'll need a high-quality personal computer with a good monitor—the bigger the monitor screen, the better. Start with at least a nineteen-inch model, and upgrade to a larger screen as soon as you can. The more generous the screen, the more grateful your eyes will be. Analyzing charts on a laptop-sized screen for any length of time stresses your vision.

If you trade more than occasionally, you will want to add extra monitors to your PC so you can keep research and extra charting capabilities nearby.

Plan to spend in the ballpark of $2,000 to $4,000 for a PC, large monitor(s), and good software. You may also want to add a high-quality surge protector. Nothing spells "gut-grinder" like discovering a high-voltage storm fried your PC internals, and your only connection to your broker is via telephone and a canned voice that says, "All of our representatives are currently on the line with other customers . . ."

This leads us to the next consideration—your Internet connection. The *minimum* connection you'll want to use is a 56K modem and an ISP (Internet Service Provider). ISP services such as AOL, EarthLink, and others vary depending on where you live, and are available for a monthly cost of about $15 to $30 a month. The challenges to using a dial-up ISP are connection slowness and inability to get online during heavy traffic.

ISDN (Integrated Services Digital Network) lines are more expensive ($40 to $100 a month), but faster. Disconnections are also possible.

Cable modems offer a reliable, higher-speed option at a reasonable price, $40 to $50 per month. The downside is that cable bandwidth can be limited (depending on the area in which you live). The more people who use the service, the slower it will operate. If you live in an area where cable is new, chances are you will encounter lightning speed. As more customers jump onboard, the speed may lag.

Depending on your level of service, DSL (Digital Subscriber Line) can cost from $40 to $190 per month. It offers good connection speed, but the speed relies on your distance from the telecom vendor and the service level you select—the higher the speed, the higher the price. DSL may not be available in all areas.

If you intend to trade more than occasionally, you'll want to think about having a backup Internet connection, just in case your primary one goes down. Why? Because the trading god has a perverse sense of humor. When Big Broker decides to downgrade the entire semiconductor industry, we're usually maxed out in semi stocks. As we frantically click on "sell" to escape with at least some of our profits, our Internet connection will inevitably crash. Unless a backup connection is available, allowing us to jump onto our online account to sell, we can end up taking nasty losses. Or, we end up morphing from short-term traders into disgruntled, long-term investors.

That's why I recommend backing up your Internet connection with an alternative connection. As a backup, I keep my laptop computer with a wireless card in my office. I know that one saved trade or rescued profit will pay for the entire year's service.

Aside from your Internet connection, you'll encounter other monthly expenses. When you start, you can use free charting services posted on the Internet (see Chapter 4). As you progress, however, you'll want to use more sophisticated charting software and trading platforms. You'll also want to calculate recurring expenses, including your Internet connection and newspaper and magazine subscriptions. Finally, remember to set aside money for your "continuing education," such as a course at a trading school, or educational materials such as books and DVDs.

CHOOSING A BROKER

There are three basic ways to buy and sell stocks: through a full-service broker, an online broker, or a direct-access broker.

The first method is to pick up the telephone and call your full-service broker. In this world of high-speed Internet connections, it's the most inefficient and costly way, but if you're comfortable with your broker and want to continue this way, by all means do so. Just be aware that you will pay the highest commission rate of all order-entry methods, and those commissions shave a hefty chunk off of your profits.

Selecting an Online Discount Broker

The next method is to open an account with an online broker and place your orders over the Internet. Find one that offers:

➤ Access to real-time quotes, which means stock prices are current when displayed. For precise entry points, real-time quotes are a must. Some companies still give "delayed" quotes, which are fifteen or twenty minutes old.

➤ A Web site that is accessible and easy to navigate, with graphics that snap on the screen rapidly and pages that appear quickly when you move from screen to screen.

➤ A well-organized order-entry screen built to guard against data entry errors. For example, are the "buy" and "sell" buttons far enough away from each other? I know lots of traders (I've done it) who, in a panic to sell a tanking stock, have accidentally doubled up on it instead of selling the original shares. That particular episode always adds excitement to the day!

➤ A quick confirmation system, account balances, and portfolio updates.

➤ Alternative ways of reaching the broker. What happens when the market plunges? Are orders accepted and filled, or does the broker's system jam? If the Web site crashes from heavy traffic, can a broker be reached by phone, and fast?

➤ Low margin rates; you'll be surprised at how they differ.

➤ A reasonable minimum dollar amount to open an account, if any.

➤ Automatic buy- or sell-stops. Ask if the buy- and sell-stops are "day" orders or if they can be "good-till-canceled" (GTC). Most GTC stop orders last for 60 days. These stop orders are particularly useful if you want to keep a core holding in your account while you go on vacation. If your stock position touches your designated stop price, it triggers a market order and the position is automatically sold.

If you want to research your targeted online brokers' background information even further, you can go to the National Association of Securities Dealers Web site, at *www.nasd.com.* Click on "Investor Information," look for "Investor Services," and click on "Check Out Brokers & Advisers."

Finally, ask other traders with online accounts which brokers they use, and whether the brokers are reliable and efficient. Take your time and do as much research as possible. Here is a selection of popular online brokers:

A.B. Watley Direct, Inc.: *www.abwatley.com* 888.733.9000

Charles Schwab & Co.: *www.schwab.com* 866.232.9890

E*Trade: *www.etrade.com* 800.387.2331

Fidelity: *www.fidelity.com* 800.343.3548

Interactive Brokers: *www.interactivebrokers.com* 877.442.2757 (within U.S.)

Scottrade: *www.discountbroker.com* 800.619.7283

TD Ameritrade : *www.tdameritrade.com* 800.454-9272

Some traders start with an online discount broker. Once they are comfortable with the markets, they transfer to the direct-access trading method we'll talk about next.

Opening an Account with a Direct-Access Broker

The final way of placing a buy/sell order is through a direct-access broker that provides customers with a direct-access trading platform. Before we venture into an overview of direct-access trading, let's define the quote systems.

Three types of quote systems are used in trading:

1. Level I. Real-time quotes issued to you by your broker. (We talked about these quotes in Chapter 1.) The quotes represent the best price for which you can buy or sell at that moment.
2. Level II. Continually updated quotes displayed on a Level II screen. In addition to the best (inside) bid and ask (offer) quoted to you on Level I, an actively traded stock may have many more participants waiting in line, hoping to buy or sell the same stock at an even lower or higher price, respectively.
3. Level III. Quote systems used by specialists and market makers to refresh their positions; they are generally unavailable to the public.

A direct-access order-entry system, using Level II screens, is the fastest way to send your order to an exchange. While we swing-and-position traders aren't as adamant about speed of execution as day traders are, it's a nice feeling to know we're in control of our orders when they're placed.

Level II screens let us see "inside the markets" on the NYSE, Amex, and NASDAQ, so it's often said that a Level II screen gives a stock "transparency." That means we can see a host of participants waiting to buy or sell a stock at that moment. As well, when you place your order directly from a Level II screen, it bypasses all intermediaries and goes straight to the designated exchange.

A Level II quote screen for an active stock moves and changes rapidly, as it is constantly being updated. Most traders add a "time and sales" screen to their

Level II screen. Time and sales displays the actual "prints," meaning the trades that are taking place—the price, share size, and the time that they were executed. We'll talk later about how to use this screen, but in the meantime, Figure 2-1 displays a Level II screen of General Electric (GE). The time and sales screen is the column on the right.

GE	34.93 ↑ +.27	100 M D 14:05						34.90	200
Bid 34.92	Ask 34.93	Vol 33706000						34.90	100
High 35.08	Low 34.65	Close 34.66 Spread .01						34.92	1400
								34.92	1600
								34.92	200
Name	Bid	Size	Time	Name	Ask	Size	Time	34.93	100
INETBK	34.92	2911S	14:05:02	INETBK	34.93	136	14:05:03	34.92	100
NAS	34.92	29	14:05:03	INETBK	34.93	5	14:04:57	34.93	200
NYS	34.92	38	14:05:03	PSE	34.93	39	14:05:02	34.93	1200
PSE	34.92	40	14:05:03	NAS	34.93	144	14:05:03	34.93	1900
INETBK	34.91	6036S	14:05:02	NYS	34.93	28	14:05:03	34.93	500
INETBK	34.90	5	14:04:57	INETBK	34.94	78	14:05:01	34.93	100
INETBK	34.90	51	14:04:57	MADF	34.95	10	14:04:54	34.93	100
INETBK	34.89	50	14:05:02	INETBK	34.95	58	14:04:57	34.92	1800
INETBK	34.88	40	14:04:57	INETBK	34.96	55	14:04:56	34.93	100
INETBK	34.87	45	14:04:54	INETBK	34.97	51	14:04:55	34.89	400
AUTO	34.86	1	14:04:57	INETBK	34.98	39	14:04:55	34.89	100
INETBK	34.86	25	14:04:59	INETBK	34.99	3479S	14:04:57	34.89	100
MADF	34.85	2	14:01:56	ETMM	35.00	1	13:46:12	34.89	200
INETBK	34.85	31	14:04:52	UBSS	35.00	40	14:03:33	34.89	300
INETBK	34.84	18	14:04:53	INETBK	35.00	3	14:04:57	—14:05—	
INETBK	34.83	16	14:04:55	INETBK	35.01	4	14:04:49	34.93	300
ADF	34.80	10	14:04:57	UBSS	35.02	750S	13:38:22	34.93	100
EDGX	34.80	10	14:04:57	INETBK	35.02	2165S	14:04:24	34.93	200
NAQS	34.80	10	14:04:57	ADF	35.02	10	14:04:57	34.92	100
ETMM	34.78	35	11:30:12	EDGX	35.02	10	14:04:57	34.93	100

FIGURE 2-1. Level II screen of General Electric (GE). RealTick graphics used with permission of Townsend Analytics. ©1986–2008 Townsend Analytics. All rights reserved.

If you intend to make short-term trading your full-time occupation, consider opening an account with a direct-access broker, as such brokers offer Level II order-entry systems. Because they cater to traders, direct-access brokers furnish their customers with comprehensive trading platforms that include customizable charts, watch lists with streaming quotes and market internals, ticker tapes, up-to-the-minute news, scans, and back-testing strategy systems.

Here's the downside: You may have to place a minimum number of trades per month, or else pay a fee for the software.

Note: A few Internet brokers now provide Level II screens and upgraded charting packages for their clients who trade frequently.

The following is a partial list of companies that provide direct-access software. The companies' Web sites list participating brokers. More software comes onto the market regularly, so check financial Web sites and magazines for new additions.

RealTick: *www.realtick.com* 800-827-0141
TradeStation Securities: *www.tradestation.com* 800.808.9336
eSignal: *www.esignal.com* 800.815.8256
MetaStock: *www.equis.com* 800.508.9180

Once you've selected direct-access sources, you may want to call the companies and ask a customer service representative the following questions:

➤ Does the company require a minimum opening balance?
➤ Is there a monthly charge for the system? Are there a minimum number of trades required per month? Are there inactivity fees? How do the number of executions you make affect the monthly charge?
➤ Is the system reliable? How often does it go down? (If the company representative chokes before answering these questions, politely end the conversation and go on to the next company.)
➤ Can the charting program access weekly, monthly, and seasonal charts? (This is important—some trading software packages do not include long-term charts.)
➤ Does it include a full menu of customizable chart indicators, such as moving averages, MACD, Commodity Channel Index, Stochastics, Relative Strength Index, Fibonacci retracements, Average True Range, VWAP (Volume Weighted Average Price), and Directional Indicators? (You'll learn about these indicators/oscillators later; for now, just inquire about the system's charting capabilities.)
➤ Can you overlay one price chart on top of another? This is useful when comparing a stock's price action to the S&P Index, for example.
➤ Does the system offer scanning abilities? (That means it can scan a certain universe of stocks and bring up those that are fulfilling designated price or indicator settings.)
➤ What's the commission structure?
➤ What are the margin rates? Does the company pay interest on credit balances?
➤ Does the system offer alarms? If so, you can set them to sound off when specified stocks hit a certain price.
➤ Does the system offer streaming news? What's the extra charge?

I encourage you to research at least three systems before you choose one. It's a good idea to talk to company representatives in person, as some of these systems require more technical knowledge than do others.

After you've ascertained that the software matches your level of technical expertise, ask the targeted companies to send you information, and then note how fast they respond. Their attitude right out of the gate will tell you something. When you call them on the phone, how fast do they answer? Does a canned voice ask you to leave a message? Are their customer representatives friendly and knowledgeable?

Finally, talk to others who have direct-access systems. Even in this electronic age, word of mouth can be the most reliable reference.

THE COMMISSION MAZE

Commissions are a necessary business expense because, by law, your trades have to go through a registered broker. The rates vary from broker to broker.

To make sense of the maze of commissions, remember that the most important service a broker can give you is to fill your orders—quickly and accurately. Generally speaking, the faster your order is filled, the better price you will receive.

The higher the commission you pay to online brokers, the more "bells and whistles" you'll be able to access, such as charts, real-time quotes, fundamental analysis, and news. One option is to pay high commission prices (assuming the company fills your orders rapidly and efficiently) and make good use of the broker's charts and research.

The bad news: Many discount brokers' charts aren't detailed enough; they don't have the customizable indicators and oscillators you need as a short-term trader for decision support.

The good news: Many fine charting software packages exist in the marketplace. As I mentioned earlier, some reasonably good Web sites offer real-time charts and updated news. If you don't mind wading through their advertisements, some offer the information at no charge. So, an alternative is to open an account with a plain-vanilla broker and obtain your charts and news from another source.

Direct-access brokers also offer a range of commission structures, which are usually more intricate than those of online brokers. If you want to open an account with one of these brokers, make sure to request a detailed list of charges.

On balance, direct-access software usually provides high-quality, intraday charts and streaming news, so you don't have to go elsewhere for these tools.

I know that's a lot of information to absorb, so let's sort this stuff out:

Option 1: If you intend to jump into short-term trading with both feet and make it a full-time business, consider opening your account with a direct-access firm that offers Level II order-entry capabilities.

Option 2: If you intend to wander into trading at a slower pace and trade on a part-time basis, an account with an online broker should be sufficient.

Option 3: You may want to venture into the market with an online broker, then transfer to a fancier direct-access system when you feel comfortable.

Know this: The least effective way to learn how to trade is to take on too much at once, then crash and burn because of information overload. Take time to develop a style that parallels your personality. Comfort is the biggest key to successful trading choices.

SLIPPAGE: WHAT IT MEANS

Slippage occurs when you put in your market order to buy or sell, and your order gets filled at a different price than the quote at that moment—higher if you're buying and lower if you're selling. A high degree of slippage can take place when you throw a market order to buy a stock that's "running" or rocketing up in price.

Slippage also chews into your profits when you place a market order to buy a "thinly traded" stock, which means a stock that trades on low volume (less than 100,000 to 300,000 shares per day). The market maker will see your lone order to buy at the market floating in, and he or she will "adjust" the price a bit to suit his or her needs. He or she will drool a little, then raise the price a fraction of a point, and fill your order. (To date, this practice seems more prevalent with NASDAQ market makers than with specialists on the NYSE, but I've seen it happen with both.)

The cure for slippage is to issue limit orders (your order will be filled at a specified price or not at all), or place your orders through a direct-access broker on a Level II order-entry screen.

To excel in short-term trading, you must learn the challenges involved. After all, the stakes are your hard-earned money. So, here's a reality lesson: The moment you enter a position, or purchase a stock, you're already "in the hole." Your broker's commission is added on to the price of the purchase. That could total anywhere from $5 to $25 or more. If you add ten cents per share slippage, you're a little deeper in the hole. On 500 shares, that equals $50. So, if you paid a commission of $15 and add that to slippage of $50, you've already got a drawdown of $65. In order for you to climb out and profit, the stock has to rise at least eleven to twelve cents per share to arrive at even money. It has to move even higher for you to profit. When you exit the trade, you once again pay commissions and experience possible slippage. Now you can understand why it's so important to plan your trades carefully.

MARGIN ACCOUNTS: HOW THEY WORK

When you open your (non-IRA) account, your broker will ask if you want to designate it a standard "margin account." The standard margin is called a "50 percent margin account." That means whatever amount in dollars you deposit into the account, your broker will match your deposit with a loan of equal value. So, if you open an account with $15,000, your broker will automatically loan you another $15,000. Suddenly, you have $30,000 at your fingertips!

Hold it. It's not time to start shopping just yet! As with any bank, your broker charges interest on the loan. The rate is usually low, however, and no interest is charged unless you actually use the money.

If you plan to make more than four round trips (open and close a position) during the space of five trading days, the SEC deems you a "pattern day trader." You'll need to open your equities trading account with a minimum of $25,000. And you **must** maintain that balance, or higher, throughout every trading day, no matter what. If the "no matter what" is violated, most brokers will freeze your account until you send them the drawdown amount. Common sense dictates that you'd better start with more than $25,000—at least $30,000—to provide a pillow for losses.

The good news is, as a pattern day trader, you can *day trade* with four times your free cash. That means if you have $25,000 in your account, you can day trade (not hold overnight) $100,000. Your overnight margin, however, usually remains double your account value.

There are two reasons to open a margin account. First, as you become more experienced, the margin gives you extra buying power. Thus, you're "leveraging" your money, or making more money (we hope) than the interest on the loan costs you. Second, the only way you can sell stocks short is to open a margin account. And believe me, in this volatile market, selling short can reap big profits.

If you're an old pro in the stock market, you may already have a margin account. If you're new to this game, your best strategy is to open a margin account, then immediately forget you have the extra buying power.

One of the riskiest things you can do as a new trader is max out your entire account, margin and all. Please understand—when a stock you are holding on margin falls, you lose twice as much money (your equity + margin equity) as you would if you were playing with just your own cash.

As a safety measure, when you first begin trading, ignore the fact that you have a margin account and use only your original equity to trade with. Keep a portion of your account in cash at all times. Sound boring? Don't worry. The market will provide plenty of entertainment and excitement along the way!

ESTABLISH REALISTIC GOALS

We've discussed your investment in your trading business, as it relates to time and money. You're probably well on your way to furnishing your trading space, and you may have your account application in the mail or sent via e-mail to your broker.

So now, let's plan for the future.

As mentioned earlier, studies confirm that those of us who establish goals, and write them down in the form of a definite plan, achieve them. Let's identify realistic goals that you can use as signposts toward an ultimate destination: success.

In the Short Term

First, we'll define short-term goals in a time frame of six months to a year.

This is the part where most rookie traders smack their lips, rub their palms together, and declare, "Let's see . . . I've opened a trading account with fifty thousand dollars. I should be able to make a thousand dollars a day."

Hmm. Really? There are about 240–250 trading days in the year. If you make $1,000 per day, you'll make about $240,000 per year, which is 500 percent. That's *not* realistic!

"Okay," the rookie trader concedes, and then continues with, "Let's say I'll make one thousand dollars a week. *That* should be more realistic."

I hate to pop your balloon, but if you trade for 50 weeks a year, and take in $1,000 per week . . . that's still 100 percent on your money. Most professional money managers turn downright giddy when they make 30 percent per annum. Add to that the fact that the rookie is just that—new to the markets. While making 60 to 80 percent a year, year in and year out, is doable for experienced traders, it's extremely rare.

When you're a novice, know that it will probably take you *at least* a year to become *consistently* profitable. So, for the sake of your trading career, please avoid promising yourself/your significant other/your kids/the dog that you will bring home a certain amount of trading or investing bacon per day, week, or year.

While you're learning to become a successful market player, your goal is to conserve your capital. Believe me, keeping your principal intact is, in itself, a challenging goal to achieve!

Once you gain some experience, then you can promise yourself and the dog that you'll make more than 50 percent of your trades "green" (winners) in a certain time period. And remember, it's far better to clear $10 on a trade than it is to lose $200. Lots of little profits add up to big profits.

Even though I've been trading for many years, I still avoid establishing daily dollar goals, such as $1,000 profit per day. A do-or-die number forces me to make questionable trades. Questionable trades equal lost money. I prefer winning percentage goals; it takes the pressure off, and I usually attain these goals, or better.

Perhaps one of the finest profit-making goals you can establish early on in your trading career is a principle I discussed in my previous book, *A Beginner's Guide to Day Trading Online, 2nd Edition*. It is: "Trade to trade well, not to make money."

If you trade to trade well, by planning your trade and then following your plan precisely, the money will follow. When you keep a running total in your head of the dollar amount made/lost at any given moment, it blurs your perception of market reality. It may even urge you to ignore a potentially dangerous situation. So, make it a goal that you will trade to trade well. Make it a forever-term goal. You'll be glad you did.

For the Long Haul

Now, let's define long-term goals that apply to a time frame of two to ten years.

First, commit to the following goal, which defines a professional trader: to consistently take profits out of the market. When you reach this goal, you can step proudly into the "arena of success."

What's your dream? A log cabin in the Smoky Mountains? A luxury cruise to Alaska? Establishing a charity? Great! Make sure to plant that seed right now. It will act as a terrific motivator, if (when) the going gets tough.

Here's a way to help you attain that long-term goal more quickly. In *The Richest Man in Babylon*, by George S. Clason, the protagonist, Arkad, reigns as the wealthiest man in ancient Babylon.

Arkad's first prosperity lesson to his followers is, "Start thy purse to fattening." Further explanation: "A part of all you earn is yours to keep." Arkad insists that when his followers earn money, they immediately put away 10 percent of those earnings into safekeeping.

From now on, when you grab profits from the market, pay yourself first. Take 10 percent and sock it away in a low-risk account. It will grow over time, and checking the balance will uplift your spirits on days the market uses you for a punching bag.

Here are some more goal-setting guidelines:

➤ Deep down inside, you must believe you are worthy of financial success.
➤ Set realistic goals. Stretching to achieve a high goal is good. Setting yourself up for failure by setting unrealistic goals is detrimental to your self-esteem.
➤ Break down your goals into small increments labeled with signposts. Once the signpost is reached, reward yourself. A perfectly executed trade, for example, deserves a treat—a new golf club, a day at the spa, or, if you really hit gold, a weekend away!

Remember, you must be able to imagine (see) yourself reaching your goal. If you can't imagine ever attaining your goals as a successful short-term trader, chances are you won't achieve them. If, however, you form a picture in your mind of yourself as a confident and competent market participant, your actions will confirm your picture, and the picture will confirm your actions.

CHECK YOUR UNDERSTANDING

Let's review:

1. Trading is a business, like any other. Begin your business plan by writing down the commitment you intend to make in time and money.
2. Make sure that your trading capital is money you can afford to lose.
3. Initial components to budget for your trading area/office: quiet, well-lit space; television, up-to-date PC, large-screen monitor(s); high-speed Internet connection and backup connection; surge protectors; and newspaper/magazine subscriptions.
4. To open your trading account, check out online brokers for these requirements: access to real-time quotes, a Web site that is accessible and easy to navigate, a well-organized order-entry screen, a quick confirmation system, account balances and portfolio updates, and reliable, alternative ways of reaching them.

5. If you choose to use a direct-access broker, make sure that the company provides intraday/daily/weekly/monthly customizable charts along with a full complement of indicators and oscillators, and news, scans, and so forth. Ask for the commission schedule in writing.

6. Slippage occurs when you put in a buy/sell market order, and get filled at a different price than the quote at that moment (higher if you're buying, and lower if you're selling).

7. The standard margin is called a "50 percent margin account," which means your broker matches your deposit with a loan of equal value.

8. "Pattern day traders," by the SEC definition, make more than four round-trip trades per week and must keep at least $25,000 in their accounts at all times.

9. Short-term goals to consider: (1) conserve your capital; (2) make a certain percentage of your trades "green"; (3) trade to trade well.

10. Long-term goals to consider: (1) consistently take profits out of the markets; (2) attain the "big-picture goal" you've always wanted!

11. Follow the advice of Arkad, "The Richest Man in Babylon": Pay yourself first by taking 10 percent of your market winnings and putting them into a separate, low-risk account.

CENTER POINT

Commit: Convert Your Dreams into Goals

> *"If one advances confidently in the direction of his dreams, and endeavors to live the life which he has imagined, he will meet with success unexpected in common hours."*

—Henry David Thoreau

Nothing jump-starts us on our roadway to success faster than making a solid commitment to our goals. When we commit ourselves to a desired result, we program ourselves to "lock on," much the same way a missile is programmed to lock on to a target. Then, magically it seems, we proceed on "automatic pilot." Our brain gives us the strategic actions to pursue the target, no matter how it tries to elude us.

Without a firm commitment to a goal, our autopilot remains in the "off" position; no basis exists for programming or locking on to a target. Perhaps only a hazy idea meanders in and out of our consciousness. Vague ideas and dreams beget vague results.

The act of commitment, however, empowers us to reach into our store of abilities and bring unused talents into our present-day experience.

We may also discover that we can cancel previous beliefs we had about our assumed lack of talent or ability. Have you ever declared a hundred times that you're not adept at a certain task, only to find that when pressured into it, you performed at a high level of competency?

The act of commitment programs us to attract new opportunities. When we make a firm commitment, things start happening. Suddenly, when we know and declare (yes, writing it down is important!) that we will achieve a certain outcome and adopt it as a fact, all sorts of opportunities start appearing in our lives.

Each time we make a new, positive commitment, we choose to begin a new experience. Suddenly, what we imagined to be a dream becomes a tangible goal, and soon transforms into an exciting new reality!

CHAPTER 3

Master a Moneymaking Mindset

"There is only one side to the stock market; . . . not the bull side or the bear side, but the right side. It took me longer to get that general principle fixed firmly in my mind than it did most of the more technical phases of the game of stock speculation."

—Jesse Livermore

The stock market is a timeless macrocosm of energy that expands and contracts as it propels itself through time and space.

Mark Douglas comments in a trading psychology classic, *The Disciplined Trader*, "The markets are always in motion; they never stop, only pause." Whether they are officially open or closed, they remain stadiums for continuous barter as perceptions of value change.

Imagine this: You purchase shares of equity in a listed company that supplies computer anti-virus software. On the evening news, the announcer reports that computer viruses are on the rise and threatening to disable entire networks. By the time the New York Stock Exchange rings the opening bell the next morning, your anti-virus software stock price has soared.

Did that company's fundamentals change in the last twelve hours? Did earnings, the product, or the debt ratio change overnight? No. The perception of future supply and demand—and thus the perceived value—changed.

Just as the opinion of value fluctuates in human minds twenty-four hours a day, actual marketplaces trade around the clock. Every moment of the day, someone, somewhere, is trading money for equity in corporations, currencies, commodities, fixed-income instruments, and more.

As the sun rises and falls on each hemisphere, the events and resulting sentiment in each market affect other markets globally, in a domino effect. In his book *Intermarket Technical Analysis*, John Murphy says, "One of the most striking lessons . . . is that all markets are interrelated—financial and non-financial, domestic and international." While we sleep, geopolitical events, economic issues, weather, and the resulting human reactions to those situations determine how our markets open the next morning.

THE MARKET AS AN UNSTRUCTURED ENTITY

Because the market is timeless, it remains unstructured to a large degree. Therein lies the challenge.

We humans like structure. We like to take a certain action with the assurance that it will produce a certain result. We understand limits, borders, and finite circumstances built on foundations of order.

As most of us find out the hard way, the market doesn't work on that principle. And, because added volatility creates wider, more erratic moves based on emotion rather than logic, the market "changes its mind" constantly. Constant change brings on a cornucopia of possibilities—some rational, and some that boggle our sense of logic.

How can we—humans who thrive on structure, order, and boundaries—survive in a mercurial market? By creating our own limits. Each time we enter the market, we must carry our own structure—meaning our own definitions, principles, and criteria—along with us.

First, assimilate all the knowledge you can that pertains to this playing field. Next, study your personal psychological reactions to various situations that trading serves up to you. Finally, armed with knowledge of how the market performs—and even more important, how *you* perform when presented with opportunities and challenges—draw up a set of guidelines that define your criteria for entering a trade.

These criteria identify *your* structure, *your* limits, and *your* boundaries, which you superimpose onto the market.

Now, you are in command of your actions. You are not reactive—you are proactive. You cherry-pick your trades by taking only those that involve the highest probability of reward tied to the lowest amount of risk. You plan your trade, and trade your plan. You assume complete responsibility and accountability for your actions. Best of all, your disciplined approach to the market speeds you to small losses and maximum profits. And that's what it's all about, isn't it?

THE STOCK MARKET IS ALWAYS RIGHT

Surely you've heard the old adage, "the stock market is always right." How true that is!

The market has no inherent sense of "right" or "wrong." Did your core holding come out with good earnings? The market sneers and slaps it down. During a televised speech, did our Fed chairman murmur that the economy isn't as recession-prone as it appears? The market puffs up in ecstasy.

Are growth stocks overvalued and their P/E (price-to-earnings) ratio blown out of proportion? The market doesn't care. That's the way it is. Like it or leave it!

I once became acquainted with a CEO from a very large organization. When I met him, he had just retired and decided to fill his spare time by actively trading in the stock market.

This gentleman epitomized success. Handsome and fit, he had a square jaw, silver hair, and drove the biggest Mercedes money could buy. And talk about a "Type A" personality! Everywhere he walked, even on an errand so trivial as lunch or the post office, he led with his chin as though he were going into battle. He spoke rapidly and allowed no time for idle comments. He was a general of people, through and through.

Just as he'd powered into everything else in life, this retired CEO powered into the financial markets, sure of his success. The market slapped him hard, and I watched, wincing. But our steely-jawed CEO licked his wounds and went back for more.

The market rolled her eyes, shook her head, and popped him in the chin. He fell, but eventually struggled to his feet and insisted on taking another swing.

Pow! The market dealt him another stinging blow.

The day came when I couldn't watch any longer. Over lunch, I said, "You're losing money, aren't you?"

He nodded glumly. "I don't understand it. My stocks never act like I think they should. I study analysis and charts. I devour books and attend lectures on finance. What more can I do?"

"It's your mindset," I replied. "You're used to being in charge. You come from a world where you're always obeyed. You've muscled through projects and deals, and if things don't go your way, you use your intellect and power to change them to your favor." I looked directly into his eyes. "You can't do that in the stock market. It won't obey you or anyone else."

I watched him flinch at the realization, but then he nodded, and I knew that he recognized the accuracy of my statement.

During the weeks that followed, he tried to alter his attitude, but it was too deeply entrenched. Once he entered a position, he zeroed in on what *should* happen, on what he *wanted* to happen, instead of *what was*. (Get the difference?) Thankfully, he finally stopped trading and decided to tackle another occupation to fill his retirement years.

People who enjoy a position of power in their own communities, organizations, or families often arrive at the market with the expectations of being obeyed. When they buy a stock, they expect it to rise. If it doesn't, frustration sets in.

Know this: The market is bigger than all of us. Few have the power to move it in any direction for any length of time. What we wish, or want to happen, makes no difference. Woe to the player who remains stuck in his or her own opinion of "the way things oughtta be."

We deal with our natural human tendencies in this direction by adapting ourselves to market movements, and by staying nimble and open-minded. We know that just because we believe the market *should* go up or down, doesn't make it so.

Now, how do we address the previous section of this chapter, which talked about applying our criteria so we're in command of our trades in a market that's always right? Like this: When we arrive at the market to trade, we observe it without greed-based or fear-based emotions. We study it without thoughts of what "should be." Once we identify the apparent trend, we choose stocks with eligible setups and apply our risk/reward criteria to them. If they fit our predetermined plan, we enter the play. If they don't, we stand on the sidelines until a better opportunity comes along.

MEET YOUR EMOTIONS—UP CLOSE AND PERSONAL

By now you've guessed what the biggest obstacle is on your pathway to taking consistent profits out of the financial arenas. You guessed it: your emotions.

As Pogo said, "We have met the enemy and he is us."

When you're new to trading, you'll probably encounter an emotional roller coaster. For example, you buy a stock that you believe will rise endlessly. Instead, it reverses sharply, swallowing not only your gains, but also a chunk of your capital. Your happiness succumbs to hope. Your hope dissolves into resentment.

The next day you enter another position. It immediately tumbles precariously close to your stop-loss point. Holding your breath and mumbling, "Not again," you watch with dread and apprehension. Suddenly, the stock bounces and soars to new highs, delivering a fat, unexpected bounty. Fear and dread convert to joy and satisfaction. You exhale, then declare staunchly that you knew it was a big winner all along!

Trouble is, riding that emotional roller coaster can get us into trouble. It also induces stress and exhaustion. At extreme levels, it causes psychological damage.

Professional traders who have been successful in this business for a long time avoid these emotional swings. They've learned how to control their reactions to unexpected market gyrations. And so can you.

That's why I'm addressing the subject of market psychology early on. Just as analysts "pound the table" on stocks they believe will outperform the market, I'm going to "pound the table" on this point. You can read every book and attend every class, hook up a wall full of monitors, and fund your account with a zillion dollars, but I promise you this: If you don't learn to master your emotions, your account will quickly slide into meltdown.

Develop a Winning Mindset—Train Your Brain

We humans instinctively build mental defenses that shield us from the pain of unfulfilled expectations. Our unfulfilled expectations may cause us to create false pictures that distort our vision, and thus our ability to see our true environment. So, emotional turmoil colors our perception of reality. And, as any psychologist will confirm, emotions are far stronger than logic.

How do we rise above these detrimental feelings? First, we identify which ones "belong" to us. (If you want to eliminate something from your life, you must first acknowledge that you "own" it.) Then, we learn to recognize those unwanted emotions and eliminate them; we replace them with positive emotions and responses. At that moment, success is ours.

As mentioned earlier, most emotions related to the stock market stem from fear and greed. What's more, the two are closely connected. Do you know what the bridge is between fear and greed? *Excitement!*

If we drag fear out into the sunlight, we'll find out exactly what it is. I once heard a psychologist say, "Fear is nothing, trying to be something."

"Sure," you reply, rolling your eyes. "Tell me that when I watch my brand-new position crash. My palms sweat, my heart pounds in my ears, and my stomach churns. You call that *nothing*?"

No. I call that fear. And fear is a feeling. Not only is it an unpleasant feeling; it causes blood vessels to constrict, which reduces the oxygen supply to our brains, thus limiting our ability to make rational decisions. And this at a time when we need to make rational decisions the most. Oh, great.

On the other hand, you can't declare, "I'm not scared," and expect fear to disappear. Nature allows no vacuums. You have to feel *something.*

In the previous situation, you bought shares of stock that your research indicated would rise in value.

The market, however, had different ideas. It took your stock and hammered it lower. As you watched that happen on your computer screen, fear and panic took over. Maybe you went into denial, maybe you rationalized, surely you justified.

Still, while your mind raced with thoughts in a frantic attempt to change your pain to pleasure, agony washed over you. You took one of two actions: You held on to the position, refusing to take the loss; or you sold, and then chastised yourself for being dumb enough to buy it in the first place.

Guess what? As long as you're a trader, the previous situations, and variations on it, can—and will—take place. Instead of the situation controlling you, however, *you'll be in command*. With practice and experience, you'll displace fear and all of its variations (from mild anxiety to stomach-grinding, head-pounding panic) with a calm confidence spawned by a concise plan that's been filtered through discipline and knowledge.

The fear of being wrong or the need to be right has surely lost more money for more people than all of the other attitudes combined.

Imagine this scene: You make every correct move; you research and plan your trade, then buy at the perfect entry point. The following day, the market goes against you. Your stock plummets and hits your mental stop-loss point.

Thoughts race through your mind. Should you sell now? Will the stock immediately rebound if you do? Will your loss be for nothing? If you hold on a little longer, will it turn into a win? Will you have to admit to others you were wrong? Feeling: anxiety, disappointment, guilt. Action: You ignore your stop-loss point and turn your back on the falling stock.

Unfortunately, Americans and most of "civilized" society are brought up with the dictum that we must always be "right." Strong, smart people are "right." Those who are "wrong," we label ignorant and empty-headed. Consequently, most of us will do anything to avoid being wrong. In the stock market, that attitude can be deadly.

Here's the cure for the fear of being wrong and the need to be right. First, banish "right" and "wrong" from your trading mentality. From now on, there are no such entities. There are only *choices*. You make a choice based on the best information available to you, with your plan at your side.

Remember, no one on this earth knows which way the stock market, or your chosen stock, will move during the next ten minutes, ten days, or ten months!

To be successful, you must make the most astute choice possible and manage the trade according to your plan. If your position moves up, you take profits at your preconceived exit point.

If the position surrenders to selling pressure and touches your stop-loss point, think, "Hmm . . . this didn't go the way I thought it would. I'll take my loss here and look for another opportunity." That thought triggers the satisfaction of protecting your capital, which in turn causes you to pull the "sell" trigger. No fear, no anxiety, no trepidation, headaches, or stomach twisting. Feels good, doesn't it?

Variations on fear's buddy, greed, are more fun to consider. Unfortunately though, they can cause just as much pain. For example, have you ever *chased* a stock?

Say the market just opened. A stock on your watch list jumps out of the gate and starts screaming skyward. "Wow!" you think, "This stock is really flying. Everybody else is paying up for it, so I will too. What's a couple of points in a stock this strong? I bet it'll fly straight up to the moon!"

Trouble is, in this scenario, you may end up buying high and selling low. Since the market is controlling you, this is the result more often than not.

Displace that thought pattern with the following: "This stock passed my entry point. No problem, I'll catch it the next time. I'll move on to better opportunities."

Bear in mind that at this moment, there are more than 9,000 stocks you can choose from. Why be a sheep that might end up shorn?

By the way, if you languish every time you leave money on the table—get over it. Just as you're going to take small losses, you're also going to watch stocks rocket to the moon the day after you sell your position. Don't drive yourself bonkers by adding up the profits you *could* have made. Learn to shrug off missed money. It's part of the business.

Another greed-motivated behavior is to "bet the ranch," especially on a hot tip. Say a cocky taxi driver told you furtively that Cranky Computers was going to be acquired tomorrow morning early by Huge Conglomerate, Inc. Out of the side of his mouth, he says, "The stock price is gonna scream!"

You run home and conduct some quick research. Surprisingly enough, Cranky has good fundamentals and a decent chart. Instead of buying a tiny lot size, you max out your account, margin and all. Yessiree, Cranky Computers is going to send your kids to college.

Cranky pops up at the open, then tanks several points to the downside, *fast.* Slack-jawed and confused, smarting from the loss and overwhelmed with guilt, you sell. Then, you slump in your chair and spend the rest of the morning berating yourself for being dumb as a box of rocks.

Stop. Get it behind you. Next, replace your "bet the ranch" mentality with the firm assertion that you are an astute trader. From this moment forward, you are far too wise to ever commit a major portion of your portfolio to any one stock—no matter what the circumstances.

When someone gives you a hot tip, and you can't resist, research it. If the stock fits all of your guidelines, buy a limited amount and set a tight stop-loss. Apply the same well-thought-out plan you assign to your other positions. Say the rumor's true, and the stock flies up. Take your profits fast. (Market mandate: Buy the rumor, sell the news.) Maybe (probably) the rumor is false. Sell quickly and tell yourself that your resolve to ignore hot tips is now firmly in place.

I will admit to checking charts on tips ever since I experienced a good one. On a flight a few years ago, I overheard two men in the row behind me talking. One man reminded the other to check out a certain stock when he arrived home; the stock had great fundamentals and was poised to rise soon.

As soon as I returned home, I called my stockbroker with the tip. (Those were the days before online brokers.) With great amusement and much clucking, my broker placated me and looked up the stock. *Huh*, he reported, *well the darn thing looked pretty good*. And, yes, he agreed I should buy a few hundred shares. Which I did. And made money.

It's not impossible to make money from hot tips—just improbable. And dangerous if done with great expectations and no analysis or discipline.

Hope, faith, and optimism are certainly wonderful attitudes to infuse into our everyday lives. But please, leave them out of your financial decisions. They can get you hurt.

Have you ever stared at a losing position on your monitor and heard yourself whispering, "Please, *please* make this stock go up"? Hope motivates us to send that prayer to the stock market god. She may not be listening.

Faith makes us declare staunchly to our friends and ourselves (when our stock is tanking), "It's a good company." (Ever heard those words before?) Optimism speaks through us, with, "It'll come back. After all, the market has an upside bias."

How do I know these words so well? Believe me, early in my trading career, I repeated them like a mantra.

Despite being such delightful characteristics, hope, faith, and optimism sure cause mayhem when they act as decision-making tools in the financial markets.

Because I know these emotions are detrimental to my wealth, I toss mine into an imagined basket each trading day, before I go into my office. I reclaim them when I leave for the day.

Is that a head game? Sure. Does it save me money? Absolutely. And I'll do it each morning until my trading days are over.

THE END RESULT: WHAT IT LOOKS LIKE

You can only achieve the self-mastery that leads to success if you know what that success looks like. Here's the picture: Wisely, you decided to learn all you could before entering the game. You crossed the market's threshold cautiously. So now, when you buy or sell a stock, you do so secure in the knowledge that you've planned for all eventual outcomes.

The feelings you experience are those of calm confidence, and detachment. You have no attachment to the outcome of the trade. Robot-like, you observe the markets, and your stock's reaction to that environment.

In addition, you know yourself. Honest introspection sheds light on the emotions you choose to replace, and those that will serve you well. Maybe you're impulsive, stubborn, and have a high tolerance for risk. Recognizing these traits, you've resolved to temper them with a mindset geared to strict money management.

On the other hand, perhaps you're a focused planner. You'll approach each entry and exit driven by the need for precision. That trait is a beneficial one, and you'll want to hone it well.

As you gain more knowledge and make more decisions filtered through your increasing self-mastery, you'll find that experience adds to both knowledge and discipline. In other words, it's a self-fulfilling circle. Each component supports the other.

After all, knowledge without discipline is dangerous. Discipline without knowledge has little value. And you won't ever gain experience without those other two.

Soon, you'll step into the market with the firm conviction of a professional who knows that the market only hurts those who allow it to. And, you'll be taking gains on a consistent basis.

R & R: DON'T GO TO THE MARKETS WITHOUT THEM

Responsibility and respect represent two of the most important constituents in our financial—and indeed, our non-financial—lives. They must be an integral part of our actions.

Ever talk to someone at a cocktail party who says smugly, "I made 25 percent on my portfolio this year"? Talk to that same person in a bear market, and he or she will whine, "The market took away 25 percent of my portfolio." Hear the difference? He or she made the brilliant decisions that increased the portfolio value. The stock market "took" money away.

You, as a confident market participant, take full responsibility for your portfolio's bottom line, no matter what market conditions reign. You are aware of the fact that you alone push the "buy" and "sell" buttons.

You also respect money, especially the money in your account. You realize that if you lose that capital, you are out of the game completely. You know that the primary objective when you compete in the financial arena is to protect your capital at all times.

Take a moment to reflect. Do you treat your money carefully? Do you pay your bills on time? Do you spend thoughtfully? Or, are crumpled $20 bills thrown on the dresser?

If you pay your bills early, spend within your budget, and keep your bills carefully organized in your wallet, those actions indicate that you respect money and the power it has to enrich your life.

SELF-RESPECT AND DESERVEDNESS

The world's most successful traders and investors believe in themselves and their ability to win. It's a known fact among top traders: The beliefs you have about yourself, as a person, will impact your bottom line to a great degree.

As Mark Douglas writes in *The Disciplined Trader*, "Contradictory beliefs cancel your energy because you have a built-in mental conflict between the validity of one belief, expressing itself only at the direct expense of another belief."

Do you state in one moment that you can learn how to take big gains out of the market—and in the next tell yourself that you'll never catch on? Do you snatch a rapid return out of a stock in one week, then "accidentally" give it back the next?

Deep down inside, you may not believe that making money rapidly, and without backbreaking labor, is honest work.

Reflect on your inner level of deservedness. Do you *really* believe you deserve to be wealthy, or at least to accumulate a lot more money than you have at the present?

Consider this: Money is a means of exchange that provides us with circumstances and experiences we could not otherwise have. There is plenty for all. When we attract prosperity into our lives, we are able to help others more fully.

Declare the truth: You deserve the best life has to offer, including abundant health, happiness, and financial freedom!

CHECK YOUR UNDERSTANDING

Time for review:

1. The market is timeless and unstructured.
2. To succeed in the market, when we trade we must bring our own structure and order with us.
3. The stock market is always "right."
4. You can fund your account with a hefty sum, buy the most expensive equipment available, and acquire reams of knowledge about the market. But if you do not control your emotions, your account will quickly dissolve.
5. Emotional turmoil colors our perception of reality.
6. Learn to replace emotions of fear and greed, and their variations, with the calm confidence born of having a plan in place, and trading according to that plan.
7. Leave hope, faith, and optimism outside your trading office door.
8. Self-mastery leads to success: You've studied and learned as much as possible before embarking on your trading career; you have an exact plan for each trade; you stay detached from the outcome of the trade.
9. Responsibility and respect play important roles in the way we feel about our money, and how we treat it.
10. The world's most successful traders believe in themselves; as individual traders, we trade with a similar confidence born of our knowledge, discipline, and experience.

CENTER POINT: MAKE YOUR CIRCLE BIGGER

"The only way to discover the limits of the possible is to go beyond them into the impossible."

—Arthur C. Clarke

As humans, our goal is to reach our highest potential. We are programmed to strive for excellence. Once we believe in ourselves, our goals are within our grasp.

Picture yourself as the center of a circle. Within the space between you and the circle's circumference is your world, meaning your friends, family, experiences, value system, career, even level of health.

Beyond that circle are the places you've never visited, experiences you've never had, belief systems you can't envision, knowledge you haven't learned, points of view you've never encountered. Also drifting outside your circle are the wonderful talents you don't realize you have, and the "distant" parts of yourself you've never explored.

Outside your circle, there are no guarantees. Indeed, this zone appears as a faraway land we gaze at and refer to as "Someday." "Someday, I'll write a book." "Someday, I'll learn to speak German." "Someday, I'll go to Europe." "Someday, I'll tell her how much I love her."

Think of all the people we honor as geniuses, people who have excelled and given spectacularly to the world. They ventured outside their circles and stepped into the unknown: Leonardo da Vinci, Albert Einstein, Mahatma Gandhi, Margaret Thatcher, Chuck Yeager, Oprah Winfrey, Condoleezza Rice, Steven Spielberg, and Bill Gates, to name a few. All left the safety of the "known" to journey into the unknown.

In order to grasp all the joy life has to offer, we have to open ourselves to new experiences. We must go to the edge of our circles and step boldly through the boundaries in order to create new and bigger personal worlds. The larger our "circles," and the more courageously we strive to stretch and extend them, the more we are filled with satisfaction, happiness, and success!

CHAPTER 4

Market Machinations 101:
The Fuel That Sparks the Energy

"I know from experience that nobody can give me a tip or a series of tips that will make more money for me than my own judgment."

—Jesse Livermore

I once overheard a renowned technical analyst state: "Trading successfully may be one of the most difficult things a human being can accomplish. Each trade is different. We never know for sure whether a specific action will produce a specific result."

That's an extremely accurate statement. No two trades are ever alike. But then, no single day in the stock market duplicates another. Every day hurtles through a profusion of different events, judged by millions of mindsets, producing a unique mixture of consequences.

And always, the final result manifests as price.

THE BUCK STOPS HERE

Imagine a giant tornado-like tunnel. At the top of this ferocious, whirling mass of energy are global events and our reactions to them. The vortex spins with supply-and-demand levels, currency fluctuations, interest rates, and cyclical industry shifts. Further down, analysts' reports, company earnings, and the public's opinion on sectors and leading equities revolves in a constant pirouette. All elements of the maelstrom converge to a single point: price.

Price is the consensus relating to value, established in a single moment of time.

Say you want to sell your current holdings in Worldwide Wireless. I want to buy shares of Worldwide Wireless. We agree that the current selling price of $60 a share is fair. So we exchange equities for money.

Moments later, the consensus shifts. For whatever reason, the perception of the value of Worldwide changes. Market players decide the stock is now worth more per share, $60.25. Once again, shares and money change hands. Have the fundamentals of the company changed in that instant? No. The change in collective consciousness—the perception of reality—dictated by those who currently participated in this stock made the change.

Also remember this: When you sell your shares of a stock to me, you believe that the value of the stock will soon shrink. I buy because I believe the value will increase. In the short term at least, only one of us will be right.

FUNDAMENTAL ANALYSIS VERSUS TECHNICAL ANALYSIS: THE TUG-OF-WAR

When I first started investing, I talked to a lot of stockbrokers. The majority of them relied solely on fundamental analysis as their decision support tool, quoting from company financial reports and earnings research for their investment advice. They fluffed off technical analysis and chart interpretation as hocus-pocus. Their standard chant: "I've never met a rich technical analyst."

Tugging on the other end of the rope were the card-carrying members of the technical analysts' club. "Who has time," they insisted, "to comb through pages of sleep-inducing company reports? A price chart tells you all you need to know."

Fundamental analysis and technical analysis are the two major methods of examining a publicly traded company to determine the health of its stock. (I've been told some folks buy stocks on the strength of a company's astrological charts and a system of sacred numbers, but for now we'll stick to standard analysis.)

Fundamental analysis is like taking an "x-ray" of a company. It examines the internal financial fitness of an organization and tells us how strong it is.

Fundamental analysts focus on supply and demand levels of the products and/or services the company produces. They study company reports, profit and loss summaries, price-to-earnings (P/E) ratios (calculated by dividing the stock's price by its earnings-per-share figure), market share, sales and growth, and brokerage analyst's ratings. Those who buy and sell on the strength of a company's fundamentals generally buy a stock "for the long haul," and ignore gymnastics performed by the market on any given day or week.

Technical analysis is the study of time, price, and sentiment of a chosen equity (or market or index) as shown on charts. The price action draws patterns on those charts. And, because human behavior can be repetitive, the price patterns are many times repetitive. When technical analysts recognize one of those patterns starting to form, it gives them a set of probabilities on which to base the stock's next move.

If fundamentals show us a company's internal financial strength, then a chart reveals that stock's personality (think: price volatility). As an added benefit, charts allow us to quickly compare price action of a specific stock to its buddies in the same industry, and to broader indexes such as the S&P 500. Obviously, charts have the advantage of speed, displaying the "picture is worth a thousand words" concept in action.

When you utilize fundamental and technical analyses together, you've got an accurate picture of a company's financial fitness and personality profile. That's why, more and more, we see technical analysts sneaking looks at a company's fundamental information, and fundamental analysts furtively peeking at charts.

As wise and profitable short-term traders, we recognize the value of both worlds. When we enter the market, we want all odds possible in our corner. To that end, the following section shows how to find the most comprehensive fundamental information about a company, in the least amount of time.

FUNDAMENTAL ANALYSIS: QUICK YET THOROUGH EVALUATION RESOURCES

In this age of information, we no longer have to spend hours wading through pages of a company's mind-numbing financial reports to find out if it's worth our time and money. Instead, we're going to look at a quick way to check a stock's fundamental health. (Later in the chapter you'll find Web sites where you can find more fundamental data about companies on your stock target list.)

The kind folks at *Investor's Business Daily* (*IBD*) have devised a rating system for stocks that I find invaluable. Under the guidance and ownership of the renowned William O'Neil, the publication provides proprietary ratings that give you a quick and reliable snapshot of corporate numbers.

You can glance at *IBD*'s stock tables, find your stock's listing, and check out the combination of six numbers and letters assigned to it. (See the following section for an explanation of the rating system.) If you want to add to your research, you can wander through the Web sites listed a bit later in the chapter and delve into in-depth reports about your target company.

IBD Proprietary Corporate Ratings

The *Investor's Business Daily* SmartSelect ratings cover the following:

SmartSelect Composite Rating. Combines all five ratings that follow into a single ranking. The stock's percentage off its 52-week high is included. Results are compared to all other companies; then the stock is assigned a rating from 1 to 99. To take a long position, I prefer a target stock to rate 70 or higher.

Earnings per Share (EPS) Rating. Tells you a stock's average short-term (last two quarters) and long-term (last three to five years) earnings growth rate. The number you see is how your company compares to all other companies; the scale goes from 1 to 99, with 99 being the highest. For long positions, I prefer a rating of 70 or higher.

Relative Price Strength (RS) Rating. This rating measures a stock's relative price change in the last twelve months in comparison to all other equities. Again, the scale runs from 1 to 99, and I look for a rating of 70 or higher.

Industry Relative Price Strength Rating. This rating contrasts a stock's industry price action in the last six months to the other 196 industries in *IBD*'s industry group list. The scale is in letters from A to E, with A representing the best-performing industries. Look for stocks with A or B rankings.

Sales + Profit Margins + ROE (Return on Equity) Rating. This rating crunches a firm's sales growth rate during the last three quarters, before and after profit margins and return on equity, into a letter. Again, the ratings are A–E. I look for companies rated A, B, or C.

Accumulation/Distribution Rating. This rating applies a formula of price and volume changes in the last thirteen weeks to determine whether a stock is being accumulated (bought) or distributed (sold). Again, ratings are A–E, with "A" indicating the heaviest buying, "C" designating neutral buy/sell volume, and "E" signaling heavy selling. This "Acc/Dis" rating is very important. Choose stocks rated A, B, or C.

These ratings are located next to the stock's listing in the *IBD* stock tables. For example, you would find your target stock and see: 99, 99, 99, A, A, A (Ratings), 72 (represents 52-week high) Cranky Computers (then the rest of the quote information with closing price, etc.). Of course, the three 99's and the three A's indicate the highest rankings possible; such a stock probably doesn't exist.

Still, you can understand how this number/letter combination gives you an instant picture of a company's fundamental health.

In addition, check *IBD*'s "Your Weekly Review," published in each weekend edition (on Fridays). This roster inventories high-quality issues within 15 percent of their 12-month high and EPS and RS (Relative Price Strength) ratings of 85 or higher. It's a great list to pull stocks from in order to formulate, and add to, your potential target list—but make sure you check the stock's intraday, daily, and weekly chart for an appropriate entry before you consider it as a trade target.

More Instant Info: CNBC and Bloomberg

Walk into any trading room, and you will no doubt see televisions perched near the ceiling tuned to the CNBC or Bloomberg financial networks. They report global events, and interview nabobs such as CEOs and securities analysts. They also take us to the floor of the NYSE and commodities exchanges.

As national and global events impact our markets to greater or lesser degrees, it's important for you to stay abreast of events that affect your portfolio.

Trading the News

Since we're on the subject of news, keep in mind that trading with the network news has disadvantages. By the time the financial networks announce a news item, the large institutions have already acted on it. (They have extensive news feeds that report events almost as they happen.)

If you *do* want to trade economic news, avoid trading the news itself. Instead, trade the market's *reaction* to the news.

How many times have you watched companies announce good earnings news only to see the stock price get driven into the ground the next day? The good news/price plummet syndrome may take place because the positive earnings news has already been factored in to the current price. Again, the old market caveat, "Buy the rumor, sell the news" remains true.

Same situation—alternative reason: In another instance, earnings might be in line with estimates, but the company's forward-looking guidance suggests slowing sales in the upcoming quarter. That can also take price lower.

Finally, if the stock's industry group is stuck in a nasty downtrend, sometimes no amount of good news will induce buyers to step to the plate.

General rules of thumb when playing earnings and even economic reports:

➤ If your target stock should go down—but it doesn't—it will probably go up.
➤ If your target stock should go up—but it doesn't—it will probably go down.

A different situation: Say Fed Chairman Ben Bernanke appears on your television screen and utters a phrase like "looming inflation." Pay attention. Before he reaches the period in that sentence, start tightening your stops and take some profits.

Use financial network news as a great overall global and market picture, and to stay aware of market sentiment. As a rule, though, refrain from basing single trades on lightning-bolt announcements.

Before we leave newspapers and networks, I want to mention the *Wall Street Journal*, first published in July 1889 by Charles Dow, and its sister paper, *Barron's*, which hits the streets on weekends. Alan Abelson's crusty opening commentary, "Up and Down Wall Street," is worth the price of the *Barron's* subscription in itself. Both publications are excellent financial resources.

WONDERFUL WEB SITES TO WANDER THROUGH

The World Wide Web offers more financial research than you could ever hope to wade through in a lifetime. In fact, if you Google "stocks," you'll see that literally millions of financial Web sites now populate cyberspace.

Here's a micro-list of well-known, well-rounded sites to jump-start your research. All display free information about the financial markets. A few offer additional subscription services and products.

Big Charts (*www.bigcharts.com*). Free interactive charts, quotes, industry analysis, intraday stock screeners, market news, and commentary. The charts offer most all indicator studies, plus you can overlay indexes on stock charts. Great charts for beginners.

BigTrends.com (*www.bigtrends.com*). A good Web site for traders that offers daily market analysis, e-mail newsletters, feature articles, and trading education by Price Headley. Additional subscription services and products available.

Bloomberg (*www.bloomberg.com*). Offers news, detailed stock lists, quotes, and more. Also, you can sign up for Bloomberg's Market Monitor, which will track stocks and indexes and give you updates on their performance.

Briefing.com (*www.briefing.com*). Great Web site for pre- and post-market analysis. Also displays updated news briefs during the trading day. A wealth of free and subscriber services offer various levels of info that include economic reports, commentaries, upgrades/downgrades, earnings reports, charts, market internals, and in-depth trading strategies.

CNBC (*www.cnbc.com*). Top stories and latest headlines in the world of finance. Streaming charts of the Dow, S&P 500, and NASDAQ Composite. News videos on demand.

DailyStocks.com (*www.dailystocks.com*). A comprehensive Web site that offers a huge menu of stock market info, including a large selection of links to financial newsletters.

Fairmark Press (*www.fairmark.com*). Tax guide for traders and investors. Offers tax forms and publications, books, and Fairmark Forum—message boards for tax questions.

Hoover's Online (*www.hoovers.com*). Includes both free info and subscription services that offer access to research, including profiles of public and private companies, IPO (initial public offering) pages, and industry information.

Investor's Business Daily (*www.investors.com*). Articles, news and analysis, educational tools, and much more. Much of the information is free, but there are additional subscription services.

Market Gauge (*www.MarketGauge.com*). In my opinion, the most comprehensive and user-friendly site on the Web for researching industry groups, and the stocks within those groups. The groups are listed in real time, whether leading or lagging, in various sorting criteria that range from short-term (on the day) to 52-week. For a free two-week trial to this subscription site, go to the home page at www.ToniTurner.com, and click on the Market-Gauge.com free trial link.

MarketWatch (*www.marketwatch.com*). Offers news and daily columns, a portfolio tracker, stock and industry screener, fund finder, upgrades/downgrades, and top gainers and losers.

Morningstar (*www.morningstar.com*). This well-known stock and fund rating service offers top stories, Market Barometer (heat map), and information on stocks, funds, ETFs, and hedge funds at no charge. Subscription services include Morningstar's buy and sell ratings on nearly 2,000 issues.

MSN MoneyCentral (*www.MoneyCentral.msn.com*). News stories and snapshots of current market activity, charts, quotes, SEC filings, company profiles, and analyst ratings.

Quote.com (*www.quote.com*). Provides real-time market information and comprehensive menu of free (delayed) charts, quote sheets, hot lists, historical time and sales data, and summary period data. Good multi-asset selection of subscription services.

Silicon Investor (*www.siliconinvestor.com*). Focuses on a host of message boards. Most are technology related.

SmartMoney.com (*www.smartmoney.com*). A great business and financial site offering commentary, portfolio tracking, customized watch list, daily market reports, and sector updates. It includes quotes, news, ETF section, company snapshots, analyst recommendations, and more.

StockCharts (*www.stockcharts.com*). Everything about charts you've ever wanted to know, and then some. Good market commentary, along with sections on "Tools & Charts" with Stock Scans, and "Chart School." Features insights from noted technical analyst John Murphy.

The Motley Fool (*www.fool.com*). Features headlines, articles and commentary, and much more. Good educational material related to investing and retirement, plus a comprehensive list of newsletters. Lively group of discussion boards.

TheStreet.com RealMoney (*www.thestreet.com*). Free analysis of the investment scene before, during, and after the trading day, plus subscription services. Columns, blogs, and alerts by noted television commentator Jim Cramer.

Toni Turner.com (*www.ToniTurner.com*). This is where you can join my community of traders and active investors. On my site you'll find information on upcoming online and live seminars, my educational DVDs and streaming videos. You'll also want to take advantage of our free content, including my monthly newletter, monthly Economic Calendar, Tutorials for various chart indicators, a Sectors/ Stocks page that helps you create a watch list, information about ETFs, active investing strategies, and much, much more.

TradingMarkets (*www.tradingmarkets.com*). Geared to traders and investors, this site includes excellent educational sections. Also, check out the blogs, commentaries, and intraday updates and look for my articles. Offers both free and subscription services.

Value Line (*www.valueline.com*). An excellent Web site from this investment research and stock subscription ratings service. Value Line University is a wonderful educational tool.

Yahoo! Finance (*www.finance.yahoo.com*). Market Summary, financial news, free stock center that furnishes comprehensive fundamental research, personal finance, and much more.

Again, there are literally millions of financial Web sites to choose from. Word-of-mouth recommendations from other traders can be a great resource.

Caveat: Traders and even investors risk getting lost in the State of Overwhelm. So much information sits at our fingertips, it can be intimidating. One way to avoid those feelings: scan a dozen sites or so, and then focus on two or three a day, maximum.

Remember, you cannot know everything that's going on in the markets—and you don't have to in order to be successful. Stay abreast of the general news and economic conditions, and then specialize in one or two sectors. That way, you can focus on news that applies to just those areas.

MAGAZINES

Three excellent magazines come to mind that target traders: *Active Trader* (*www. activetradermag.com*), *Stocks & Commodities* (*www.traders.com*), and *SFO* (Stocks, Futures and Options) *Magazine* (*www.sfomag.com*).

Active Trader arrives each month filled with articles that educate traders about everything from market psychology to pattern analysis. Its "Trading Basics" section speaks primarily to novice traders, and is well worth the read.

Stocks & Commodities does a great job of explaining various indicators and how to use them, among other topics. It also gives sector (industry) reviews and interviews industry gurus.

SFO Magazine features a wide range of topics that delve into global and economic issues. It also includes educational, "how to" articles geared to traders and investors.

Of course, a host of magazines geared to investors and the U.S. business world line the newsstand shelves. Most are treasure troves of educational material, but because of the time lag between the writing and go-to-press dates, these periodicals are not to be depended on for short-term buy/sell decisions.

CHECK YOUR UNDERSTANDING

1. Price is the consensus on a stock in a single moment.
2. Fundamental analysis and technical analysis are the two major methods of examining a publicly traded company to determine the financial health of its stock.
3. Fundamental analysts study supply and demand levels of the products and/ or services the company produces. They also study company reports, profit and loss summaries, price-to-earnings (P/E) ratios (calculated by dividing the stock's price by its earnings-per-share figure), market share, sales and growth, and brokerage analyst ratings.
4. Technical analysis is the study of time, price, and volume of a chosen equity (or market or index) as shown on charts.
5. Investor's Business Daily (IBD) newspaper provides proprietary ratings that give you a quick and reliable snapshot of corporate fundamentals.
6. CNBC and Bloomberg television networks are used as great overall global and market resources and to stay aware of market sentiment. As a rule, though, refrain from basing single trades on network announcements.
7. Active Trader, Stocks & Commodities, and SFO Magazine are great educational tools for short-term traders and active investors.

CENTER POINT: INVITE SPONTANEITY INTO YOUR LIFE

"Not life, but good life, is to be chiefly valued."

—Socrates

The stock market is a rigid mistress. Those who meet with success in her playground must proceed each day armed with exacting guidelines and principles, a structured mindset, and unyielding discipline. Human traits including optimism, hope, and spontaneity must be avoided at all times.

Once we leave the market arena, however, it's important to rebalance and refresh the way we look at the world. To that end, we can shift our perspectives and mindsets to the opposite end of the emotional spectrum, and invite spontaneity into our world.

Spontaneity means to take action on the spur of the moment, just because it promises to be an enjoyable experience. The actual experience may even turn out differently than you imagined it might, but that's part of the enjoyment. Besides, impulsive actions can produce surprising results that change your life for the better!

If you act spontaneously, and especially if those around you don't expect it, you may be labeled as irresponsible. Good! Wouldn't you rather be the one experiencing the adventure, rather than those who stayed behind and gossiped about it?

We all know "higher-ups" who get stuck on their thrones, and miss out on the laughter, pleasure, and sometimes heightened productivity that result from spontaneity. They march through their lives with ramrod backs, noses held high, and blinders in place. When presented with a new suggestion, their retort is, "We've never done it that way before, and we're not changing things now."

On the flip side, what do you want to wager that the zipper, the paper clip, and the Hula-Hoop flew out of nowhere to zap their open-minded inventors with a spontaneous bolt of genius?

We spoke in an earlier Center Point of the "masks" we wear that disguise our inner light. Spontaneity chips off those masks and reveals the true spirit of lightheartedness that's layered just beneath.

Just for laughs, indulge yourself in a spontaneous act, or two (three?), this week. Grab the phone and call someone you haven't talked to in years. Jump up from your desk in the middle of the day and take a fast walk around the block. Better yet, call in sick and take someone you love on a day trip. Invite one of your kids to go to a Disney movie. Tell someone who doesn't expect it how much you respect them and appreciate their support.

Remember, sometimes acts of spontaneity produce unexpected blessings that last a lifetime!

CHAPTER 5

Market Machinations 102: Cycles as the Foundation of Technical Analysis

"My plan of trading was sound enough and won oftener than it lost. If I had stuck to it I'd have been right perhaps as often as seven out of ten times."

—Jesse Livermore

Chapter 4 showed you where to find quick yet comprehensive fundamental information. Now, it's time to begin learning the basics of technical analysis. I realize that the term "technical analysis" intimidates the bejeepers out of most people. Taken one step at a time, however, the subject matter is not as daunting as it sounds.

Keep this in mind: The moment you start absorbing the charting essentials in this chapter and those that follow, you will be way ahead of most market players—and on your way to earning consistent trading profits.

First, let's take a quick look at how cycles play a role in the way the financial markets pulsate through time.

CYCLES: THE WORLD'S OPERATING SYSTEM

Our world, indeed our universe, operates on a system of cycles. The earth, along with her sister planets, orbits around the sun. A complete orbit completes a cycle, which we refer to as a "year."

Predictable weather patterns create four seasons within that year, each with its own cycle. Tides flow in and out on exact cycles. Humans and all living creatures experience cycles of life, including birth, childhood, puberty, adulthood, and passing on.

Industrialized economies progress through cycles of expansion, peaking, trough, and expansion again. It follows then that the major industries propelling those economies pass through four phases during their existence: introduction, growth, maturity, and decline. Those industries consist of several companies; the prices of the securities issued by those companies tend to anticipate business cycles. That's why the stock market cycle leads the business cycle by approximately three to six months.

When you look at a stock chart, especially a long-term chart that encompasses a time span of several years (Figure 5-1), you can observe its price history and the cycles—or series of peaks and troughs—that it's completed.

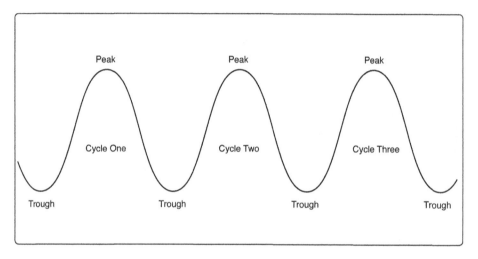

FIGURE 5-1. Economic cycles.

If you observe a monthly or weekly chart, where each bar or candlestick (we discuss candlestick charts in Chapter 6) represents one month or one week, respectively, you can see a stock's price history for an extended duration of time, such as five to ten years. Although the price cycles may not form as uniformly as those drawn in Figure 5-1, they will still etch a bell curve, or cycle formation, consisting of peaks and valleys, or troughs.

These cycles take place from the macrocosm to the microcosm. Each large cycle consists of many smaller cycles, and each small cycle is formed by a sequence of even tinier cycles.

Here's an analogy: This book is made of many chapters. Within each chapter are separate sections that, when strung together, create that chapter. The sections are made of a series of paragraphs; the paragraphs are built of sentences, which are formed by words. Each word, sentence, paragraph, and section is a complete unit in and of itself. And, when looked at as a whole, they form the complete book.

You will find complete cycles occurring on monthly, weekly, daily, and intraday stock charts, where one bar or candlestick may represent a time frame of one month, one week, or one day. On intraday time frames, each bar or candlestick designates a certain period of time, such as sixty minutes, thirty minutes, five minutes, one minute, or any increment in between.

HOW CYCLES MOVE: BASIC STAGE ANALYSIS

A "close-up" of a cycle, whatever the time frame, reveals that it's constructed of four different movements, or stages. We call the study of these stages "stage analysis."

When you learn how to identify which of the four price stages (Figure 5-2) your target stock currently inhabits, you've made the first step to keeping your losses small and your profits large.

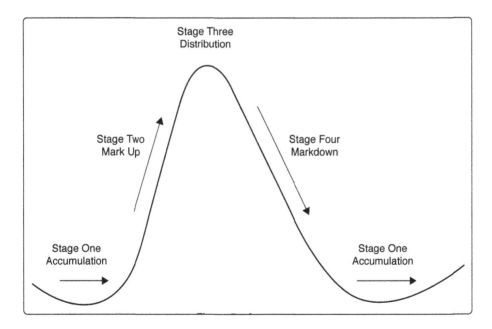

FIGURE 5-2. Four stages of a cycle.

Stage 1 represents the valley, or trough, of the cycle. This is when the stock prices are at their lows of the cycle. During these times—which on weekly and daily charts could last from weeks to months—the stock price moves sideways in a range between an approximate high and low price, and increments in between. You'll hear gurus and analysts talk about a stock in Stage 1 as "basing." That means the stock is forming a new price base from which it will (sooner or later) start to rise again.

What is the collective mindset of market players participating in a Stage 1? *Indecision*. Buyers support the price up each time it falls to the bottom of the base's price range, and sellers push it down each time it rises to the top of the base's price range. Equal pressure from buyers and sellers cause the stock to oscillate sideways, sort of like a snake swiveling through a drainage pipe.

When the stock bases for a period of time new buyers will come in, responding to market conditions, industry rotation, or good fundamentals. A portion of these buyers may be institutional buyers, meaning portfolio managers and fund managers. Thus Stage 1 also becomes the "Accumulation" stage. As strong volume gives the stock momentum to the upside, more buyers step in and agree to pay higher prices.

When price "breaks out" of its base and shoots into an uptrend, or Stage 2, the collective mindset is optimism. This mild form of greed creates more and more demand, which absorbs supply and drives the stock higher. As long as it remains in Stage 2, which we also call the "mark up," price rises, then pulls back, then rises again, riding on the wings of optimism and finally euphoria.

Finally, at its peak, buyers refuse to continue paying higher prices, and the uptrend slows to a halt. Euphoria and demand dissipate. Supply increases as worried stockholders put their shares on the market to avoid a loss. Stage 2 is broken, and the stock drifts sideways into a Stage 3.

During Stage 3, which forms into the peak of the cycle, buyers support the price when it falls. Sellers press the price down when it rises. The bulls and bears engage in an emotional tug-of-war, which can cause extreme price volatility.

We also call Stage 3 "distribution." Institutional money may decide the stock has run as far as it's going to at the present time, and consider it overpriced. If they start dumping shares on the market, they are "distributing" stock. This dose of supply pushes price lower. Now, fear steps in. (If it doesn't, and the stock breaks out to new highs, it resumes a Stage 2.)

When increased selling pressure becomes evident, buyers refuse to support the stock any longer. Result: The stock tumbles into a downtrend, into a Stage 4.

Now the stock "heads south." In a Stage 4, the stock dives to lower prices, rebounds a bit, and then dives again (think: "rubber rock"). Supply floods the market, as fear goads terrified sellers into unloading their long positions.

The only happy campers who hold a Stage 4 stock are short-sellers. As you may remember, short-sellers sell the stock at a high price. Then, they buy it back at a lower price and pocket the difference as profit. (We'll go into selling short later.)

Stage 4 is also the place where frustrated investors, who are watching their stocks tank and their principal shrink, "average down" by buying more of the losing issue.

Because averaging down lowers the average price paid for the stock, their fervent hope is that when the stock rebounds, losses will recoup faster.

Maybe. Maybe not. Some beat-up stocks stay down for the count, or at least for weeks and months. Hanging on to these supposed "Blue Light Specials" ties up money that could be spent on a strong stock that makes money. We sometimes call capital invested in such issues "dead money."

Since we're on this subject, if you have the "averaging down" mentality, please ditch it. There's a correct way to average down that's based on sound money-management principles; then there's the desperate averaging down method that usually leads to bigger losses. In the pages that follow, you'll learn how to average down properly.

When stocks experience a Stage 4, you're better off to stand on the sidelines, cash in hand, while others hold losers or run screaming to the door. Then, when the selling is over, you can step in and buy high-quality bargains that are ready to recover.

At some point, a stock in a Stage 4 will slow its descent. Hot and furious selling evaporates, and buyers start stepping up to the plate. Now the stock turns back into a sideways, basing pattern—a Stage 1—and the cycle begins anew.

DIFFERENT STAGES CALL FOR DIFFERENT REACTIONS

With a little practice looking at charts, you'll start to recognize which stage of a cycle a stock is experiencing. This in turn will initiate your selection process for buying stocks.

We use Stage 1 to scan for stocks that are currently creating a base. The best bases are those that take four to eight weeks to form. Again, these basing stocks are in the first stage of a new cycle, and usually coincide with a market or industry correction. This is when a stock is "on sale." We monitor stocks in Stage 1, and when (if) they break out of their base, if all other conditions of our criteria are met, we enter a position.

Stage 2 is where you, as a short-term trader, will spend most of your time and make most of your profits. When you're position trading, or want to buy a stock for a core trade, you spot a stock breaking out of a solid Stage 1 base into a Stage 2 uptrend. You buy it and ride it for weeks to months, taking profits when it completes its entire Stage 2 uptrend.

HOT TIP

As a general rule, stocks fall three times faster than they rise. Why? Fear is stronger than greed. Panic causes traders and investors to sell even more quickly than optimism entices them to buy.

If you opt to swing trade, you play Stage 2 by buying the breakouts and selling before the stock pulls back, taking multiple-point profits out of 2- to 5-day holds. With practice, you may decide to do a combination of both position trading and swing trading. This is a great method for capturing optimum profits.

When a stock rolls over into a Stage 3, we stand aside. During this stage, price patterns tend toward the volatile and unpredictable, and a stock may lurch sideways in a haphazard pattern. It's risky to hold a Stage 3 stock overnight—or for any length of time.

Again, stocks that fall into a Stage 4 are doomed to suffer lower and lower prices. There are two ways to treat a stock in a Stage 4 downtrend.

Sell Short

First, if you are relatively new to the stock market and have no prejudices against selling short, that's good news. When you arrive at Chapter 12, which talks about shorting, you'll want to thoroughly study the information presented there to maximize your profits. Or, perhaps you've been in the market for a while and already realize the profit potential in selling high and buying low. You may even hedge your account by selling short.

Avoid Trading

The second way to approach a stock in a Stage 4 downtrend is to avoid it completely. If shorting a stock—or even the thought of it—makes you break into a sweat, then sidestep stocks in crash and burn mode. During times when major market indexes plummet to new lows, as they did in the bear market of 2000–2002 (and as some indices are doing in 2008), you can keep the majority of your assets in cash, hedge, or diversify with ETFs.

One of the most important lessons any trader or any investor can learn is when to stay out of the market altogether. Remember, when you stand on the sidelines—that's a position!

HOT TIP

While a stock in a Stage 3 price pattern experiences the same basic movement as a Stage 1, the length of time that a stock stays in a Stage 3 can be much briefer, and is usually much more volatile. Emotions run higher in a Stage 3, where the bulls keep buying to defend their "territory," and the bears sell every bounce to drive the stock lower.

ADDITIONAL CYCLE COMPONENTS

Now that we've identified the stages inherent in cycles, let's zoom in even closer to analyze the action.

In the illustration that follows (Figure 5-3), you can see motivating factors in each stage. (Keep in mind that it takes many cycles to form the larger stages and cycles.) It's interesting to note that while a stock experiencing a Stage 2 uptrend on a daily chart may be soaring on the wings of optimism, greed, and euphoria, a glance at an intraday chart may reveal short-term intraday price action—not apparent on a daily chart—where apprehension and outright panic prevail.

Aside from emotions, Figure 5-3 also shows various levels of supply and demand. As discussed in Chapter 1, greed and fear act as precursors to these two dynamics.

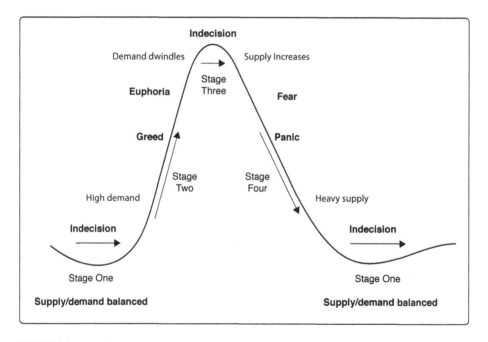

FIGURE 5-3. Supply/demand cycle.

In Stage 1, indecision causes supply and demand for a stock to alternate in the short term, pushing it sideways. When optimism (mild greed) triggers a stock to break out of a Stage 1 into a Stage 2, hunger for the stock at that price causes increasing demand. The greed amplifies as more and more buyers absorb all available stock (supply) at each higher price level.

HOT TIP

Swing and position traders who stare at intraday charts of their holdings many times get "shaken out" of their positions early. A better plan: Once you're in a trade, enter an automatic, trailing stop order with your broker. Then, check the stock's progress at intervals during the trading day.

When the price gets "frothy," or "toppy," at the height of a Stage 2, demand will shrink as increased supply, provided by sellers taking profits, arrives in the marketplace.

As the stock rolls over into a Stage 3, indecision reigns again. Just as in Stage 1, supply and demand remains in relative balance, although volatile, roller coaster–like price swings are the norm.

Sooner or later, buyers turn their backs on a Stage 3 stock and decide to take profits. Supply floods the market. When no one steps in to buy, these buyers-turned-sellers must lower their prices to attract new buyers.

This initiates a Stage 4. Now, apprehension turns to fear, causing even more sellers to join the ranks, which pushes more and more supply onto the market at each lower price level. Just as greed initiates demand, so does fear initiate supply. It becomes a self-perpetuating action and reaction.

Finally, when the falling price reaches a support area established weeks, months, or even years before (as seen on a weekly or daily chart), supply begins to be absorbed by tentative buyers. As these bulls continue to buy up the supply, the stock ceases making lower lows. Selling volume dries up, and buyers start to step in. Supply and demand even out, and the stock reverts to a Stage 1 to begin a new cycle.

Figures 5-4 through 5-7 show daily, weekly and/or monthly charts (each candle represents one day, one week, or one month, respectively) of stocks that have made complete cycles. Check out how fear and greed incite supply and demand to drive stock prices up and down.

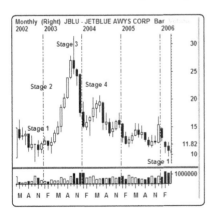

FIGURE 5-4. JetBlue (JBLU) monthly cycle. RealTick by Townsend Analytics. Here's a very straightforward, yet drawn-out cycle in JetBlue (JBLU). The monthly chart takes roughly 3.5 years to complete, but conforms very well to the four-stage cycle by the time it finds Stage 1 support from its prior lows. Notice, too, how quickly the Stage 4 top forms and how well the overall pattern conforms to the bell-curve shape to complete the four cycles.

FIGURE 5-5. Autodesk (ADSK) weekly cycle. RealTick by Townsend Analytics. This chart shows a weekly cycle of Autodesk (ADSK). The stock also shows the familiar bell-curve shape in completing the four cycles. However, notice its more volatile personality as compared to the monthly chart pattern of JetBlue. By volatile personality, we're referring to the more jagged movements within its stages. This is very apparent as ADSK moves abruptly from a Stage 3 top and continues to move with volatile behavior throughout Stage 4.

FIGURE 5-6A. Empire Resources (ERS) daily cycle. RealTick by Townsend Analytics. This name might be a bit less familiar to some, but for growth stock traders, Empire Resources (ERS) is certainly a memorable stock. This issuer of semi-finished aluminum products vaulted up *IBD*'s 100 list to the number one spot during early 2006, only to fall back into obscurity and off the radars of the momentum/growth crowd as the stock's price pattern created a very steep and quick cycle completion. It's also a great example of how smaller capitalization issues do adhere to the same principles as their larger capitalized peers. However, price moves can be lightning fast. In this instance see how Stage 3 turns into a Stage 4 downswing after only one session. It's a great example of how important it is to set protective stop orders soon after you enter a trade!

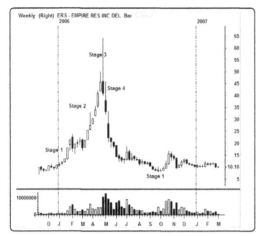

FIGURE 5-6B. Empire Resources (ERS) weekly cycle. RealTick by Townsend Analytics. This weekly chart of Empire Resources (ERS), in which every candle represents one week, shows how cycles move on a long-term basis.

FIGURE 5-7. Google (GOOG) daily cycle. Real-Tick by Townsend Analytics. Many traders are well versed by now in Google's (GOOG) heady price swings. The Internet search engine behemoth has a very large stock price. It's also a "darling" of institutional traders (brokers, portfolio managers, and hedge fund managers), who have fat wallets. Together, this indicates a combination of factors likely to shift the crowd's perception and their buy and sell efforts at lightning speed. With that said, look how uniform Google can be when adhering to the cycle principle.

SUPPORT AND RESISTANCE, OR ACTION AND REACTION

Now we're going to add the final, yet mega-important components to the cycles: support and resistance. These two factors are the result of the interaction between fear and greed and supply and demand. Recognizing how they all work together, both in the short and long term, is like appreciating a magnificent, orchestrated dance. It also gives you an enormous advantage in the world of trading and investing.

As you read, keep this statement in the forefront of your mind: for every action, there is a reaction.

Support and resistance will form the foundation for every trading decision. You can trade without oscillators and indicators and moving averages. You can even eliminate charts altogether from your financial decisions (although I wouldn't recommend it). But even floor traders in the pits mentally compute where price resistance and support lie, even as they shout and use hand signals (called "open outcry") to get their orders filled.

The concept behind support and resistance is a simple one, and once you digest it, you will have absorbed the basic premise underlying market moves.

I used the following analogy in my previous book, *A Beginner's Guide to Day Trading Online, 2nd Edition*. We'll use it again now, because it gives such a clear image of support and resistance in action.

Picture this: You're standing in the living room of a house, on the first floor. In your hands, you hold a ball. This ball equals the price of a stock. You toss the ball over your head. It soars upward, and hits the ceiling. The ceiling keeps it from rising higher, so the ceiling equals resistance. Now, the ball falls back down and bounces on the floor. The floor stops it from falling further, so the floor equals support.

Next, you spot a hole in the ceiling. You throw the ball as hard as you can, and it flies through a large hole in the ceiling. It sails up to the second-story ceiling and hits it. That ceiling equals resistance. Then, the ball falls to bounce on the second-story floor, which now forms support. Understand that the first-story ceiling supports the second-story floor. Result? Resistance becomes support.

Continue by running upstairs and grabbing the ball. Throw it back down the hole, down into the first-story living room. When it drops through the hole in the floor, it breaks through support. It falls to bounce on the living room floor, or previous support.

Then, it rises to hit the ceiling, or previous resistance.

Run back down the stairs. Take the ball and toss it through a hole in the floor. The ball descends to the basement floor, which forms support. Then, it rises to the basement ceiling. That stops the balls bounce, because that ceiling acts as resistance. Just above the basement is the living room floor, which formerly provided support. So now, previous support forms resistance.

Figure 5-8 illustrates support and resistance. You'll see support and resistance (buying and selling pressure) form on *every time frame*, from minutes to years.

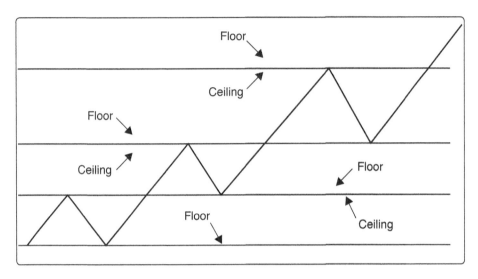

FIGURE 5-8. Support and resistance. When the ball, which we'll now think of as a stock price, bounces off of support or resistance, we refer to it as a pivot point (Figure 5-9). In technical analysis, a "pivot high" is established when price makes a new high that remains higher than the pivots just prior and just after it. A "pivot low" is created when price hits a new low that is lower than the pivots established just prior to, and just after it.

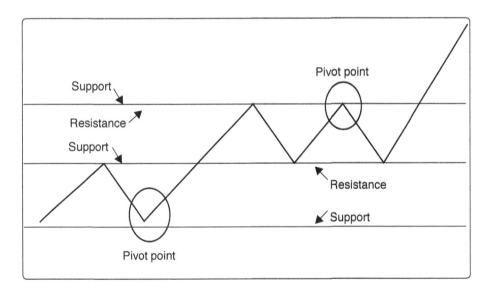

FIGURE 5-9. Pivot points.

As you study support and resistance, remember, they are *price areas,* or *zones.* You will have to find a specific price to refer to, for example $54, but give it a little leeway.

Imagine yourself jumping on a trampoline. The trampoline supports you when you land on it, but the depth of your bounce varies a little each time. Also, just as heavier people stretch the trampoline base lower when they land, more volatile stocks need a little extra latitude in their resistance and support areas.

Since you now know what support and resistance look like, let's quickly find out how they actually form.

Go back to imagining the ball bouncing from floor to ceiling in the basement. Now, apply that to a stock in a Stage 1, or basing price pattern. The basement floor is support, and we call it that because buyers are supporting the price. Were it to start lower, buyers (greed + demand) step in and accumulate, thus keeping the price from sinking lower.

When the price rises to the basement ceiling, it hits resistance. Resistance equals buyers who jam their hands in their pockets and refuse to pay a higher price for the stock. Resistance also indicates supply. At this point, some previous buyers, as mentioned before, revert into sellers. Afraid (fearing) the stock will rise no higher, they offer their stock for sale, thus flooding the market with supply. If the stock falls here, the next time it rises to return to this price area, it may sell off again. The reason? We humans have memories.

Say the stock shoots through the resistance (supply is absorbed). Maybe the sector it inhabits is in a favorable spotlight, the bulls are in control of the market, or the company itself enjoys a spurt of good news. The price will continue to rocket—maybe for hours or days—until a new factor suppresses it. When it "sells off," that pivot point creates fresh resistance. The stock then falls to the earlier resistance area, which is now the "floor," or support. It will hold there if buyers absorb the supply, and in so doing, "support" it.

Support and resistance levels apply on every chart you'll ever see, whatever the time frame. In fact, you may have guessed by now that nearly all the applications you'll learn about charts hold true on all time frames. That means the concepts you find in these pages pertain not only to swing and position trading, but also to styles such as active trading and investing.

Figures 5-10, 5-11, and 5-12 show support and resistance areas on a weekly chart, a daily chart, and a 15-minute intraday chart. As you study these charts and observe support and resistance levels, you may be amazed at how accurate these levels are when price comes back to retest them.

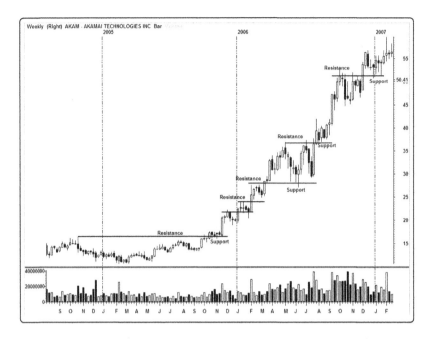

FIGURE 5-10. Akamai (AKAM) weekly cycle. RealTick by Townsend Analytics. This weekly chart of Akamai (AKAM) shows a stock well into Stage 2 by the early part of 2007. Notice how well the stock consistently uses prior resistance as an area of support on price pullbacks within the rising trend.

FIGURE 5-11. Toll Brothers (TOL) daily Stage 4 support/resistance. RealTick by Townsend Analytics. Notice in this Stage 4 downtrend how support, once broken, becomes overhead resistance. You can see the resistance in action as both holders of long stock and short-sellers act as supply (selling) and effectively push Toll Brothers lower.

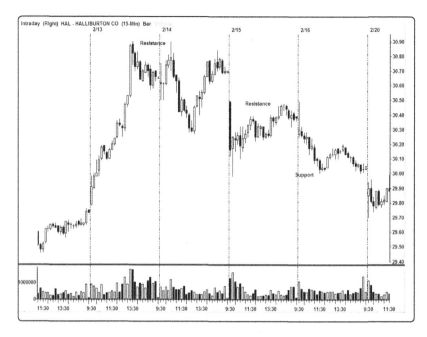

FIGURE 5-12. Halliburton (HAL) 15-minute cycle with support/resistance. RealTick by Townsend Analytics. As this 15-minute chart of Halliburton (HAL) shows, price patterns on all time frames move in cycles and thus encounter support and resistance zones. In this case we're looking at a 15-minute chart spread across four days of trading. Notice how an early retest of the prior highs on February 14 served as resistance, setting up a confirmation for Stage 4. Look at how prior highs and lows act as both resistance and support within the downtrending price action.

From this chapter on, you'll find a quiz at the conclusion of each chapter. Remember, in the high-stakes game of trading, the more knowledge you bring with you to the market, the more money you'll make. Here's your chance to find what you've absorbed, as well as points you may want to review.

HOT TIP

When a stock pivots off of a support or resistance level three times or more, we call that "major support" or "major resistance."

QUIZ
IIIIIIIIIIIIII

1. Name the different stages in a typical stock price cycle, and describe in which direction each stage moves.
2. Specify the collective mindset that applies to each stage.
3. True or False? The trading method known as "averaging down" is the best way to recoup your losses when you're holding onto a falling stock.
4. Briefly name options available to short-term traders in each stage of a stock's cycle.
5. Which emotion fuels supply—greed or fear? Which one fuels demand?
6. Referring to the "ball bouncing between the floor and ceiling" analogy, what does the floor represent—support or resistance? Which of the two does the ceiling represent?
7. Continuing with the same analogy, when the ball soars through a hole in the ceiling and bounces on the floor above, what does that depict on a stock chart? What if the ball drops through the floor, then bounces up to hit the ceiling?
8. What denotes major resistance or support?
9. What is a "pivot point"?
10. Define a "pivot high." Define a "pivot low."
11. True or False? Support and resistance levels apply on every chart, regardless of the time frame.

Answers
1. Four stages create a stock's price cycle. Stage 1 forms in a horizontal, or basing, movement. Stage 2 represents the uptrend. Stage 3 is the peak, or topping action, in which the stock moves sideways. Stage 4 is the downtrend. When the downtrend ends and the stock turns up again, it initiates a Stage 1 and the cycle repeats itself.
2. The collective mindset in a Stage 1: indecision. Stage 2: greed. Stage 3: indecision. Stage 4: fear.
3. Very big False!
4. Stage 1: We monitor stocks in this basing action, ready to spot a buying opportunity when they break into a Stage 2 uptrend. Stage 2: As swing and position traders, we spend most of our time playing stocks in a Stage 2; we work the uptrend, with the intention of grabbing multiple-point profits. Stage 3: We avoid stocks experiencing this stage. Stage 4: We either take advantage of short-selling strategies, or stand aside until the stock assumes a more positive price pattern.

5. Fear fuels supply. Greed fuels demand.

6. Floor represents support. Ceiling represents resistance.

7. Prior resistance becomes support. Prior support becomes resistance.

8. Major resistance or support is noted when a stock bounces off a support or resistance area three times, or more.

9. Basically, a "pivot point" is when a stock price reverses direction.

10. A "pivot high" is established when price makes a new high that remains higher than the pivots just prior and just after it. A "pivot low" is created when price hits a new low that is lower than the pivots established just prior to, and just after it.

11. True.

CENTER POINT: DEVELOP A PROSPERITY MINDSET

"Seek not proud riches, but such as thou mayest get justly, use soberly, distribute cheerfully, and leave contentedly."

—Francis Bacon

Believe it or not, we each create our own financial picture. How we think and feel about our financial affairs determines our experience with them.

When we first encounter it, this is a difficult concept to grasp. It's far easier to blame someone else or outside circumstances for the lack in our lives. The truth is, "as within, so without." The image we hold of ourselves and our financial situation is reflected onto our external world.

Let's check out this premise. Do you entertain thoughts like these? *There's always too much month left at the end of the money. I have to grab mine before someone else does. Opportunity probably won't knock on my door. It never does.*

HOT TIP

When a pivot is higher than the pivot directly prior to it and directly after it, we call the high pivot a "pivot high," or a "relative high." It follows that when a pivot is lower than the pivot directly prior to it and directly after it, we call the low pivot a "pivot low," or a "relative low."

If you take time to rethink these statements, they all focus on scarcity. They define a world of lack and shortages.

Since we receive what we focus on, when we dwell and speak about scarcity and lack, that's exactly what we produce.

Conversely, we attract abundance and prosperity into our lives when we discard thoughts of lack and limitation and replace them with statements like: *I have everything I need right now to experience abundant prosperity.*

True affluence requires us to live from the inside out. When we accept that we are complete right now, and when we develop an inner knowing that limitless abundance can be ours just like the air we breathe, then we discover that everything we need and desire is within our reach. We can draw it to us like a magnet, using our consciousness, our beliefs, and our actions.

We cannot control global events, or the stock market, or the behavior of those around us. We can, however, command our own thoughts. The minute we truly know that we have within us the potential to prosper and succeed in all areas of our lives, then innovative ideas, resourcefulness, and opportunities will appear!

CHAPTER 6

Jump-Start on Chart Basics

"If a stock doesn't act right don't touch it; because, being unable to tell precisely what is wrong, you cannot tell which way it is going. No diagnosis, no prognosis. No prognosis, no profit."

—Jesse Livermore

You know how each one of your friends has a different personality? So do stocks! Just as some of your friends are quiet and dependable, some stocks—mostly those listed on the NYSE—move in mostly polite, conservative price patterns. I think of Goodyear Tire (GT) and the Monsanto Co. (MON) in that way. Mild-mannered stocks typically move in single-digit price increases or decreases during the course of a day, and so move through their cycles in measured, orderly paces.

In contrast, do you have friends who are moody, and you never know from one day to the next which frame of mind they're going to exhibit? I call stocks that mimic this behavior "sleeping manics." Residing on either the NYSE or NASDAQ, they can nap for days, weeks, or even months, then snort themselves awake and explode into action.

Still other stocks continually bounce up and down all over their charts, resembling kangaroos on steroids. Most of these stocks thrive on the NASDAQ, represent growth (versus value) stocks, and are referred to by pundits as "high-flyers."

Many of these stocks behave in wild and crazy patterns. I think of them like friends who act in a similar manner—you can't rely on them. Yes, they're fun to spend time with occasionally, but if you hang out with them for any length of time, they drive you bonkers.

When you learn to analyze a chart with a trained, discerning eye, it won't take long before you'll be adept at assessing the setup's risk/reward, and thus moneymaking possibilities of any stock you choose.

One glance at a chart will show you whether a stock has an orderly or erratic personality. And from now on, the operative word is *orderly*. Memorize it, set it to music, and write it on the back of your hand. From this day forward, for our purposes of trading multi-day and multi-week holds, we will focus on stocks that exhibit orderly price personalities.

Disorderly stocks are undependable; they exhibit little or no follow-through. Playing an erratic stock skyrockets the risk involved and greatly diminishes odds of a reward. That's called "gambling." Traders who gamble have short trading careers.

Orderly, more predictable stocks may be boring to monitor and trade, but a low risk/high reward setup aligns itself with our goal to take consistent profits out of the market. And I think you'll agree that consistent profits are never boring.

CHARTING ESSENTIALS: LINE CHARTS AND BAR CHARTS

Technical analysts use three types of charts: line charts, bar charts, and candlestick charts.

Line Charts

Line charts typically connect a stock's or index's closing price into a single line, during a designated period of time.

For example, look at Figure 6-1. The daily line chart of Bear Sterns (BSC) illustrates the daily closing prices of that issue from August 2006 to February 2007, drawn into a single line.

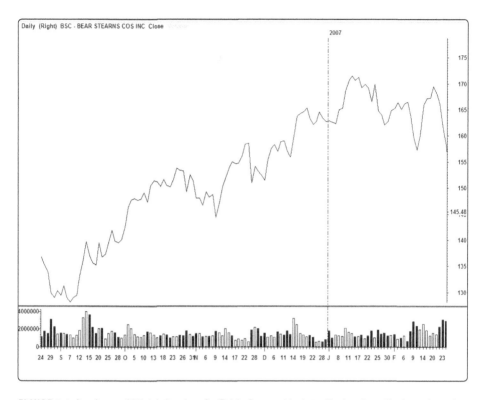

FIGURE 6-1. Bear Stearns (BSC) daily line chart. RealTick by Townsend Analytics. This line chart of brokerage house Bear Stearns (BSC) illustrates the closing daily prices connected by a single line, from late August 2006 to the tail end of February 2007.

Line charts are handy for comparing stocks to other stocks or indexes, such as the benchmark S&P 500. If you overlay a related index over your stock's chart—such as the biotech index (BTK) over a chart of Amgen, Inc. (AMGN)—you can instantly measure the stock's strength as compared to the overall industry group where it resides, as indicated in a single, straightforward line.

Many chart indicators, especially overbought/oversold oscillators, are customarily displayed as line charts. We'll discuss those in Chapter 8.

Bar Charts

Bar charts use single, vertical bars to illustrate a stock's price range and opening/closing prices for a designated time period. Figure 6-2 displays the same daily chart of Bear Stearns (BSC), but this time it is shown as a bar chart. Because it is a daily chart, each bar represents a single day's price activity in BSC's history.

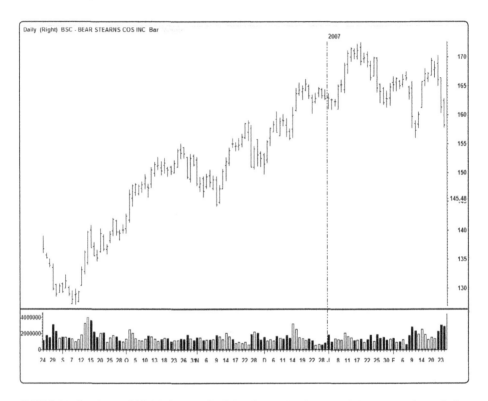

FIGURE 6-2. Bear Stearns (BSC) daily bar chart. RealTick by Townsend Analytics. Here's the exact price history for Bear Stearns (BSC) shown in Figure 6-1. However, this time the price action is shown by using a daily bar chart.

Figure 6-3 interprets the components of a single price bar. The top of the bar indicates the stock's "high," or the highest price for the day. In this case, we're using the price high of 50. The bottom of the bar represents the stock's lowest price for that period; in this illustration, 40. The small, perpendicular bar on the left designates the stock's opening price (42). The one on the right shows the stock's closing price (48).

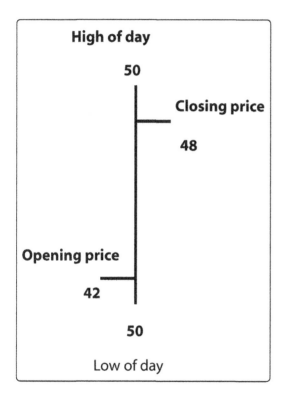

FIGURE 6-3. Single bar.

Although some traditional technical analysts still prefer bar charts, most have switched to candlestick charts. For the remainder of this book, we're going to use candlestick charts. They definitely shine more light on the subject.

CANDLESTICK CHARTING BASICS

We owe a debt of thanks to a legendary seventeenth-century Japanese rice broker, Munehisa Homma, who was one of the first Japanese traders to use price history to predict price future. Referred to as "the god of the markets," Homma amassed a huge fortune. Legend tells us he made 100 consecutive winning trades.

Homma's trading theories and principles evolved into the candlestick charting techniques we use today.

Candlestick guru Steve Nison, president of CandleCharts.com (*www .candlecharts.com*) who wrote the foreword to this book, earns our applause for bringing this ancient and highly effective technique to the United States, and indeed much of the rest of the world. I highly recommend Nison's books, *Japanese Candlestick Charting Techniques* and *Beyond Candlesticks: More Japanese Charting Techniques Revealed* as thorough, reader-friendly texts that explain candlestick charting in depth.

Basic Candlestick Patterns

We're going to explore some important candlestick patterns that, when interpreted properly, can produce winning trades. For example, Figure 6-4 is the previously shown chart of Bear Stearns (BSC), this time in candlestick form.

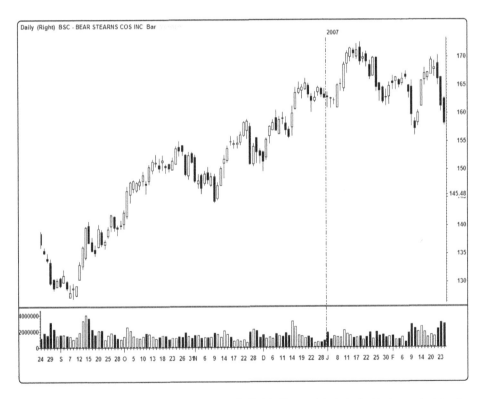

FIGURE 6-4. Bear Stearns (BSC) daily candlestick chart. RealTick by Townsend Analytics. In this chart, we've taken the same price history for Bear Stearns (BSC) one step further by using candlesticks. You can see how the same price information produces more impact and meaning for technicians when candlesticks are used.

Just as a bar chart uses the top and bottom of its bar to indicate high and low prices of the time frame indicated, so does a candlestick. With candlesticks, however, we draw in a "real body" to connect the opening and closing prices. This gives us a quick and complete picture of the stock's action and displays prevailing sentiment.

Candlestick patterns indicate that a change in the direction of a trend may be imminent. That means that a stock in an uptrend/downtrend could begin moving sideways, or it could make a U-turn.

The real body shows the opening and closing prices with a white, or a dark, rectangle. The bar that extends above and below the real body is called the upper and lower "shadow."

When the rectangle or real body is white, it means that the stock closed above its opening price. When the real body is dark, it means that the stock closed below its opening price.

These white/dark real bodies give you an instant picture of a positive or negative close. Those of us who stare at charts for hours at a time find that candlesticks are not only easy on the eyes, but they also convey strong signals sometimes missed on bar charts.

Please note: From now on, "candlestick" and "candle" will be used as interchangeable terms.

Figure 6-5 shows basic candlestick formations.

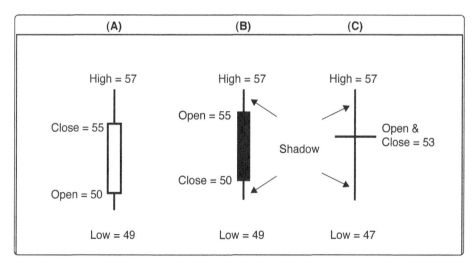

FIGURE 6-5. Basic candlestick formations. In (A), the candle opens at 50, closes at 55, with a high of 57 and a low of 49. In (B), the candle opens at 55, closes at 50, and again has a high of 57 and low of 49. In (C), the candle opens and closes at 53, with the same high and low.

Candlesticks, like bars, each represent a specified time frame. For example, on a weekly chart, each candlestick represents one week; on a daily chart, each candlestick represents one day; and on a 15-minute intraday chart, each candlestick represents a 15-minute unit of time.

Now, notice the long, clear real body in formation (A) in Figure 6-5. The long, clear real body, showing the closing price multiple points above the opening price (in this case, 5 points), indicates extremely positive or bullish sentiment. In (B), the long, dark real body, with the closing price multiple points below the open, reveals negative or bearish sentiment.

Note (C) in Figure 6-5. This formation, where the stock opens and closes at the same price (or very close to it), is called a "doji." Also, please note that the plural of "doji" is "doji." With a doji, no real body is present. Because buyers could not apply enough bullish pressure to close the stock higher than the open, and sellers could not force enough bearish pressure to close the stock lower than the open, it reveals a collective mindset of indecision.

Please memorize the doji. It is a very important candlestick, as it many times presages a shift in, or even a reversal of, a current trend. As short-term traders, we need to stay on top of trend changes and reversals at all times. Why? Because these changes in momentum act as our most valuable entry, exit, and money-management signals.

Candlestick reversal patterns can be read alone, but are extremely powerful when used in conjunction with other charting indicators. Therefore, key patterns are detailed in the next few pages. In the chapters that follow, you'll learn how to combine them with other indicators to recognize buy and sell signals.

Single Candle Patterns

The doji is a single candle pattern. The candlesticks illustrated in Figure 6-6 are also single candle patterns known as the hammer and the hanging man. Their real bodies are small, and can be either clear or dark. Their lower shadows should be twice the length of the real body. They should have "shaven heads," meaning that no (or short) upper shadows protrude from the real body.

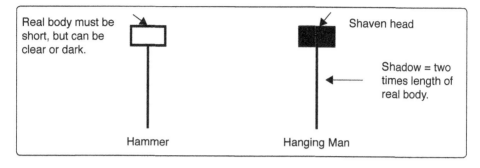

FIGURE 6-6. Hammer and hanging man.

When you see a hammer form in the context of a downtrend, it may signify that the downtrend will slow and change direction by moving sideways or reversing to move upward. Think: Hammer it back up. The next candle's formation will tell you whether or not the hammer is a true reversal signal.

If a hanging man appears in an uptrend, the connotation is evident right away. Still, you'll have to wait for the next candle to form before the signal is established. When/if the subsequent candle confirms that the hanging man is valid, take partial/all profits. Figure 6-7 illustrates these two patterns.

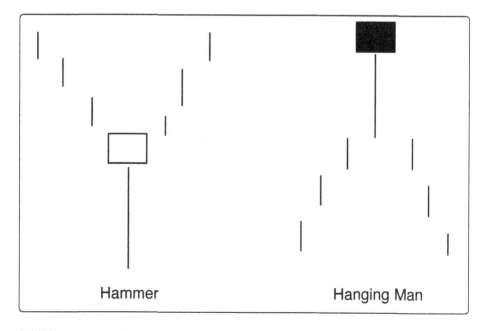

FIGURE 6-7. Hammer and hanging man as reversal signals.

Two-Candle Patterns

The next pattern that presages trend change is an "engulfing pattern." It's a two-candlestick pattern consisting of opposite-color real bodies. The second real body must completely "engulf" the first real body. Translation: The opening price of the second real body must be lower than the closing price of the first, and the closing price of the real body must be higher than the opening price of the first. That's called a "bullish engulfing pattern." The flip side of this is a "bearish engulfing pattern." Figure 6-8 shows these two patterns in action.

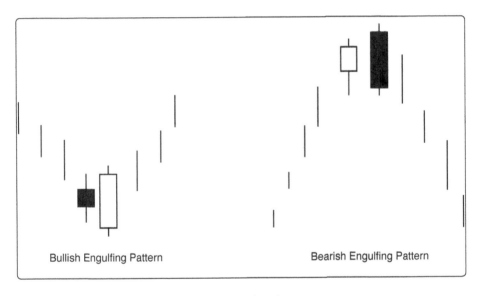

Bullish Engulfing Pattern   Bearish Engulfing Pattern

FIGURE 6-8. Bullish and bearish engulfing patterns as reversal signals.

Bullish and bearish engulfing patterns are similar to Western "key reversal" patterns, in which a stock opens at a new high (or low), then closes lower (or higher) than the previous day's low (or high).

Another important reversal pattern is the dark cloud cover. Also a two-candlestick pattern, it portends change when it appears at the top of an uptrend, or toward the top of a congestion (sideways) move. The first candlestick is a long, clear real body. The second real body opens above the close of the first, then closes near the low of the range and deep within the price range of the first candlestick. The deeper into the first real body (range) the second real body closes, the more bearish the signal. Dark cloud cover indicates exactly what the name conveys: a storm is brewing—take cover.

The reverse of the dark cloud cover is the bullish piercing pattern. Resembling the bullish engulfing pattern in that the second candlestick (real body) opens below the previous candlestick's close, the piercing pattern shows that the second real body should rise at least halfway into the previous dark

The dark cloud cover pattern is very reliable and shows up as a warning signal on virtually all time frames.

real body. The greater the second real body pierces the first, the greater the chance that it is a strong reversal pattern. When this two-candlestick pattern takes place at the bottom of a downtrend, look for a change in direction to begin.

Figure 6-9 illustrates dark cloud cover and bullish piercing patterns. Since these both are powerful patterns, be sure to commit the simple formations to memory.

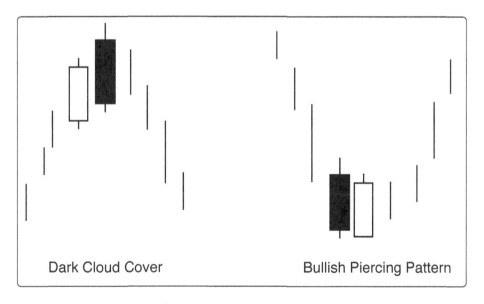

Dark Cloud Cover   Bullish Piercing Pattern

FIGURE 6-9. Dark cloud cover and bullish piercing patterns.

The harami and the harami cross are two-candlestick patterns that also indicate a trend change. Harami means "pregnant" in Japanese—the pattern consists of a long real body that engulfs the subsequent small candlestick. The long real body is the "mother" candlestick and the smaller real body is the "baby."

In this pattern, the long real body must occur first, with the short real body appearing second. (The reverse of this pattern is the bullish engulfing pattern.)

The colors of the real bodies need not be opposite, but you will find they usually appear that way. Figure 6-10 illustrates the harami and the harami cross.

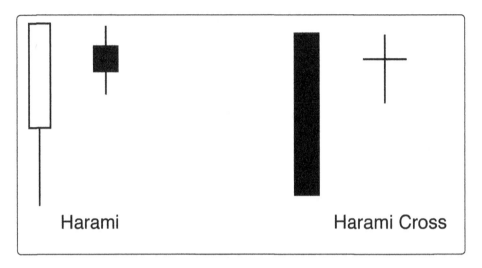

FIGURE 6-10. Harami and harami cross patterns.

If you're comparing this formation to the "inside day" in Western technicals, you're right. A Western inside day, however, demands that the second session keep its highs and lows within those of the preceding one. The harami does not. As long as the first real body is relatively longer than the second, and the second is short, the shadows (session high and low) of the second real body can extend above or below the first.

The harami pattern warns not so much of a dramatic reversal in a trend as it does that the current trend may slow or drift sideways for a while.

A harami cross forms when the second candlestick (baby) is a doji. This means that definite opinion—strong bullish for a tall, white real body, or strong bearish for a tall, dark real body—has dissolved. A doji, as mentioned before, translates into indecision and uncertainty. Thus, a harami cross can be a potent reversal signal. When you spot this pattern during an uptrend or downtrend, take note.

Three-Candlestick Patterns

The following patterns consist of three candlesticks that include "stars." Star patterns represent strong and valuable reversal warnings.

As Steve Nison says, knowing how to identify strong reversal patterns in the making not only alerts us to potential setups for entries; they also offer efficient profit-taking signals. Why? Because if you're long (own) a stock, and you see a reversal pattern forming that indicates the stock may make a U-turn soon, you can grab your gains quickly, while buyers are keeping the price aloft.

To qualify for "star" billing, the candlestick should appear at the top (or bottom) of an uptrend (or downtrend), have a short real body, and gap away (open higher in uptrend, or lower in downtrend) from the previous candlestick.

The co-stars: In the context of an uptrend, the first real body should be long and clear. The third real body should be long and dark, penetrating the real body of the first candle. In a downtrend, the first real body is long and dark; the star appears next. Finally, the third real body moves up, well into the first dark real body.

The Japanese call the first star an evening star and the second a morning star. When the star emerges as a doji, it's an even more powerful warning that a reversal may be impending.

Figure 6-11 depicts the evening and morning stars and evening and morning doji star patterns.

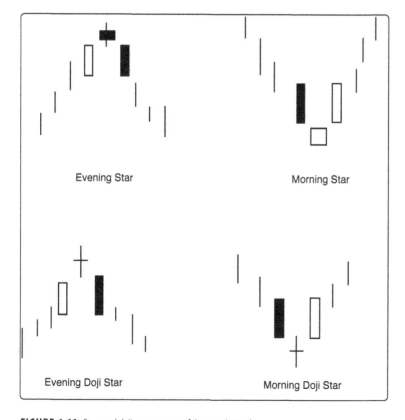

FIGURE 6-11. Stars and doji stars as powerful reversal signals.

While we're looking at doji, let's check out variations on this extremely powerful candlestick. When you spot a doji—and remember, its most potent forecasting position is at the top of an uptrend or bottom of a downtrend—the following points should be taken into consideration:

HOT TIP

These three-candlestick patterns promise to pack more of a punch when the first candlestick forms on relatively low volume, and the third candlestick forms on high volume.

➤ Traditionally, the doji opens and closes at the same price. But if you spot a "near-doji," where the prices are within a few decimal points of each other, it's still a significant signal.

➤ A doji that appears in a sideways consolidation move, accompanied by other doji and short real bodies, is not a powerful beacon of change. These candles must appear at the top or bottom of a price pattern to emit a strong reversal signal.

➤ Doji can be viewed as more powerful at stock/market tops, rather than bottoms. This holds especially true when preceded by a long clear candle, such as in the doji evening star pattern. Think: Long, clear real body equals strong bullish opinion. Then, a doji develops. Doji equals indecision by market players to pay a higher price. Result? Possible pullback or profit-taking may soon follow.

➤ Doji that confirm trend tops or bottoms many times turn into support or resistance areas.

➤ When a stock in an uptrend pulls back to support and then forms a doji, it indicates the stock may be ready to turn and resume its uptrend. The same is true of a stock in a downtrend; a rebound to resistance, followed by the formation of a doji, may indicate the stock will drop back to the downside. Notice the operative word here is *may*. Always wait for the next candle to confirm price direction. Figure 6-12 shows two additional distinctive doji formations.

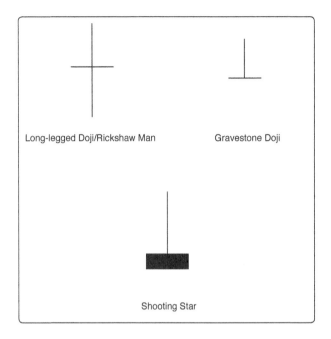

Long-legged Doji/Rickshaw Man   Gravestone Doji

Shooting Star

FIGURE 6-12. Long-legged doji/rickshaw man, gravestone doji, and shooting star patterns.

The long-legged doji has long upper and lower shadows, and its appearance at stock/market tops should definitely grab your attention. When a long-legged doji opens and closes in the middle of its session, it's referred to as a rickshaw man.

If you think through what actually happened to form one of these doji, you'll realize why their emergence is so meaningful. Imagine a stock opens at a certain price, say 50. Buying pressure pushes it strongly higher, then selling pressure shoves it much lower. Still, it closes at or very near the session's opening price of 50. Conclusion? *Total indecision.* Neither the bulls nor the bears have the strength to raise or lower the price above or below the open. Can you see how that may cause bulls to shrug and take profits during the following session? Remember, the market dislikes indecision.

When you see a gravestone doji form in an uptrend, and you're long that stock, take partial or all of your profits immediately. At the very least, tighten your protective stop.

In *Japanese Candlestick Charting Techniques*, Steve Nison writes, "As we have discussed, many of the Japanese technical terms are based on military analogies, and in this context, the gravestone doji also represents the graves of those bulls or bears who have died defending their territory."

As you can see in Figure 6-12, a gravestone doji opens and closes at the low price of the day. If the price rises to a new high, drawing a long upper shadow, that spells even more gloom and doom for bulls. Translation: No matter how much the bulls absorbed supply, the bears squashed the price down to the low, and closed it there. Remember, the point at which a stock or market closes on the day is a very significant signal in itself.

Because they signal indecision in the minds of market participants, doji, spinning tops, and high wave candlesticks can act as potent price reversal indicators when they emerge in an uptrend.

Spinning Tops and High Wave Candlesticks

The final candlesticks we'll discuss are spinning tops and high wave candlesticks (Figure 6-13). Candlesticks with small real bodies, of either color, are referred to as "spinning tops." The length and range of their shadows may vary. Think of spinning tops as slightly "kinder, gentler" versions of doji. Their siblings form as "high wave" candlesticks, which are spinning tops exhibiting very long upper and/or lower shadows.

A single high wave candle indicates massive confusion, and appears mostly on daily charts. When you own a stock that endures this pattern, please take strong risk management action. Although rarely seen, a group of high wave candlesticks usually forecasts a trend reversal.

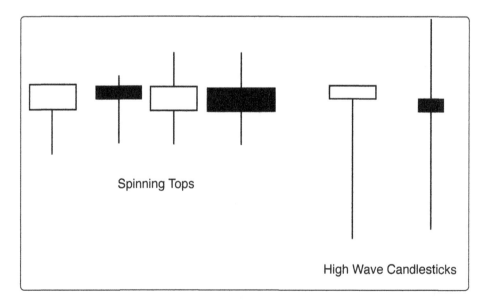

Spinning Tops

High Wave Candlesticks

FIGURE 6-13. Spinning tops and high wave candlesticks.

In the previous pages, you've learned major candlestick formations and patterns that will alert you to changes or reversals in trends. Many more exist, and as previously mentioned, you can study books and educational DVDs by Nison for additional examples and explanations. I find candlesticks an invaluable source of information. If you continue to study them, it will be time well spent.

In the following chart examples, you will see examples of the candle patterns we just discussed. Observe how price trends can slow or reverse when certain formations occur.

FIGURE 6-14. Google (GOOG) daily candlestick chart. RealTick graphics by Townsend Analytics. The daily chart of Google (GOOG) from November 2006 into March 2007 details several candlestick patterns: 1. Evening Star topping pattern. 2. Harami bottoming followed by a doji confirmation. 3. A shooting star candle. 4. Dark cloud cover, which doesn't play out, but check out the pattern that occurs next. 5. Bearish engulfing candle. 6. Three-candle morning star pattern with bullish piercing. 7. Evening star. 8. Bearish engulfing pattern. No one chart tool is going to predict future price action 100 percent of the time, but we can see that learning the basics of candlestick analysis for further price confirmation is certainly worth the effort.

After looking at those charts, I'll bet my duck slippers you pointed to a doji that appeared after an extended downtrend and said, "Hey, there's a doji in a major downtrend, but the downtrend didn't reverse. It just kept going." Or, "I see a dark cloud cover in the middle of an uptrend, but the stock kept going up."

Remember, when you see what appears to be a candle reversal pattern forming, you must wait for the *next* candle to form and follow through. If you don't want to wait for the follow-through candle, go to an intraday chart and note how that candle is forming on the day. That short-term candle action can offer clues as to price strength or weakness, and the probabilities of closing price.

Also remember: No candlestick pattern, indicator, oscillator, or analyst's report can tell you where your stock—or the market—is going to go in the following hours, days, weeks, or months. What these prognosticators *can* do is give us possibilities and probabilities of price movement based on history.

FIGURE 6-15. streetTRACKS Gold Shares ETF (GLD) daily chart. RealTick by Townsend Analytics. 1. Shooting star top. 2. Hammer low. 3. Multiple topping patterns/candles: A. Evening doji star. B. Bearish harami. C. Two gravestone candles. Some traders might see the last three candles as spinning tops. Labeling aside, the bearish-looking candles finally result in the GLD shares cracking to the downside. 4. Hammer low. Notice how the reversal candle finds support with the unlabeled hammer several sessions prior. 5. Bearish dark cloud cover. 6A. Evening star. 6B. Dark cloud cover confirms the top of this move in progress. 7A. Bullish, two-candle harami. 7B. Hammer confirmation still inside the first long real body candle of first pattern. 8. Bullish piercing pattern.

FIGURE 6-16. Marvell Technology (MRVL) daily chart. RealTick by Townsend Analytics. This daily chart of Marvell Technology (MRVL) shows more reasons why candlestick patterns are such an important tool for traders for spotting trend reversals. 1. Bearish dark cloud cover. 2A. Harami. 2B. Bearish engulfing to confirm. 3. Wide-range hammer complemented with an inside bar sets up a bullish harami. 4. Three-candle bullish morning star. 5. As I mentioned, nothing is perfect. Here we find a two-candle harami followed by a very large bearish engulfing pattern—ultimately, to no avail. 6. An evening star does a bit better in its bearish forecasting, but you had to be quick! 7. Dark cloud cover and a "third time is the charm" in this case, as price proceeds lower. 8. Here's an interesting low. 8A. Two gravestone doji, but this isn't a bearish signal, as the sequence occurs after an extended move lower and should be interpreted as a potential sign of weakness by the bears to take prices even lower. B. This sequence forms a high wave candle, bullish piercing, and three doji that ultimately result in a fast catapult higher. 9. Harami top followed by a second inside gravestone and a subsequent bearish move lower.

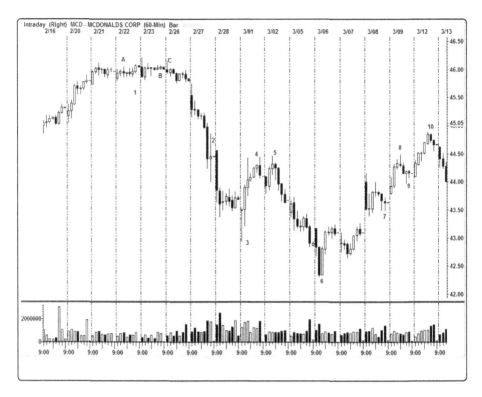

FIGURE 6-17. McDonald's (MCD) 60-minute chart. RealTick by Townsend Analytics. While we've been focused on the daily chart in our analysis of candlestick patterns, they work equally as well on any time frame. This is a 60-minute chart of McDonald's (MCD), where the price activity is stretched across three weeks. 1. A, B. Here we're faced with indecision by traders, as multiple spinning tops and/or doji keep price activity bound in a very tight trading range. C. This gravestone doji could be an early indication of which way the price is going to move next. 2. As it turns out, the stock moved dramatically lower. Here we see a real tug-of-war between bulls and bears as a high wave candle is forged. 3. A very bullish hammer after the bears aren't able to make good on the breakdown from a series of indecisive doji. 4. Bearish engulfing 5. Evening star and hanging man top. 6. Bullish piercing low. 7. Bullish harami. 8. Gravestone top. 9. Bullish harami. 10. Dark cloud cover topping pattern.

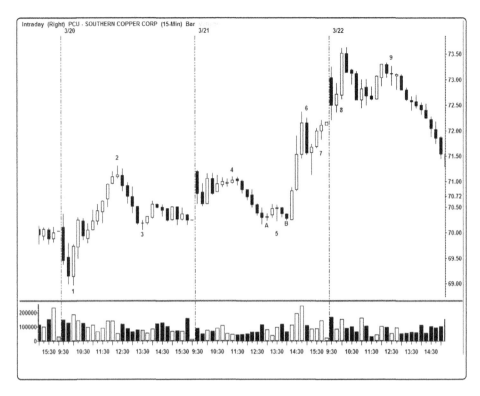

FIGURE 6-18. Southern Copper (PCU) 15-minute chart. RealTick by Townsend Analytics. Let's drill down on our time frame even further, to a 15-minute chart. Here we're looking at three days of price activity in Southern Copper (PCU), using the 15-minute chart. 1. Bullish engulfing. 2. Evening star. 3. Possible doji low. 4. Indecision by traders courtesy of doji/spinning tops. 5A. Harami pattern. 5B. A second harami followed by a powerful bullish engulfing resolution. 6. Dark cloud cover and ultimately a failed warning. 7. A quick reversal in the form of a hammer. 8. Another warning, this time as a bearish harami. Again, to no avail, but . . . 9. A final dark cloud cover and doji prevails, and prices move lower.

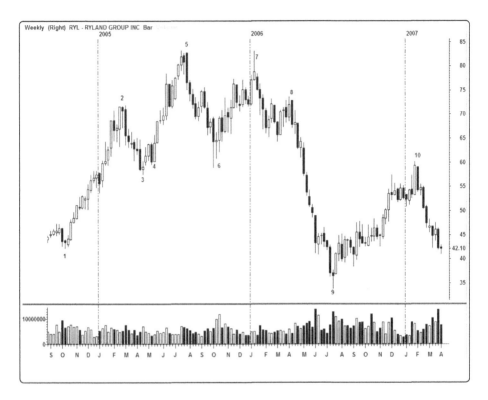

FIGURE 6-19. Ryland Group, Inc. (RYL) weekly chart. In this final example, we're going to leave in a big way, by way of a weekly chart. Above is the weekly of Ryland Homes (RYL) from late 2004 all the way into 2007. 1. We start off with a three-candle morning star pattern. 2. A two-candle harami high (could also be labeled a hanging man) is followed immediately by a bearish engulfing confirmation. 3. Morning star. 4. Bullish piercing. 5. Bearish engulfing. 6. Bullish harami. 7. Shooting star. 8. Bearish engulfing. 9. Hammer/morning star formation. 10. Dark cloud cover. Finally, I didn't label all of the patterns, so you'll want to go over the chart and locate additional examples. No one tool is perfect when it comes to predicting price moves, but on an overall basis, candle patterns are among the most valuable indicators we can use.

QUIZ

ıllıllıllıllıllı

1. True or False? When presented with a stock chart that displays a disorderly, erratic price pattern, you disregard it completely and go on to the next.
2. A line chart shows a stock's _____ prices, drawn in a single line.
3. In bar charts, the top of a vertical bar indicates the stock's _____ for that session. The bottom is the _____. The short, perpendicular bar extending on the left shows the _____ price, and the corresponding one on the right displays the _____ price.
4. What does the rectangle on a white candlestick, referred to as a "real body," indicate? What does a dark real body indicate?
5. Define "doji."
6. What prevailing opinion or emotion does a long, clear candlestick suggest? A long, dark candlestick? Which one implies supply? Which implies demand?
7. The plural of "doji" is _____.
8. What does the candlestick referred to as a "hammer" look like, and where, in a price pattern, might it forecast a trend change or reversal?
9. Describe a "bearish engulfing" candlestick pattern. What is its counterpart in Western technical analysis?
10. Give one common characteristic of all "stars."
11. If you're long a stock and you see the current trading day is closing in a gravestone doji, what action might you take?
12. What collective opinion do "spinning tops" and "high wave candles" indicate?

Answers
1. Very true!
2. Closing.
3. High, low. Opening, closing.
4. On a white candlestick, the lowest point of the real body is the opening price of that session; the high represents the closing price. On a dark candlestick, the top of the real body is the opening price and the lowest end designates the close.
5. A doji is a candlestick formation consisting of upper and lower shadows intercepted by a single "crossbar." That means that stock (or index, or market) opened and closed at the same price.

6. A long, white candlestick translates into a strong bullish opinion. The collective emotion equals greed. Implication equals demand. A long, dark candlestick displays a firm bearish opinion. Collective emotion equals fear. Implication equals supply.

7. Doji.

8. The candlestick referred to as a "hammer" consists of a small real body with a lower shadow that extends at least two-thirds the length of the real body. Resembling the common carpentry tool, when it appears in the context of a downtrend, it implies a possible slowing and reversal to the upside, as in "hammer it up."

9. The bearish engulfing pattern is a two-candlestick pattern of opposite colors that appears during an uptrend and warns of a possible reversal. The second candlestick's real body will completely engulf the prior candlestick. The Western counterpart is the "key reversal day."

10. All "stars"—whether morning, evening, or doji stars—must open away from (meaning higher or lower, whether in an uptrend or downtrend, respectively) the previous candlestick's real body.

11. Take some or all profits; if holding, tighten protective stop.

12. Indecision and uncertainty.

CENTER POINT: REACH FOR YOUR HIGHEST POTENTIAL

"What lies behind us and what lies before us are tiny matters compared to what lies within us."

—Ralph Waldo Emerson

Our planet, born of stellar debris, came together billions of years ago and has continued to evolve ever since. As part of that evolution from one-celled plants and animals to conscious beings of expression, we are a unique part of life unfolding, always in the process of moving to greater expression.

Because the urge to achieve our highest potential is innate and ever present (even though at times, we may try to ignore it), it offers us the opportunity to participate in the creative process in our own lives, to develop our special talents.

Indeed, each of us is born with special gifts that if brought to the surface, developed, and polished, are meant to take us to new levels of personal growth, fulfillment, and happiness. In the best-case scenario, we use our gifts to make the world a better place.

Many times, we believe—even fear—that our dreams are selfish, egotistical, or impractical. Consider the child who longs to grow up to be an actor, and his parents, who pooh-pooh that dream as selfish and impractical.

The truth is that by entertaining us in a stage play or film, actors and actresses encourage us, the audience, to "suspend our disbelief" and accompany them into a wonderful world of feelings and experiences we otherwise could not access. They transport us to a time and place that transcends our everyday environment. The experience may invite us to laugh, offer a life lesson, or simply alleviate our stress.

What a wonderful gift these performers give to us. Selfish? No. Impractical? Certainly not! Good actors and actresses are paid for their work.

What does your heart want to undertake? What makes your soul sing? What is that inner talent that longs to assert itself? Are you ready to bring it to the surface of your life and make it a reality?

If the answer is *yes*, form a mental image of yourself expressing your special talents right now. Then take the first step that will make it a current reality. When you do this, you are taking action toward achieving your highest potential.

CHAPTER 7

Chart Close-Ups: The Pieces of the Puzzle

"A trader gets to play the game as the professional billiard player does—that is, he looks far ahead instead of considering the particular shot before him. It gets to be an instinct to play for position."

—Jesse Livermore

Want to hear really good news without the usual "bad news" tacked on? Stock prices only move in three directions—up, down, and sideways. Why is that such great news? Because it underscores the simplicity of actual price moves.

The up, down, and sideways news gets even better. If you keep your wins larger than your losses, you can afford trades to go against you more than 50 percent of the time—and still make money. Trading is probably the only business on the globe where that dynamic applies.

We talked in previous chapters about uptrends (Stage 2), downtrends (Stage 4), and sideways price movements (Stages 1 and 3). Now let's dissect them to find moneymaking buying and selling signals.

ANATOMY OF YOUR FRIEND: THE UPTREND

An uptrend is defined as a price pattern making a series of higher lows and higher highs.

As I said in the last chapter, trading stocks in strong, well-defined uptrends is where you and I will spend most of our time. Swing traders target the 2- to 5-day breakouts in a stock that initiates an uptrend. Position traders scan for stocks breaking out of a Stage 1 base, and then buy and hold for the duration of the uptrend. That uptrend may last for weeks to months. You can also define position trading as "core trading," meaning that these trades form the long-term core positions of your account.

Stocks break out of bases and into uptrends for several reasons: Institutional buyers (such as managers of mutual funds, hedge funds, and managed accounts) suddenly show interest, the related industry or sector gains favor, or the stock comes out with positive news and good earnings. The added buying pressure (greed plus demand) shoots the stock out of its base and above previously formed resistance.

Figure 7-1 shows how a stock breaking out of a base and into an uptrend will appear.

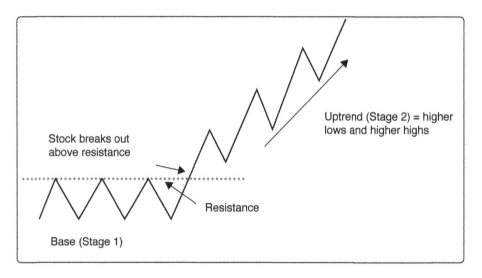

FIGURE 7-1. Typical price action when a stock breaks out of a base and into an uptrend.

If you show a tennis pro a tennis racket, he or she will show you the "sweet spot" on the racket face; it's a small area in the center of the strings. Hit the ball perfectly on the sweet spot, and you'll deliver your shot with power and accuracy.

As a swing trader, your goal is to capture multi-point "sweet spots" in the upswings of a strong uptrend. The sweet spot translates into the "middle" of the upswing.

"*Middle*?" you ask. "What do you mean, 'middle'? I want more than the middle points. I want to buy at the bottom and sell at the top!"

I wish it were that easy, but it isn't. Here's why: When you buy, you want to make sure the breakout is a healthy one, so you wait for price confirmation provided by the breakout. This ensures that people are willing to pay more for the stock than the price at the prior high.

When you take profits, you sell when you can, *not when you have to.* In other words, you should sell when the stock is nearing resistance on a daily chart (the prior pivot high) but is still moving higher on the wings of greed. Will you sometimes leave a point or more on the table? Sure. Do you care? I hope not. It's much better to take some or all profits when the stock is still moving higher than to hold too long and end up riding a winner into a loser! If you've planned your trade well and traded your plan, consistent profit-taking paves the road to trading success.

Figure 7-2 gives you a quick glance at the potential swing and position trading opportunities in an uptrend.

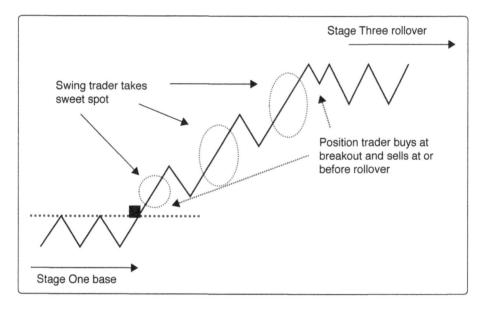

FIGURE 7-2. Swing and position trading opportunities in an uptrend.

I've already anticipated your next question: "How can I make the most money, by swing trading or position trading?"

Answer: In a muscular bull market that propels market leaders skyward, a talented swing trader can jump onto stocks rocketing in uptrends and take multipoint profits. In a market rising in a meandering uptrend, where breakouts take more savvy and skill to capture (and the discipline to jump out when they fail), a position trader who quietly plods through the higher highs and higher lows, pulling a trailing stop-loss behind, may actually come out ahead.

The best of both worlds: Take a position in a stock when it breaks out; then, depending on market conditions, swing trade a portion of the position, and keep the remainder in position or core trade mode.

Here's an alternate way of accomplishing the same goal. Choose a sector or industry group that's moving in an orderly base with the potential to break into an uptrend. Check the exchange traded funds that match that sector or industry group, and find one with good average daily volume of at least 200,000 to 300,000 shares. When/if it breaks above resistance, buy a position in that fund. You can swing trade the strongest stock(s) in that group to add to your profits.

BUY SIGNALS: WHAT TO LOOK FOR

This section shows optimal buy signals for swing trading and position trading. The basic pattern forms the foundation of all trading entries you make. You can use this pattern on day trading setups as well.

Figure 7-3 illustrates three key buy signals. Read them like this:

1. Breakout over base resistance.
2. Breakout after the stock pulls back to support and resumes its uptrend.
3. Best used as an add-to-position point. It takes place when the price rises over the previous high's pivot (resistance) price. If the price has trouble overcoming that resistance price, either take profits or raise your protective stop to guard profits.

HOT TIP

A chart is a chart is a chart. Whether it's a daily chart or a 3-minute intraday chart, as pertains to breakouts, the buying criteria for entering a trade remain basically the same.

• • •

The 1, 2, 3 pattern works on all time frames, whether intraday, daily, or even weekly. Traders must be aware, however, of overall market conditions before taking any trade—no matter how well the pattern appears to evolve.

HOT TIP

Professional traders utilize the scale-in and scale-out method. They scale into a position when buying, and then scale out when selling. This tactic minimizes risk, which is always a wise tactic to employ.

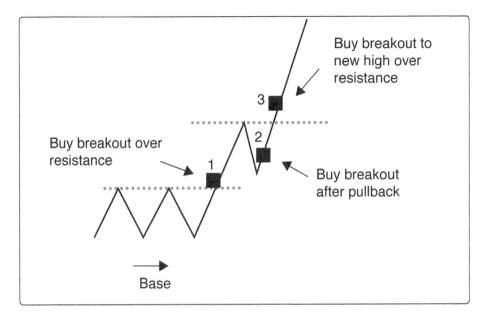

FIGURE 7-3. Three key buying entries.

In the following chapters, we'll add indicators to our charts as decision support tools that confirm buy/sell signals. For now, though, please memorize the basic price pattern. At the end of the day, price *always* has the final word.

Typically, both swing and position traders will buy the first breakout over resistance (see 1 in Figure 7-3). Swing traders take quick profits by selling half or all of their position while greed and demand remain strong, and before the first pullback begins.

Position traders will watch the stock pull back to support, and when it "bounces," or trades over the high of the lowest pullback day, they may add additional shares to their original position (see 2). This gradual accumulation of shares is called "scaling in."

Swing traders, who bought at the first breakout and sold before the first pullback, will now watch the stock for the next entry—the bounce subsequent to the pullback (see 2).

Okay, stay with me. Say both swing traders and position traders are long the stock as it continues its uptrend and heads for its previous high. Both traders watch how it approaches this point of resistance. If it falters, swing traders may want to take profits in one-half or all of their position. Or, if the market and relevant sector is flying to the upside on the wings of strong momentum, traders should tighten their stop-loss prices and tune into how the stock handles supply (resistance) that comes its way.

Position traders should hold tight, and look for the next opportunity to raise their stop-loss point. You'll learn how to set stop-loss points in Chapter 11.

Note: From now on, when your target stock gives you a buy signal, you'll enter the stock from three to ten cents above the previous day's high price. (This will be explained in further detail as we go.)

Figures 7-4, 7-5, and 7-6 show stocks that have broken out of their bases and into uptrends. Check out the 1, 2, 3 entry points.

HOT TIP

You've heard the old saying, "The trend is your friend"? It's the absolute truth. Going against a prevailing trend is like trying to win on the defense. It's a lot of work and you may get beat up!

FIGURE 7-4. RTI International Metals, Inc. (RTI) 1, 2, 3 daily pattern. RealTick by Townsend Analytics. This daily chart of RTI International Metals, Inc. (RTI), the titanium producer, is a classic tight, flat base pattern and is very suitable for locating 1, 2, 3 setups. In this case we see that a heavy volume breakout took place in mid-October 2006, which is our buy signal number 1. The number 2 buy signal occurs four sessions later and after a successful test of support, which is defined by the hammer pivot low. In this instance, that same candle acts as an entry for signal number 3 as the prior highs are taken out by twenty-three cents.

FIGURE 7-5. IAC/Interactive Corp (IACI) 1, 2, 3 daily pattern. RealTick by Townsend Analytics. Here's a solid flat base breakout of IAC/Interactive Corp (IACI). While the results don't go on to provide the same stellar gains shown in the last example involving RTI, a couple of good technical points of interest are demonstrated. Notice how the development of Interactive's base finds support above prior resistance. Second, I've labeled a gravestone doji as being "False & Short" with regard to being signal number 1. The first breakout attempt looked uncertain at best, as it formed the bearish candle by the day's close. Further, the duration of the base at that time was less than four full weeks, so it was "short" in length. A couple of weeks later, in early October 2006, the number 1 buy signal is achieved with greater success. A pullback that develops with a spinning top low then sets up the number 2 signal, which lines up fairly well with the original buy point decision. Several days later, the number 3 add-on, or buy point, is realized as the price action sufficiently crosses the prior highs of 30 a share, which took place in the second session after the breakout.

FIGURE 7-6. Lam Research (LRCX) 1, 2, 3 daily pattern. RealTick graphics by Townsend Analytics. This daily chart of Lam Research (LRCX) is another great example of the power of the 1, 2, 3 entry system. The number 1 buy signal is generated in a price breakout that takes place after a 2-month flat consolidation during the late summer of 2006; the breakout counters the prior steep downtrend. The number 2 buy signal occurs on the confirmation of LRCX's successful hammer pullback, which tests prior resistance. The number 3 signal occurs the same session as a strong rally clears the prior highs of 46.51 set four sessions back. I've labeled another potential number 1 buy signal several weeks later. This particular one ended up failing after struggling to hold on to multi-year highs of 53.74. With that said, gains of 8 percent were available before Mother Market decided to smack down Lam Research and many of its semiconductor peers.

How to Draw an Uptrend Line

Okay, get out your crayons. It's time to connect the dots.

Now that you're playing a stock that's broken out of its base and into an uptrend, it gives you a good sense of the stock's ongoing health if you draw a trendline as soon as it has established two (higher) lows. First, when you draw a trendline defining an uptrend, you connect the lows of the pivot points, then extend the line a bit farther than the price action to get an idea of the path it might take ("might" being the operative word). Technically, you can draw a trendline connecting any two pivot lows (or any two pivot highs), but the following method is a bit more precise. Start your line at the first low after the breakout high, and then connect subsequent lows. Figure 7-7 shows an uptrend line.

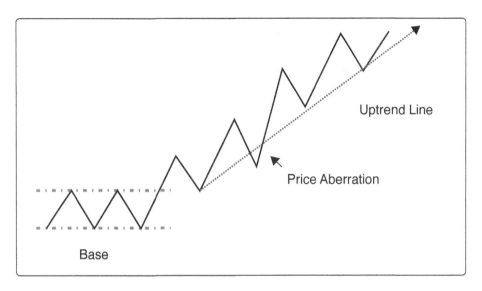

FIGURE 7-7. Draw an uptrend line.

Now, I already know your next comment. "Wait a minute," you say. "You ignored a pivot low and drew the trendline right through the price pattern. What's up with that?"

Heck, they're my crayons. ☺ Seriously, when you see three or more pivot lows that connect in an orderly trendline, it's permissible to use those pivots for your trendline and ignore a price aberration. Now and then you'll see a low that doesn't coincide with the general channel line of the others. As long as it has not made a lower low than the previous low, you can draw right through it.

Here are some trendline tips:

➤ For our purposes, the best uptrends are formed at about a 45-degree angle. Any angle steeper than that can result in a gut-grinding trade. A price pattern that crawls up a shallower angle may bore you silly.

➤ When you connect three or more lows in a trendline, it's considered a "major" trendline. Position traders may want to use the line as a stop-loss point; that is, if your stock closes below it, you take profits.

➤ The trendline is broken the first time the stock pivots to a price lower than the prior one.

➤ Can stocks in an uptrend roll over, make a lower low, then shoot back up and start making higher highs? Sure. And, if you were long that stock and sold it when it broke the trendline, you may want to buy it back. If you do, treat it as a brand-new trade, holding it to your usual criteria.

TRADING IN A RANGE, CONGESTION, AND CONSOLIDATION

As mentioned earlier, stocks move in three directions—up, down, and sideways. The sideways moves can be divided into three basic categories: trading in a range, disorderly congestion, and consolidation.

When we say a stock is "trading in a range," that means it is moving up and down between a low price area, or support, and a higher price area, or resistance in a horizontal range. Many stocks trading in a range are experiencing a Stage 1 or Stage 3. Another term for trading in a horizontal range is "bracketing."

In former times, before current levels of volatility infiltrated the market, it was easier to pinpoint stocks that traded in orderly horizontal ranges. Traders called them "rolling" stocks. Playing these securities produced tidy profits, as traders bought the dips and sold the rallies.

These days, most trading ranges tend toward the unpredictable, even in dignified listed stocks. Follow-through, meaning a smooth transition in a continuous move to the upside or downside, may be rudely interrupted by market or sector antics.

Gary Anderson, veteran market analyst and author of the weekly market advisory service, Equity Portfolio Manager (*www.equitypm.com*), says, "Congestion areas tend to be 'hot-war zones,' where strong and weak hands engage in active battle. At bottoms, scared traders sell into the waiting hands of strong buyers. At tops, the reverse is true. Strong sellers offer shares in size to late-adopters of the bullish trend."

Figure 7-8 depicts how a stock trades in a range.

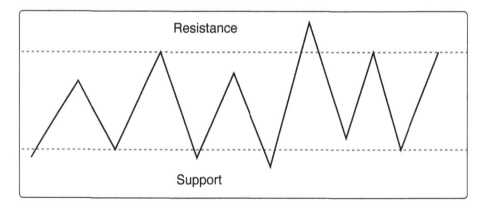

FIGURE 7-8. This stock is trading in a range, held captive by support and resistance. When a stock trades in a range, buyers support it at the bottom of its price range. When it reaches the top area of its range, however, buyers refuse to pay higher prices, so it falls again. This is one of the most uniform examples of rotating supply and demand.

The following chart, Figure 7-9, shows a stock trading in a range.

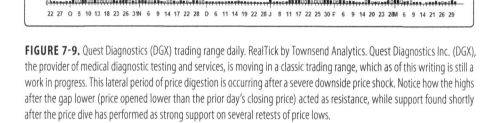

FIGURE 7-9. Quest Diagnostics (DGX) trading range daily. RealTick by Townsend Analytics. Quest Diagnostics Inc. (DGX), the provider of medical diagnostic testing and services, is moving in a classic trading range, which as of this writing is still a work in progress. This lateral period of price digestion is occurring after a severe downside price shock. Notice how the highs after the gap lower (price opened lower than the prior day's closing price) acted as resistance, while support found shortly after the price dive has performed as strong support on several retests of price lows.

The second way a stock trades in a sideways price pattern is "congestion." Think back to the last time you had a cold or the flu. Remember how your nose was stuffed up, and you couldn't breathe?

In the same way, a stock in a congestion pattern gets stuck moving laterally, in an erratic, disorganized fashion, with very little follow-through, as though it can't breathe. You'll see this many times in a stock experiencing a Stage 3.

Congestion patterns form resistance and support. If a stock falls under a ragged congestion pattern, that congestion will act as resistance. Why? Because all those who bought at the high price area are annoyed and are just waiting for the stock to bounce near enough to what they paid for it so they can dump it without too big a loss. That creates supply. Conversely, if the stock rises above the congestion area, the congestion forms support. Figure 7-10 shows how a stock trading in a congestion pattern might look.

Please avoid entering or holding stocks moving in a congestion pattern. Day traders may play them intraday, but for our purposes of holding overnight, an unpredictable congestion pattern usually produces losses. As I said in my previous book, "You don't kiss a friend with a cold, and you don't trade a stock in a congestion pattern."

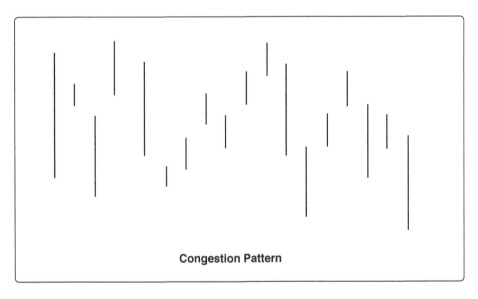

Congestion Pattern

FIGURE 7-10. Avoid stocks trading in congestion patterns.

Check out the stocks experiencing congestion patterns in Figures 7-11 and 7-12, so when you spot the disorderly congestion pattern in the making, you'll know to steer clear.

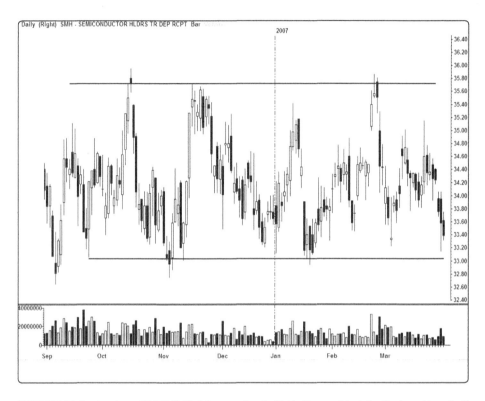

FIGURE 7-11. Semiconductor HOLDRS (SMH) daily congestion. RealTick by Townsend Analytics. Check out this work still in progress. Talk about erratic! This congestion pattern in the Semiconductor HOLDRS (SMH) proxy has been a graveyard for any would-be momentum players during the last seven months. The best advice that I can give traders: Avoid entering into similar situations until resistance or support is cleared for two sessions, or more.

FIGURE 7-12. KLA-Tencor (KLAC) daily congestion. RealTick graphics by Townsend Analytics. Here are a couple of similar congestion patterns in the semiconductor stock, KLA-Tencor (KLAC). KLAC is somewhat notorious for producing these formations; if you trade this volatile stock, trade cautiously.

Unlike the congestion pattern, the next sideways pattern will become our best friend. It's called a "consolidation" pattern, and it presents profitable opportunities when observed and played appropriately.

A stock in a consolidation pattern moves sideways in a very tight price range. You'll see this pattern most often in a basing pattern, or when a stock is in an uptrend and decides to go into a "resting" mode.

Picture a pressure cooker—a big pot placed on a hot stovetop with its lid clamped on so it becomes airtight. The superheated steam in the pot cooks the food. If you turn up the heat under the pot, the steam expands. If you open the vent in the lid, the steam escapes with a loud "whoosh." Were you to lift the lid with the heat still burning on high, the steam and food would erupt into the air.

HOT TIP

Stocks in uptrends correct in one of two ways—through price or time. They either pull back (down) to previous support, or consolidate laterally.

Just so, a stock moving in a tight sideways consolidation pattern heats up in a pressure cooker. Simultaneously, bulls lift, bears squash. At some point the pressure cooker builds up so much steam, the lid bursts off and the contents explode into the air. In other words, a jolt of rising volume—caused by good/bad news or market activity—explodes the stock price to the upside or downside. When you're playing a stock breaking out of a consolidation pattern (assuming you're on the right side of the price move), you can profit mightily from the price explosion.

Figure 7-13 displays a typical congestion pattern. When a stock breaks above or below the congestion area (think "ledge" or "shelf"), accompanied by high volume (you'll learn volume signals in the next chapter), it many times produces a buy or sell signal.

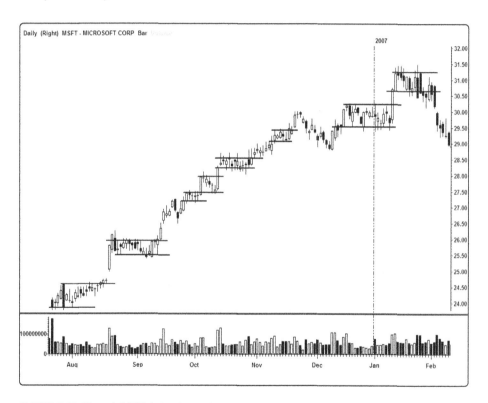

FIGURE 7-13. Microsoft (MSFT) daily tight consolidations. RealTick by Townsend Analytics. This daily chart of Microsoft (MSFT) shows how well tight consolidation patterns can act as springboards, as well as diving boards, for price thrusts once resistance or support is cleared respectively. Also note too, how stronger resistance and support can be found by lining up the real bodies of the candles. While this method results in drawing through some shadows, it often enough gains us a better entry point than the absolute high or low of the consolidation. Finally, notice how many black or bearish-looking candles developed in MSFT's most recent consolidation during early 2007. It's easy to see the difference from the daily action within the tight patterns on the way up. As of the moment, MSFT has entered into a Stage 4 downtrend.

The longer a stock stays in a consolidation period, the more explosive the move to the upside, or downside, when it finally occurs. That's why you'll often read in *IBD* that optimum breakouts shoot up from bases that take at least four to six weeks to form.

Figure 7-14 shows additional consolidation and breakout patterns. Once you learn how to recognize them, bring up charts from your own source and scan for more consolidation patterns. Each time you find one, note the strength of the subsequent move to the upside, or the downside.

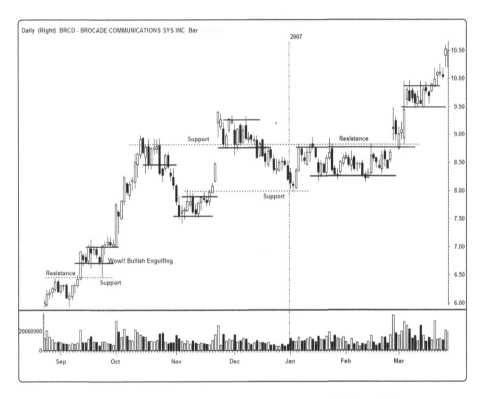

FIGURE 7-14. Brocade Communications (BRCD) daily effective consolidations. RealTick by Townsend Analytics. This daily chart of Brocade Communications Systems, Inc. (BRCD), the data storage networking and data management company, is another great example of how tight consolidations act as coiled springs for a period of price thrusting or direction. You'll see many of these tight areas put in multiple doji and spinning tops. If you think about it, it's quite logical, as these patterns represent indecision among both the bulls and the bears. And it's also no coincidence that once the technical tug-of-war is broken decisively, the subsequent price move can often be a very fast and profitable one (as long as you're trading the right side of it!). Finally, look at how well those prior consolidations act as both support and resistance for fresh pattern development. It's certainly a testament to how price action develops a good "memory." We can certainly use this understanding of support and resistance to our advantage.

Remember, once a stock breaks down from a tight consolidation pattern, the consolidation forms major resistance—think "glass ceiling"—and the stock may struggle when it tries to rise above it.

ANATOMY OF A DOWNTREND

The definition of a downtrend is a price pattern making a series of lower lows and lower highs. Although you will probably spend most of your time trading stocks in strong uptrends, if you learn how to sell short properly, you can grab multiple points out of a stock in a Stage 4 downtrend. In Chapter 12, you'll learn how to sell short safely and profitably.

Since we usually jump out of short trades faster than we do those to the long side, swing traders targeting breakdowns in the initial or early stages of a downtrend will expect to take the sweet spot out of two- to three-day holds. Position traders will scan for stocks breaking down from a Stage 3, and then sell short and hold for the duration of the downtrend, possibly weeks to months.

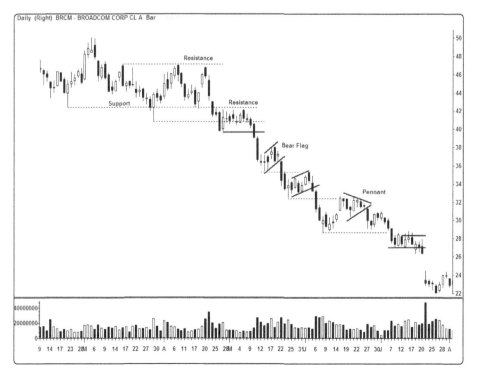

FIGURE 7-15. Broadcom Corp. (BRCM) daily downtrend with consolidations. RealTick by Townsend Analytics. What goes up must come down, as the Broadcom Corp. (BRCM) might attest too. Despite a great 2006 for the broader market and a

wonderful 2005 for this particular semiconductor heavyweight, BRCM went into a Stage 4 downtrend during much of that year. And once the move was under way, it seems the only thing holding it back, before the trend resumed lower, were short and tight consolidations. Notice that I've labeled a couple of variations of this pattern. Bear flags slope slightly higher, but have the same lateral feel to them, while a pennant formation contracts into a small triangular consolidation. Further, look at how these consolidations, once formed and broken, act as resistance to any subsequent price action.

HOT TIP

Most professionals I know would rather "go short" than take on a long position. Why? By selling short, they make more money faster. Remember, fear is much stronger than greed. That's why stocks many times fall much faster than they rise.

Stocks break down from Stage 3 rollovers for several reasons, including overall negative market conditions; institutional buyers' disenchantment with a stock's industry or sector; company reports that show weak earnings, sales, or high inventory; or other negative news. You can always count on a stock to fall into a tailspin when the company reports "accounting irregularities."

So when a stock tops out, rolls over, and heads south into a downtrend, it's because fear goads sellers (supply) to lower prices at every level in order to entice reluctant buyers. The fewer the buyers, the faster the fear floods the market with supply, and the more rapidly the stock falls.

Figure 7-16 shows how a stock breaks and falls into a downtrend.

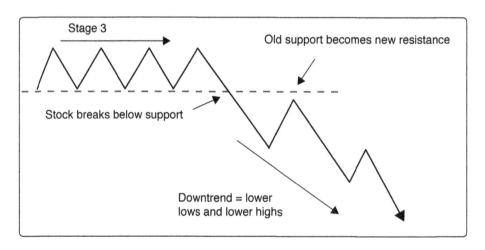

FIGURE 7-16. Stock breaks and falls into a downtrend.

OVERVIEW OF SELL SIGNALS: WHAT TO LOOK FOR

Since we'll delve into selling short in Chapter 12, the following presents only a brief overview of shorting signals in a downtrend. As you can see, the setups resemble buying signals in an uptrend. There are, however, subtle differences that we'll discuss later on. Figure 7-17 illustrates three key shorting signals. Read them like this:

➤ Number 1 is the breakdown from support.
➤ Number 2 is the breakdown after the stock rebounds to resistance (supply), then drops back into its downtrend.
➤ Number 3 is the add-to-position point for position traders. Here, the price collapses below the previous pivot low, or support.

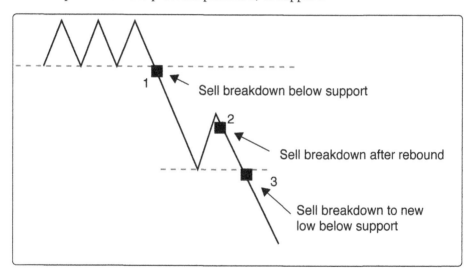

FIGURE 7-17. Key shorting signals. Typically, both swing and position traders will sell short the first breakdown below the support area established in the rollover phase (see 1 in Figure 7-17). Swing traders will buy the shares back to "cover their short" within a day or two, depending on the price action and the next level of support (probable profit target).

Position traders will watch the stock rebound to resistance. When it hits that resistance ceiling and resumes its downtrend below the low of the highest rebound day, traders may add additional shares to their original position (see 2).

Swing traders, who sold short at the first breakdown and closed the trade, or "covered" the trade before the first rebound, can also sell short again at (2). Both traders can add to their position at (3), as the stock falls below the support of the last low and continues its tumble. If the stock/industry/market shows signs of rebounding at that support level, swing traders might want to take profits.

The following three charts show stocks breaking down from their Stage 3 tops and dropping into downtrends. Check out the 1, 2, 3 entry points.

As you'll see in Figure 7-18, signals 2 and 3 may come at one time. A stock falling into a downtrend can push up to previous resistance, then gap down multiple points. It can break down from the rebound and pass prior support—all in one candlestick.

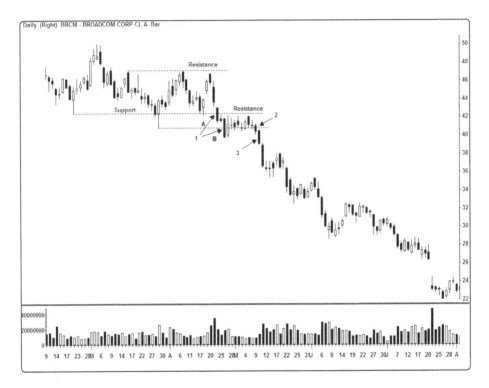

FIGURE 7-18. Broadcom Corp (BRCM) daily downtrend 1, 2, 3 entries. RealTick by Townsend Analytics. Here's the same chart of Broadcom (BRCM) shown earlier, sans the labeled consolidation patterns in its Stage 4 downtrend. Now, we'll focus on the available 1, 2, 3 opportunities for shorting out of the Stage 3 top. The number 1 sell short signal might be open to two entries. However, the preference is the short labeled "A," as that line of support was tested more times prior and affords a slightly higher entry than does "B," a more obvious spot for potential trapping of fresh short initiation. In fact, the tight price consolidation that follows finds its support at hammer lows, frustrating "B" shorts (somewhat) before confirming a number 2 short signal and then a number 3 short through the prior lows in the very next session.

FIGURE 7-19. Ryland Group (RYL) daily downtrend 1, 2, 3 entries. RealTick by Townsend Analytics. The trader's "American Dream" is to have shorted this wonderful Stage 4 downtrend, which begins with the 1, 2, 3 shorting opportunities in homebuilder Ryland Group (RYL). The number 1 short is triggered out of a very nice trading range that had acted as support. That short did occur on a price gap (price gap: stock opens higher or lower than the previous day's closing price) and made for potentially a more difficult trade decision. The reason: Quite often smaller price gaps will get filled or tested before proceeding. Since our method for shorting looks to incorporate that type of price action, that also means a potential opportunity for a number 2 short to set up. A bit more than a week later, the gap is filled, which also acts as pattern resistance due to all the trapped longs from the prior consolidation. Our entry is in the next session as the lows of that testing candle (a doji) are broken. A day later, the number 3 short is available as pattern lows also are broken. And from there, the shorts get to "nail down" some serious profits! Two months and roughly 40 percent later, a second "late" Stage 4 and number 1 short are offered.

FIGURE 7-20. Comcast Corp. (CMCSA) daily downtrend 1, 2, 3 entries. RealTick by Townsend Analytics. After enjoying a wonderful Stage 2 bull run during 2006, cable operator Comcast Corp. (CMCSA) spent 2007 unwinding some of those gains. A brief Stage 3 gave way to a number 1 short entry as supports were broken on February 1. Shortly thereafter, a same-day number 2 and number 3 short was delivered to traders looking to enter the early downtrend. And—a profitable one at that! Notice, too, that a couple of more entries developed, offering strong shorting opportunities as the trend rolled lower. Finally, I've extended prior support/resistance lines, so you can see how well this methodology takes advantage of prior support/resistance price levels.

How to Draw a Downtrend Line

Still got your crayons handy? Just as with an uptrend, you can get a good sense of the possible direction of a stock if you start drawing a trendline as soon as it establishes lower highs in a downtrend. Connect the tops of the lower highs, beginning at the first one. Figure 7-21 shows a downtrend line.

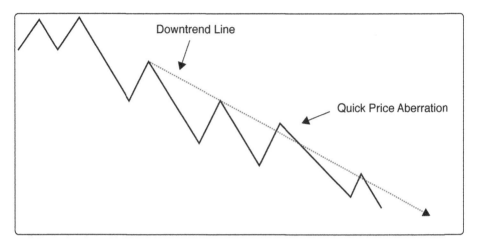

FIGURE 7-21. Draw a downtrend line. Remember how I drew a trendline in the uptrend right through one of the lows? It's sort of like when a piece of your hair sticks out in a weird direction right before a big night on the town—so you get out your scissors and cut it off.

I did the same thing in Figure 7-21. I drew through the high that sticks out beyond the rest of the pattern. Notice that the price aberration is not a higher high. It didn't break the downtrend.

When the stock does break the downtrend line by making a higher high and higher low, then that trend is considered finished, or "broken."

I'll stress the following point more than once: A high-quality, orderly stock can rise in a stair-step uptrend that gladdens the hearts of swing and position traders everywhere. But once that stock reaches the trend's peak and rolls over into a downtrend, watch out! Downtrends are usually very volatile, with the stock's price bouncing like a rubber rock. That's why, as you'll learn later, when you sell short, you may hold the position for a briefer time period than if you were long.

QUIZ
IIIIIIIIIIIIIIII

1. Stocks move in what three directions?
2. Give one reason why stocks break out of bases and into uptrends.
3. Define "uptrend."
4. Briefly describe buy signals 1, 2, 3.
5. What is a swing trader's strategy when presented with a stock breaking into a strong uptrend? What is a position trader's strategy?
6. Name three distinct patterns in which a stock moves sideways.
7. True or False? It's fun and profitable to play a stock trading in a congestion pattern.
8. Stocks correct one of two ways: (1) _____ or, (2) _____.
9. The longer a stock marches sideways in a tight congestion pattern, the more explosive or less explosive the breakout/breakdown?
10. Give the definition of a downtrend.

Answers
1. Up, down, and sideways.
2. A stock may break out of its base and into an uptrend because an institutional buyer(s) starts to accumulate it. Also, the stock's industry/sector may come into favor, or the company issues good news, or announces higher-than-expected earnings.
3. An uptrend is when a stock's price pattern makes a series of higher highs and higher lows.
4. (1) Buy breakout above resistance, (2) buy first breakout immediately after first pullback (consolidation) to support, (3) buy breakout to new high over previous high.
5. When presented with a stock breaking into an uptrend, a swing trader will buy the initial breakout and sell on or before the first pullback takes place. The swing trader will then strive to take the sweet spot, or middle, out of the upswings in the trend. The position trader buys the initial breakout, and while he or she may add to the position along the way, the trader will hold until the prevailing uptrend slows or is broken.
6. Trading in a range, congestion, consolidation.
7. Don't you dare say true!
8. Stocks correct (1) by pulling back to support, or (2) by consolidating.

9.More explosive.

10. A downtrend is a price pattern that makes a series of lower highs and lower lows on a chart.

CENTER POINT: THE POWER OF SYNCHRONICITY

"The moment one definitely commits himself, then Providence moves too. All sorts of things occur to help one that would never otherwise have occurred. A whole stream of events issues from the decision, raising in one's favor all manner of unforeseen incidents and meetings and material assistance, which no man could have dreamed would come his way."

—W. H. Murray (Climbed Mt. Everest)

If a single miracle takes place of which I have no doubt, it is the existence of synchronicity. Some choose to call the perfect timing of seemingly unrelated events and people coming into our lives as "coincidence." Not me. Too many situations in my life have been touched by synchronicity.

One cold winter evening, only an hour lingered before fifty guests would arrive at my home for a holiday party. It occurred to me that I'd forgotten to bring the ice chest up from the storeroom downstairs. Once in the storeroom, I found the Styrofoam container damaged and broken. I had no time to go to a store and buy another.

Frustrated, I returned upstairs. Suddenly, an inner voice insisted I take a load of newspapers back down to the recycling bin. "Later," I argued with myself. "Newspapers to the recycling bin are not a priority. I have a problem! What am I going to use for an ice chest?"

Take the newspapers down now, the voice insisted. Grudgingly, I grabbed an armful of newspapers and went back downstairs. When I opened the recycling bin, my jaw dropped. On top of the stack of newspapers sat the cleanest, newest Styrofoam ice chest a hostess could ever want! Evidently, someone had given it as a gift, filled with frozen desserts. Now it had been "delivered" to me with perfect timing.

Have you ever spontaneously thought of someone one minute, and he or she called the next minute? Have you ever wished for an answer to a question, and then tripped over it in a book, movie, or conversation with a friend?

Underlying these connections between seemingly random events flows a grand and harmonious plan. It weaves through our lives, offering us exactly what we need, when we need it. Can you imagine how empowered we would be if we learned to access it and trust the outcome?

When we believe in synchronicity, we know that an efficient and miraculous rhythm reverberates through our lives. As we give thanks for it, this intelligence supports every part of our lives with flawless timing and grace.

CHAPTER 8

Fitting the Puzzle Together

*"The professional concerns himself with doing the right thing rather than
with making money, knowing that the profit takes care of itself if the other
things are attended to."*

—Jesse Livermore

Certain things in life are givens. At Thanksgiving, serving turkey, stuffing, and cranberry sauce is a given. Then, according to our own family traditions, we add the sweet potatoes, mashed potatoes, vegetables, and pumpkin pie.

Swing and position traders need certain chart "givens." Once you interpret those with ease, according to your personal preferences, you'll plot additional indicators and oscillators that agree with your trading speed and style.

Before we go on, allow me to briefly climb on my soapbox. Traders' e-mail inboxes become stuffed with messages making bizarre promises like this one: "Make $15,000 a month in the stock market by working just thirty minutes a day."

Sure. You betcha. And I'm Tinkerbell. These glowing reports go on to show you charts with red arrows and green arrows, without explaining the reasoning behind them. They tell you "It's SO EASY to trade with *our* special software! We'll do *all* the research for you. You'll make buckets of money. When you see the green arrow, all you have to do is BUY!"

Never mind that you are risking your hard-earned money in a trade where you have no clue what's really going on. Never mind that they don't teach you how to monitor market conditions or economic data. Talk about driving without brakes!

Guess you can tell by this huffy discourse that we're not going to trade blindly in this book. Will we give specific buy/sell signals? *Yes, indeed.* Are you going to know why you're following them? *Absolutely.* That way, if a freight train is headed in your direction with its whistle turned off (stock market surprise), you'll have the savvy to jump off the tracks before it arrives. Those traders blindly following green arrows may not enjoy the same fate.

Now, back to trading givens: candlesticks, volume, and moving averages. As soon as you understand how they work in a buy/sell setup, you can add additional indicators/oscillators as decision support tools.

We've already discussed candlesticks, so let's move on to volume and moving averages.

VOLUME: A MEGA-IMPORTANT INDICATOR

Volume is one of the most important indicators traders use to predict future price direction. The ability to read volume signals accurately will be one of the most valuable tools in your toolbox.

Have you ever gone to a party where only a few people showed up? Not very exciting, was it? In the same way, when you're buying a stock, you don't want to be the only person at the party. You want a crowd of people to attend so that the stock skyrockets right out of the gate (breakout).

Think of high volume as energy being directed at a stock. This energy may be positive or negative.

Can you hear your dentist telling you, "Only floss the teeth you want to keep?" Makes sense. Keeping your teeth extra-clean means your teeth and gums will stay healthier, longer.

When you water and fertilize a plant, it flourishes happily. If you don't, it withers. When you deposit money into your checking account, you have the funds to pay your bills. No deposit, no bill paying. Conclusion: Positive energy directed at an entity—human or otherwise—causes it to flourish. Low or negative energy causes it to stagnate or atrophy.

Stock prices, especially, respond to energy. Human energy translates into volume, or the number of shares traded in a specified period of time. By now you've spotted the volume spikes that appear in the lower scale of our charts. The spike below the candlestick represents the total number of shares traded during that session.

 **HOT TIP**

While a climactic volume spike many times slows a stock in an overextended uptrend on a daily chart, that same volume spike may only temporarily slow the fall of a stock in a violent downtrend.

When you're entering a trade or managing your risk in a trade, you'll find that volume will serve as one of your most telling indicators. Why? Because volume is one of the only predictive charting tools available that are not *derivatives of price.*

Moving averages, momentum indicators, oscillators, Fibonacci retracement lines, and most other charting tools derive from various price calculations and formulas. Volume does not. Volume is a separate "voice" in and of itself. Think of it as getting a second opinion—apart from other chart components—on possible upcoming price direction. Know that the time you spend studying volume and the signals it gives will be time extremely well spent!

HOT TIP

Joe Granville, a well-known market technician who created the popular On-Balance Volume indicator, said, "Volume precedes price."

Two Key Volume Rules:
1. When volume expands, price expands higher or lower. When volume contracts, price contracts. We say volume confirms price action.
2. When volume expands and price does not, it's referred to as "price/volume divergence." We say volume shows a non-confirmation. Expect that volume expansion to show up shortly in upcoming price movement.

Please note: From now on, I'm going to be talking about signals to the buy side, not to selling short. So, please keep that in mind. (We'll discuss shorting signals in Chapter 12.)

Now, as swing and position traders, you initially look for high volume on the breakout, when the stock trades over its first resistance area (lots of people at the party). As the stock continues to the upside on subsequent days, strong volume (if not quite as strong as the breakout day) is desirable.

When the stock tops off and begins to pull back, or retrace, make sure the pullback takes place with decreased volume. Why? Because you don't want the selling pressure (energy) during the pullback to be as strong as it was on the move up.

If pullback volume is low, it means that most previous buyers are holding on to their positions. If pullback volume is high, buyers are selling just as hard and fast as they bought. That means the stock will surely drop *not only* to its previous resistance, but also perhaps below it. You shouldn't stay at that party. If you are long the stock when it tops out and begins its pullback or retracement, and you see heavy selling pressure coming in via high volume, take profits.

Figure 8-1 shows ideal breakout and pullback volume patterns.

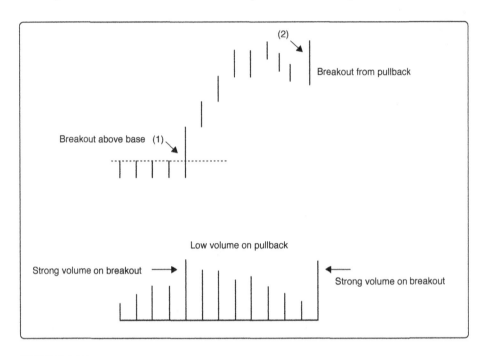

FIGURE 8-1. Volume patterns.

Attention swing and position traders: If interpreted accurately and used with appropriate risk management, the following volume signal can significantly add to your profits.

When you're scanning charts to find stocks' building bases, closely observe the volume spikes and locate a stock experiencing increasing volume, while at the same time, *the stock continues to trade in the same tight price range.*

This particular pattern indicates a strong possibility that institutional buyers are quietly accumulating the stock—and hoping no one will notice. A mutual fund, for instance, might have instructed its broker to purchase limited share lots per day, at odd hours of the day. That way, the accumulation remains invisible until the order is filled.

Of course, this game can only be played until all the shares offered at the low price levels are absorbed (supply). After that happens, the stock may shoot out of its base. If you're tracking the stock like the stealth trader that you are, you'll have your finger on the buy button.

In fact, this is one time (as you become more experienced) when you might take on a small lot size (100 shares) early on, while the stock is still in the base.

You'll set your protective stop order (protective stop settings are discussed in Chapter 11) to keep risk at a minimum. Then, if the stock jumps out of its base, you can add to your position. On the chance that the volume fizzles out and no breakout occurs, you jump out with a loss of only commissions.

Another volume signal for swing traders: After two to three days up, if the current day made a new recent high and appears to be ending in a doji, star, or spinning top (short real body) on low volume, that's a good time to take profits. Why? Any one of those three candlesticks translates into "indecision" on the part of market players.

Remember, low volume means "low conviction." Indecision plus low conviction equals falling prices. Figure 8-2 illustrates this point.

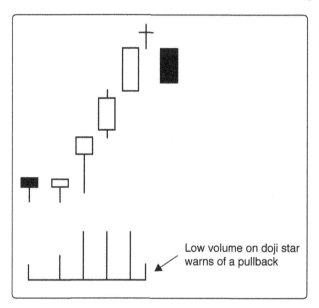

FIGURE 8-2. Low volume on doji star.

Low volume on doji star warns of a pullback

The final volume signal for both swing and position traders: When climactic volume (highly extended volume spikes) appears at what could be an overly extended uptrend or downtrend, it often indicates that the current trend may soon slow or halt. By "highly extended," I mean several times the usual average daily volume. If you trip over a mega-spike like this (you'll see examples in the charts that follow) and you're holding a position, take partial or all profits.

On the chance that the climactic volume reversal warning doesn't play out, and the stock continues in a strong uptrend, you can always buy it back if presented with a good opportunity. (You're better off, though, scanning for a stock that's in early stages of an uptrend. The older the uptrend, the less steam it has left.)

Conversely, just because a climactic volume spike forms on a stock that's fallen for several weeks in a downtrend, don't take this as an automatic trend reversal and start bottom fishing. These patterns sometimes take a few days to play out. Occasionally, they even misfire. However, if you're convinced the stock is about to move higher, you can place the stock on your watch list and monitor it for a future base/breakout.

Figures 8-3, 8-4, and 8-5 illustrate the volume signals we've just discussed. Study the price action that takes place immediately after the volume signal occurs.

If you're interested in learning more about volume signals and how you can use them to support your entries and exits, please go to my Web site, Toni-Turner.com, and check out the downloadable webinar: Volume Signals: How They Make You Money.

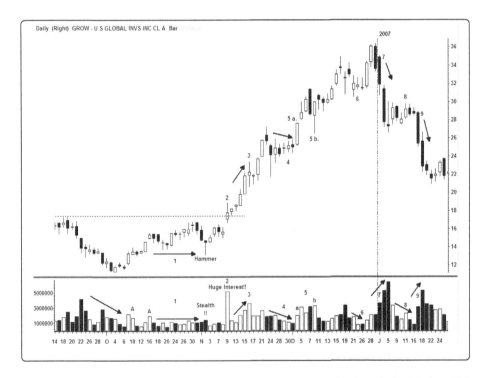

FIGURE 8-3. U.S. Global Investors (GROW) volume analysis. RealTick by Townsend Analytics. In this daily chart of U.S. Global Investors (GROW), an investment services company, we can see how important the role of volume is. 1. During its basing or Stage 1 cycle, notice how volume drops off dramatically. However, notice accumulation marked by "A" and a stealth hammer with buyers stepping up to the plate. 2. Breakout on huge volume. 3. Notice how volume tapers during two days of "inside" action and then increases as the uptrend resumes. 4. A pause in price with multiple doji/spinning tops and much lighter volume. 5a. Price expansion through the prior highs and a rally see above-average volume to confirm buyers. 5b.

Increased volume on a wide hammer. 6. Another consolidation filled with doji/spinning tops and lighter volume representative of indecision. 7. 2007 got off to a bad start after ending 2006 in an engulfing bearish candle. Increased participation by sellers results in a couple of very volatile days in a quick-to-form Stage 4 downtrend. 8. A technical pause on lighter volume. 9. By late January, a range expansion and breakdown of support on heavier volume keeps the bears in control.

FIGURE 8-4. Titanium Metals (TIE) volume analysis. RealTick by Townsend Analytics. Here's another chart that validates how important volume is for trend-following and for confirming signs of exhaustion. The Titanium Metals Corp. (TIE) began showing accumulation clues (label "A") in early 2006 while still basing laterally. Where I've labeled the volume "R," I'm seeing additional "tells" of buyers, this time in the form of a two-bar candle pattern that's very much in the spirit of the bullish piercing pattern. Notice how the bulls showed equal and above-average force! 1. The breakout on higher and above-average volume. 2. These candles point to "2 & 3" setups for swing longs. While each ended up working, notice how difficult the road higher was, because volume didn't confirm the triggers. 3. Now here's a show of force: a near 5-week breakout on higher and above-average volume. 4. Another "2 & 3" set up on the same candle, but this time with strong volume! See how much easier trading is when volume confirms? 5. Further confirmation of the uptrend's strength. 6. Good grief!! Now they want it? On the year's strongest volume, but well-extended past any appropriate swing or position entries, this enthusiasm is climactic in nature. 7. High-volume gravestone doji followed by a confirmation thrust down on record volume quickly puts TIE into a Stage 4 downtrend. 8. Evening doji star pattern. Do you see how it retests the prior final stages of the uptrend when it shot into a near parabolic feeding frenzy? Then fear and that overhead resistance took TIE down, once again.

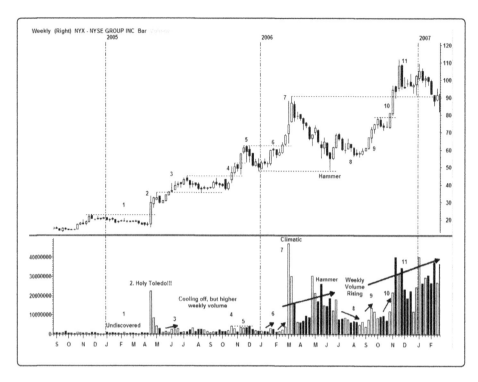

FIGURE 8-5. NYSE Euronext (NYX) weekly volume analysis. RealTick by Townsend Analytics. Let's close off our study of volume analysis with the weekly chart of the NYSE Euronext (NYX), the NYSE Euronext stock exchange holding company. With Stage 1 breakouts typically taking weeks to develop properly, this higher time frame can come in very handy. You'll find that many position traders, like those who study *IBD*, use weekly charts as their bread and butter. With NYX being a relatively new IPO when we captured this chart, and as most of those issues take time to develop into story stocks, we can really see via this chart where investor awareness picks up—and how! 1. Shhh! We're napping. 2. Investors wake up and start to buy NYX. In the form of increasing volume, awareness spikes in a dramatic upturn. 3. A second, albeit smaller breakout on increased volume levels. 4. Base breakout on biggest volume since point 3 and pattern inception. 5. Trouble brews. After more than 17 points from point 4 breakout, volatile and heavy trade starts showing lower weekly closes. 6. A classic weekly handle (from the cup-with-handle formation—we'll study this pattern later) and a bona fide breakout on increased volume. 7. Climactic buying, and more than 28 points are tacked on from the buy point at 6. Time for a rest! A black candle, but hammer low suggests buyers are regaining control. 8. Lighter volume pullback. 9. Volume picks up handily to the upside. 10. Another breakout on increased volume and price thrusting. 11. More than 30 points later, dark cloud cover on increased volume suggests that at a minimum, lateral movement is likely as buyers show exhaustion.

MOVING AVERAGES: WHAT THEY ARE, HOW TO USE THEM

Another important tool you'll keep tucked into your trader's toolbox is the moving average (MA). Moving averages come in three basic calculations: simple, weighted, and exponentially smoothed averages.

For our purposes, simple moving averages work perfectly. We're going to use them as one criterion of our buy signals.

A moving average plots just that: a stock's average price over a designated period of time.

A simple moving average is a line constructed from the closing prices of a stock (index, market) assigned a specified time period. For example, a 20-day moving average equals the sum of the last twenty days of a stock's closing price divided by twenty. The procedure is repeated each day and finalizes as a line plotted on our chart's price pattern.

Moving averages are called "lagging" indicators, because they use information that has already taken place. Because of that, they are also called "trend following" indicators. They work best as predictive indicators when the price pattern is rising in the context of an uptrend or downtrend.

Major moving averages can act as strong support areas. Think of them as magnets for price patterns. Over and over, you'll see a stock in an uptrend rise high above its 20-day moving average line, only to fall and dip back down to it. Price will use the line for support, and then bounce and rise again.

Moving averages can also act as potent resistance. Once a stock trades under a major moving average, that line can serve as a ceiling, or resistance, to hamper the stock's future price rise. This is especially true with a stock that's fallen below the 200-day moving average. A stock that's slid beneath this "power line" usually puts up a struggle before clawing its way back through. This is especially true when the stock has traded below this long-term line for weeks or months.

Conversely, a stock that dips to its 200-day MA many times finds support on it.

The term "major" moving average usually refers to the brawniest ones used by technical analysts. You'll hear them mentioned on CNBC and other financial networks. They are the 20-day, 50-day, and 200-day moving averages. Other effective moving averages are the 10-, 30-, 40-, and 100-day MA. Everybody develops their favorites—I've heard traders swear by the 12-, 18-, 21-, and 67-day MAs.

On our charts, we're going to start with the 20-, 40-, 50-, and 200-day MAs. You may want to experiment with others as you gain experience, but hold yourself to a limit. Ever seen a mass of tangled fishing line? That's what moving averages look like if you plot more than three or four on a chart. At that point they don't give signals. They give heartburn.

The 20-, 40-, and 50-day MAs will provide decision support tools for our buy signals. The 200-day MA maintains as a thermometer.

Note in which order we want moving averages to appear on a chart. When we look for buying signals, optimally we're looking for the 20-, 40-, 50-, and 200-day MAs layered in that order, from top to bottom. Figure 8-6 illustrates this point.

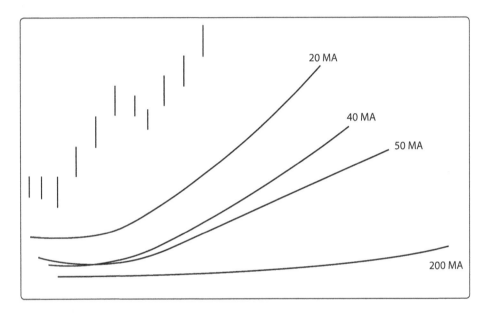

FIGURE 8-6. Optimal moving average layering.

Now, after reading my warnings about stocks trading under their 200-day MAs, consider this scenario: Some years present a volatile market game, to say the least. These volatile times have the power to drive stocks far beneath their 200-day MAs.

As such, these stocks can offer good buying opportunities, especially in the "orderly base with rising volume" situation we talked about in the volume section.

Were we to ignore these stocks because their price pattern remains under their 200-day MAs, we would miss juicy profits delivered by high-momentum breakouts from tight bases. So . . . am I contradicting my previous warning? Not exactly.

Always take overall market conditions into consideration when you trade. Use common sense. Stand back and look at the big picture.

In a raging *bull market* where healthy stocks abound, a stock trading under its 200-day MA should be observed and traded with extra caution and extra risk management. There's a reason the stock has not done well when others around it have soared.

When stocks start basing after a *bear market*, many good companies trade under their 200-day MAs. The market trough that drove them down represents an inevitable part of the unending business and stock market cycles in action.

In this case, would I buy a fundamentally strong company (healing from a bear market) breaking out of a steady base with increasing volume—with its 200-day MA sloping down from high overhead? I might. First, I'd check for sound fundamentals. Then I'd scale in, set hard protective stops (order placed with broker—not a mental stop), and closely monitor market movement.

What I would *not* do is buy a stock trading under its sloping 200-day MA that's within a few points of touching it. The downward sloping 200-day MA can form a powerful ceiling, or resistance. Most stocks will falter and even pull back as they near this bully from underneath. If your stock climbs to a point near the 200-day MA, take some profits off the table. After it rises above the MA, re-enter only if it meets your buying criteria and resumes a solid uptrend. Remember to use wisdom and common sense in all trading situations.

We will, however, not fudge with the other moving averages I listed. We will only target stocks to buy when they trade above their 50-day MAs. The 20-day and 40-day should be layered above the 50-day MA, as previously mentioned.

As I said at the beginning of this section, we're going to add moving averages as a component of our 1, 2, 3 buy signals:

➤ When our uptrending target stock pulls back to the 20-, 40-, or 50-day MA for support, then bounces.
➤ When a faster moving average rises from below a slower moving average to cross and climb above it. This is called a "moving average cross" or "crossover."

Let's consider the first point. Think of a moving average rising like a staircase. Your feet, moving up the staircase, are the stock. Your foot rises above the step, and then moves lower to use it as support before rising again. The moment your foot lifts off the staircase equals the stock rising off its moving average. That's the buy point, and as you will soon learn, it will correlate perfectly with volume and our 1, 2, 3 signals.

Now let's look at an example of the second point. A 20-day MA is inverted and trading under the 50-day MA on a daily chart. (Naturally, both are below the price pattern.) As the stock rises out of its base, the 20-day MA starts curving up, will cross over the 50-day MA, and rise above it. When you see a faster MA (the shorter the time frame of the MA, the "faster" it is) cross above a slower MA, it's a very bullish sign. Depending on how the stock fits the other buying criteria we will establish, we may use the crossover as an add-on signal.

Figure 8-7 illustrates both points.

To clarify this explanation, the following charts show examples of moving averages, how stocks use them for support, and bullish crossover signals.

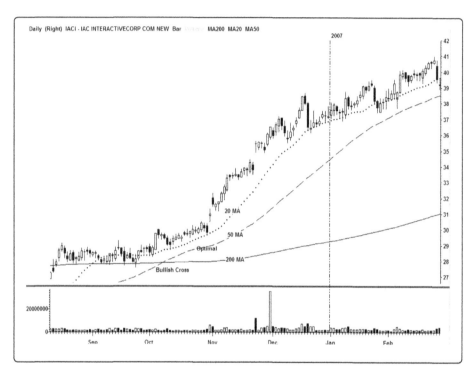

FIGURE 8-7. IAC/Interactive Corp (IACI) cross and MA alignment. RealTick by Townsend Analytics. You might recall part of this daily chart of IAC/Interactive Corp (IACI) from our study of 1, 2, 3 setups. By now, you can spot the setups without the labels. In this view I've expanded the daily to show how the power of moving average crossovers and optimal alignment of those trendlines helped influence those entries and developed into a healthy uptrend. Notice after the bullish crossover of the faster 50-day MA through the 200-day MA, all three moving averages are in optimal position, with the 20-day MA already taking charge on top. In fact, the "2" entry from our earlier exercise finds support off the 20-day MA, right after the crossover. A second test of this trendline occurs right before an explosive upside gap. That results in a very strong trend that has the 20-day MA acting as support, but offers no real testing of that line until late December and nearly two months later.

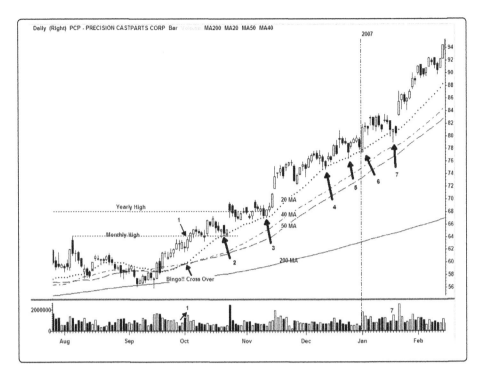

FIGURE 8-8. Precision Castparts (PCP) daily crossover and 20-day MA support. RealTick by Townsend Analytics. On this daily chart of Precision Castparts Corp. (PCP), a manufacturer of metal components and products for engines, we've added a fourth and final moving average, the 40-day MA. In this case, though, after the initial moving average crossover and alignment of our trendlines, we could actually erase everything but the 20-day MA and use that as our trading guide. 1. The 20-day MA crosses the 40- and 50-day MAs. Incidentally, this lines up with a 4-day consolidation breakout on heavy volume. That's no accident! The referenced arrows (numbers 2 through 7) show how amazingly well the 20-day MA defines PCP's uptrend. On six separate occasions the moving average is used as support and a possible buy signal for entries. Notice how number 2 and number 3 also occur at powerful price pivots. And finally, number 7 is interesting, as it's the first sign of real trend weakness. Intraday action results in a long shadow and a closing hammer that closes just above the 20-day MA on heavy volume, adding conviction that the buyers are still in control after a slight bout of well-deserved profit-taking.

FIGURE 8-9. Coach Inc. (COH) daily uptrend. RealTick by Townsend Analytics. This daily chart of Coach (COH), the trendy women's handbag manufacturer, is a slight reality check after the picture-perfect 20-day MA trend in Figure 8-8. Here, the 20-day MA is still the dominant trend for the bulk of our support entries, but the higher the price moves, the more volatile those entries become. Coach is a great example of why we use volume and candle analysis as added confirmation to a moving average trigger. 1. The 20-, 40-, and 50-day MAs are properly aligned, while the 200-day MA is far enough away as to be a non-issue. This is a high-volume hammer test that finds support by the close, above the 40-/50-day combo. Perhaps Coach will find enough buyers to move higher. 2. A high-powered price breakout of the 20-day MA. 3. The 50-day MA crossover of the 20-day MA; now the moving averages are perfectly aligned. Again, notice the high volume enthusiasm! 4. Our first pullback entry to the rising 20-day MA with strong volume on a bullish engulfing candle. 5. A pullback of nearly three weeks and a second 20-day MA buy signal from a doji. And once again, stronger volume is apparent. Nice! 6. Here's a great reason why we look for technical confirmation. 6A. After a 2-day test, a bullish candle reverses cleanly above the 20-day MA, but where's the volume? 6B. A second breach and closing reversal of the trendline on equal volume makes the potential case for this buy signal. However, notice that these two entries are right before the Christmas holiday. This time period is associated with increased risk due to lower volume levels. 7. Welcome in 2007, higher volume, and a trigger that ends up seeing a handful of points before faltering from a shooting star top. 8. Coach's first test of the 50-day MA on a huge volume hammer! Sign me up! 9. While this isn't a trend entry, I wanted to point out a decent "trend exit" based on a couple of factors. First, after a multi-point run up, Coach establishes a dark cloud cover top on increased volume. That's a nice signal to book at least partial profits. Second, after also setting all-time highs, notice too how stretched the price pattern is from the 20-day MA trend, which supported the bulk of the ride up; there's little or no support for quite a few points before buyers might step up to the plate. 10. An ugly (for trapped longs) wide-range hammer on a bearish price gap. Please keep in mind that these violent price gaps many times take place on negative earnings announcements. After a very nice trend higher and now, potential overhead resistance, risk-to-reward is greatly reduced.

As you work through these charts and study them, you'll see how price patterns, volume, and moving averages all move in harmony, just like a well-directed orchestra.

In the next chapter, you'll learn how to add one more instrument to the symphony in the form of momentum indicators, also called overbought/oversold oscillators. And in the chapter after that one, we're going to go shopping.

QUIZ
‖‖‖‖‖‖‖‖‖‖‖‖

1. True or False? A higher-than-average volume spike indicates strong emotion on the part of market participants.
2. In the context of an uptrend, a profitable price pattern on a chart will show _____ volume on the breakout and subsequent rising candles, and _____ volume on the pullback.
3. You're swing trading. Your stock has risen three days in a row. The current day appears to be closing in a doji, on decreased volume. What action do you take?
4. How would you calculate a simple 40-day moving average?
5. Moving averages act as _____ and _____.
6. We will use the _____ -day, _____ -day, and _____ -day moving averages as decision support tools for our buy signals.
7. True or False? If a healthy bull market is in force, it's fine to scan for stocks trading far below their 200-day moving averages as buying targets. After all, if they fall that low, they're a great bargain.
8. Many institutional managers use the _____ -day MA as a buying and selling tool.
9. When you see a fast-moving average crossing over and moving above a slow-moving average, is that bullish or bearish?
10. If you add moving averages to our buy signal criteria, what will you look for now when targeting a stock to buy?

Answers
1. True.
2. Strong, decreased.
3. Take partial or all profits.
4. Add the closing price of a stock for each of the last forty days, then divide the sum by 40.
5. Support and resistance.

6. 20-day, 40-day, 50-day.
7. False, false, false.
8. Many institutional traders and money managers monitor the 50-day moving average.
9. Bullish.
10. Look for a stock breaking out of a base, pullback, or consolidation that's bouncing off of the 20-, 40-, or 50-day moving average on strong volume.

CENTER POINT: THOUGHTS ARE "THINGS"

"A man is what he thinks about all day long."

—Ralph Waldo Emerson

Every single tangible and intangible reality in this world began with a thought. The chair you sit in, the book in your hands, the computer on your desk, indeed your best friend, originated with a thought.

A thought plus a feeling equals an action. Pure, simple, and accurate. Our thoughts are energy, and we are the product of our thoughts!

I once spoke with a friend who had accomplished a masterful feat in an amazingly brief period of time.

"How did you achieve such a momentous goal so quickly?" I asked.

He shrugged. "It never occurred to me that I couldn't do it." He zeroed in on his goal, held it in his consciousness as a fact, and did it!

What kinds of thoughts are you holding in your mind right now? Are you focused on anxiety, frustration, or even failure? Or, are you centered on ideas reflecting happiness, confidence, and peace?

Indeed, in our hectic lives, we rarely stop long enough to realize the truth: *We create and choose our thoughts.*

Furthermore, when we hold thoughts of ourselves as inept, lazy, or stupid, our conscious mind says, "Okay. You got it. Clumsy, stoic, and dumb you are." Robot-like, our actions follow suit, and those in our world see the person who is all of the above.

Why not rewrite that mindset? Why not mentally live in a consciousness that accepts and believes you are poised, dynamic, and sharp? Your consciousness will work to produce that image and make it a reality.

Since our thoughts are energy, our resultant words and actions emerge as that energy in motion. When we focus on the truth of ourselves as prosperous, loving, and successful human beings, we become that—*and more.*

CHAPTER 9

Additional Chart Indicators: Techniques for Using Them Successfully

"To learn that a man can make foolish plays for no reason whatever was a valuable lesson to me."

—Jesse Livermore

N ow that we've covered charting basics, including important candlestick patterns, the 1, 2, 3 setups, and how volume and moving averages play a major role, it's time to add momentum indicators. The following pages discuss the most reliable and popular oscillators and indicators, and easy-to-understand methods of incorporating them into your chart analysis as money-making tools.

At the end of the chapter, we'll focus on price gaps and techniques for playing them to your advantage.

OSCILLATORS: WHAT THEY ARE

An "oscillator" is not a cubicle you step into and ride up to the third floor of Macy's. An oscillator is a chart momentum indicator that tells at a glance whether a market, index, or equity currently trades in an "overbought" or "oversold" condition.

Mostly plotted as line charts, you'll position oscillators near the bottom of your charts, above the volume.

When a stock is overbought, this means it is trading at the upper extreme of its current price range and may be vulnerable to a correction. A stock that's oversold is scraping the bottom of its current price range and is due for a bounce higher.

A variety of momentum indicators is available for study and use, each with its own benefits and quirks. Those discussed in the following sections—the RSI (Relative

Strength Index), Stochastics, and MACD (moving average convergence divergence)—represent popular oscillators commonly found on most charting software.

THE RSI: WHAT IT IS, HOW TO USE IT

Relative Strength Index is a misleading moniker for this overbought/oversold indicator. When we speak of a company's "relative strength," many times we refer to its health as it relates to the broad market index, the S&P 500. Or, we may be comparing it to the industry index where its stock resides, like the semiconductor index (SOX.X) or the pharmaceutical index (DRG.X).

The RSI, however, does not compare a stock to an index. Introduced by Welles Wilder in the June 1978 issue of *Commodities* (now *Futures*) magazine, and in his book published in the same year, *New Concepts in Technical Trading Systems*, the RSI operates as a single-line oscillator that measures a particular stock's current relative strength as compared to its own price history.

When Wilder first introduced the RSI, he recommended using a 14-day time period. Now, the 9-day and 25-day RSIs are also used by traders.

The RSI is a reliable oscillator, and we're going to use it in our buying criteria. For multi-day to multi-week holds, the 14-day default period works well (and is standard in most charting software). Please stick to that default period for now. As you become more familiar with the RSI, you may want to tweak the default setting to a faster, or slower, time period.

As a price-following oscillator, the RSI is plotted on a vertical scale numbered from 1 to 100. It's considered to be oversold when it falls below 25, and overbought when it rises over 75.

Features of the RSI:

➤ The RSI forms chart patterns, such as a double top or head-and-shoulders (see Chapter 10), which may not show up in the stock's price pattern.

➤ The RSI may indicate support and resistance levels more clearly than the stock's price pattern.

➤ The RSI is a valuable buy/sell decision support tool when it diverges from the stock's price action. For example, the stock price may make a new high, but the RSI does not. That's bearish. Or, the price may tumble to a new low, while the RSI moves sideways or up. That's bullish. Prices usually follow the direction taken by the RSI.

 **HOT TIP**

The shorter the time period you use to calculate moving averages or oscillators, the more volatile these indicators become. For example, an RSI set to a 9-day period gives much faster signals than an RSI set to a 25-day parameter.

To incorporate the RSI into your buy/sell criteria, you'll add it to the signals we already have in place, meaning the 1, 2, 3 entries, strong volume on the breakout, and price bouncing off a major moving average (such as the 20-day, 40-day, or 50-day MAs).

Now add the RSI to these criteria. When you enter a position, you want it to appear in one of these ways:

> ➤ Oversold, and hooking up from below 25 to 30.
> ➤ Hooking up from below 25 to 30 and in an uptrend (making higher lows and higher highs).
> ➤ Making a bullish divergence by rising when the stock price is consolidating, or pulling back, in the course of an uptrend.

Figures 9-1 and 9-2 show the RSI in action. Note the different ways it can support your buy/sell signals.

FIGURE 9-1. Microsoft (MSFT) RSI analysis. RealTick by Townsend Analytics. On this daily chart of Microsoft (MSFT), note that the RSI is added in the scale above the volume. I've drawn in horizontal dotted lines at 25, 50, and 75 on the RSI scale for additional clarity. 1. Notice how as price trends higher, the RSI has started to diverge negatively from price; it's reading above 75 and in overbought territory. That's a classic bearish divergence and in this instance does lead price, which moves into a two-and-one-half-week pullback. 2. An engulfing bullish candle on strong volume off a test between the 40 and 50 MA, with the RSI hooking back up from below 50 is good confirmation for a long entry. 3. A similar development and

opportunity, but this time, a hammer candle acts as the reversal bar. 4. A push up to 75 after two days of rallying is a nice spot to take partial profits or get ready to do so. 4A. A retest of the highs is met with a negative RSI divergence, bearish dark cloud cover candle, and heavy volume. Yikes! 4B. A lower high in the form of a bearish harami and a plunging RSI the next session. 5. Bullish piercing test of the 200-day MA embedded within a large bullish hammer. This time the RSI signal is oversold and hooking up from below 30.

FIGURE 9-2. U. S. Steel (X) RSI analysis. RealTick by Townsend Analytics. This time we're looking at a daily chart of U. S. Steel (X). Once more, we see how well RSI can lead price movement and give us an extra heads up. 1. RSI shows a stronger positive divergence while price puts in a double-bottom pattern. Look at that volume confirmation as the candle clears moving average resistance. Without alignment of the moving averages, the signal doesn't have that important confirmation, but does illustrate many important trade characteristics. 2. This is a classic pattern: MAs optimally aligned, a test of the 40-day MA, strong volume, and the RSI quickly hooks up from the 30 oversold level. 3. A doji test of support on a pullback, while the RSI shows positive divergence. 4. By the highs, it appears as though we've hit an overbought reading, but also notice the price versus RSI negative divergence. Further, a light volume harami serves as a nice signal to book profits. 5. This is similar to the price and RSI pattern in number 1, but here the breakout candle clears all three slower moving averages. 6. Hey longs —lighten up! Note the topping candles culminating in a gravestone doji, with mostly lighter volume during the several sessions leading into the highs. Plus, look at that negative RSI divergence. Great signal! 7. Here, RSI shows positive leadership as it pushes quickly through its 50 level, while a higher-volume doji close above the 20-day MA acts as nice confirmation to the hammer low set three days prior. 8. Price forms a double top on lackluster volume, a gravestone doji kicker, and negative divergence from overbought levels (a downward sloping triple top) in the RSI. This is yet another great signal for booking profits before they quickly disappear!

As I mentioned earlier, in our final buy criteria, we'll use the RSI as our main momentum indicator. Still, you'll want to read over the descriptions of the remaining momentum indicators, as they have alternative styles and benefits.

STOCHASTIC OSCILLATOR: WHAT IT IS, HOW TO USE IT

Traders sometimes refer to the Stochastic (pronounced sto kas' tik) Oscillator as "Stochastics," because it employs two lines to give a single signal.

An overbought/oversold indicator developed by Dr. George Lane, the Stochastic Oscillator compares where a stock's price closed to its price range over a specific period of time.

The driving principle: As a price rises in an uptrend, the closing price moves to the upper end of the recent price range. In a downtrend, closing prices usually sink to the bottom of the range. We won't study the actual formula here. If you ever see it, you'll be glad we didn't!

Again, the Stochastic Oscillator is displayed in two lines. The major line is called the "%K." The second line, which is the signal line, is referred to as the "%D." The %D is a 3-day moving average of the %K. Many times you'll see the %K as a dotted line, and the %D as a solid line.

Stochastics come in two speeds—fast Stochastics and slow Stochastics. The one described in the previous paragraph is fast Stochastics. In slow Stochastics, the slow %D is plotted as a 3-day average of the fast %D.

If you plot either fast or slow Stochastics, your charting software understands the equations needed to calculate the display.

I call this indicator "the drama queen," because it tends to fly and fall in dramatic swings. That's why I prefer slow Stochastics. Slow Stochastics has a somewhat smoother flow than fast Stochastics and reduces herky-jerky signals that can whipsaw traders.

The %K and %D lines rise and fall in tandem, on a scale of zero to 100. Readings above 80 are considered overbought, and readings below 20 are oversold.

Stochastics Buy/Sell Signals:
➤ Buy—when the lines are below 20, and the faster %K line crosses above the slower %D line.

HOT TIP

Stochastics have one drawback. When a stock stays in a strong uptrend (or downtrend) for an extended period of time, the oscillator will rise (fall) to the overbought (oversold) position, and then stay "glued" to the top or bottom of the scale while the trend continues. This condition renders the stochastics neutral until the trend changes and the lines move below 80 (sell signal) or above 20 (buy signal).

(Beware of short-term crossovers. Use additional price indicators to confirm the reversal.)

➤ Sell—when the lines are above 80, and the %K crosses the %D to the downside.

➤ Look for divergences, just as you do with the RSI. An example: Bossy Bank's price makes a new high. At the same time, Stochastics moves sideways or hooks to the downside. That's called a "bearish divergence." The price will potentially follow Stochastics south. Or, while Bossy Bank experiences a normal consolidation period in an uptrend, the Stochastics suddenly hooks up. Referred to as a "bullish divergence," it tells you to prepare for a continuation of Bossy's uptrend within the next few time periods.

➤ Stochastics quirk: A stock carves an orderly base and Stochastics issues a bullish divergence. As the stock climbs out of its base and shoots higher, Stochastics quickly signals an overbought condition. As the stock moves higher in a strong uptrend, Stochastics continually pops against its upper scale, at the 90–100 levels. In other words, the indicator remains overbought for the duration of the stock's uptrend. Point: Like many momentum oscillators, Stochastics issues valuable buy/sell signals when the stock is basing in Stage 1, or rolling over in Stage 3. When the stock is trending, however, Stochastics may lose its predictive value if it continually gives overbought or oversold readings.

Figure 9-3 shows Stochastics on a daily chart of U. S. Steel Corp. (X).

HOT TIP

Limit your oscillators to one per chart. Choose a single oscillator and get to know it, up close and personal. Study how it relates to the price and moving average action with which it correlates. As you gain experience, replace it with another oscillator, and try that one out.

FIGURE 9-3. U. S. Steel (X) Stochastics analysis. RealTick by Townsend Analytics. We're looking at the same daily chart of U. S. Steel Corp. (X), but using fast Stochastics in this example. Much like RSI, Stochastics can offer positive and negative divergences to help confirm our setups. When the %K (dotted line) crosses over the %D (solid line) after they hook up from the bottom (oversold), a buy signal occurs. Similarly, when %K crosses over the %D after topping and hooking down, a sell signal takes place. The arrows represent these signals. Notice too, in this uptrend, the buy signals are more robust and "overbought" stays overbought, negating the indicator's momentary usefulness; it also flashes more false sell signals. Further, flip back to Figure 9-2 and see how this compares with our RSI indicator. Although slower to react, at times the RSI does a better job at providing fewer false entries and exits.

THE MACD: WHAT IT IS, HOW IT WORKS

Traders refer to the MACD as "the mac-dee." The acronym stands for "moving average convergence divergence" indicator.

Developed by Gerald Appel, publisher of *Systems and Forecasts*, the MACD is a trend-following momentum indicator/oscillator that tracks the relationship between the 26-day and 12-day exponential moving averages of a price pattern. A 9-day exponential moving average, referred to as the "signal line," accompanies the MACD and indicates buy/sell setups.

The MACD usually acts as a "lagging" indicator, meaning it delivers signals from price information that's already taken place. Therefore, the MACD is best used in strongly trending markets.

At times, however, the MACD will diverge from price and move in the opposite direction. This indicates a potential weakening in the current price trend.

Because the traditional MACD issues signals a bit more slowly than its more hyper collegues (RSI and Stochastics), short-term traders may leave money on the table by adhering strictly to its signals. To obtain faster signals, I recommend using the MACD histogram, available on most charting programs.

The MACD histogram (MACD-H) represents the difference between the MACD and its 9-day exponential MA. The MACD-H will snake above and below its zero line, moving into positive (above zero) or negative (below zero) territory.

MACD-H Signals:

➤ Crossovers. Buy signal (bullish) equals when the MACD-H rises above its zero line. Sell signal (bearish) equals when the MACD-H tumbles below the zero line.

➤ Overbought/oversold indicators. As an overbought/oversold oscillator, when the MACD-H rises to the top of its scale and resembles a majestic mountain, the stock may be overbought and ready to pull back. When the MACD-H edges below the zero line and digs a deep scoop to the downside, the stock is oversold. When the histogram bars shorten and edge back up, the stock should be preparing to bounce.

➤ Trading idea: Use a MACD-H on a weekly chart to generate a long-term buy/sell signal. Then, go to a daily chart of the same stock, and trade only in the direction of that longer-term signal.

Figure 9-4 illustrates the MACD-H. Check out the buy/sell signals it gives as it moves above, then dives below, the zero line.

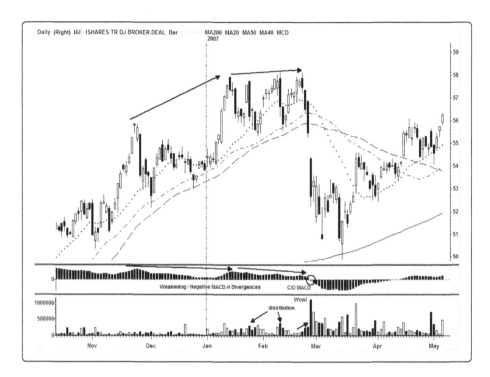

FIGURE 9-4. iShares Trust DJ Broker-Dealer (IAI). RealTick by Townsend Analytics. This daily chart of the iShares Broker-Dealer Trust (IAI), which is an ETF, illustrates the use of the MACD-H (histogram) indicator. In this instance, note that while price made a higher high from late November into early January 2007, the MACD-H was weak during most of that period. In fact, the IAI only managed to approach its prior highs due to the rapid multi-day upmove in early January, but still fell short. From there, with the IAI putting in a series of three slightly higher highs ("triple top" in advanced technical talk) through February, we have a solid negative divergence with the MACD-H. The actual sell signal when MACD-H crosses its zero line is "a day late" for most short-term traders. However, the divergence, the distribution characteristics of volume, the last two tops being confirmed by engulfing bearish candles, plus the breakdown through moving averages certainly gave traders ample signals for a short entry, as well as warnings to take profits in long positions.

ON-BALANCE VOLUME: WHAT IT IS, HOW TO READ IT

The On-Balance Volume (OBV) represents another decision support tool we'll use for our buying criteria.

Originally developed by market technician Joe Granville, the OBV is a momentum indicator that integrates volume and price change. Take a quick glance at this single line superimposed onto a chart's volume spikes, and you can gauge whether money's flowing into—or out of—a stock.

The OBV works like this: Say Bargain Biotech closes higher than the previous day's close; the OBV considers the total volume on this day to be positive. When Bargain closes lower than the previous close, the OBV records the volume as a negative. Therefore, the OBV tracks the cumulative volume of a stock and assigns it positive or negative value. The line can trend higher or lower, depending on the stock's volume momentum.

HOT TIP

Remember, you want to go long with stocks receiving positive (buying) energy. The OBV represents a snapshot of the energy—positive or negative—that drives your stock's price.

The basic theory behind the OBV is that volume precedes price moves and is, in itself, a leading indicator. If you're scanning charts and see that the OBV has bottomed out and then hooks back up, you can assume money is flowing back into the stock.

Read the OBV like price patterns. That means it moves just like price: up, down, and horizontally. For our purposes, we want the OBV hooking up, or in a solid uptrend, just like the corresponding price pattern. As it can be a short-term indicator, the OBV only needs to be moving up to give us the signal we need.

Points to learn about the OBV:

➤ When the OBV reverses from a downtrend by hooking up near the bottom of the volume spikes, the downtrend may have been broken. You may see this happen in a basing stock. As this event normally precedes a price breakout, quickly check out your remaining buying criteria (we'll establish buying criteria in Chapter 10) for a possible entry point.

➤ Conversely, if price movement precedes OBV action, we call this a "non-confirmation." This occurs at the conclusion of extended uptrends or downtrends. Think "divergence," and if you're holding the stock, consider taking a portion or all of your profits.

The following charts (Figures 9-5 and 9-6) show how the OBV displays its signals.

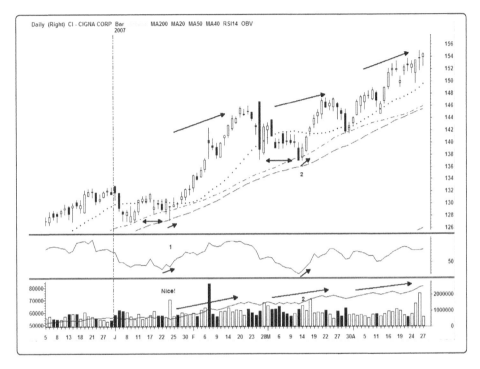

FIGURE 9-5. Cigna (CI) daily and OBV. RealTick by Townsend Analytics. This daily chart of the Cigna Corp. (CI) shows a consistent uptrend of higher highs and lows and an equally convincing and confirming OBV. In conjunction with two upward hooks from the RSI indicator, Cigna offers two moving average/double-bottom tests on strong volume. Point 1 is further confirmed by its hammer finish, while point 2 develops as a bullish piercing setup. Nice!

FIGURE 9-6. Caterpillar (CAT) daily OBV with RSI. RealTick by Townsend Analytics. This is a daily chart of Caterpillar Inc. (CAT). I've removed the volume indicator to emphasize the OBV confirmation of trend, as well as the key divergences that act as solid secondary evidence for trade decisions. 1. Notice how well OBV confirms the uptrend through February 2006, while RSI puts in a stable, but overbought reading, which will occur in trending markets. At this juncture, a higher high in price is not confirmed by OBV. And, note how RSI drops rapidly too; that's a definite heads-up of waning strength. 2. Two higher highs and higher lows are established in CAT into mid-May. However, once more, we can see highly evident negative divergences. And at this time in the established trend, it's no longer our friend, because an evening star pattern marks the beginning of a Stage 4 situation. 3. Here, and at much lower levels, CAT puts in its first test of the 200-day moving average. A couple of days later, with a hammer low in place, secondary confirmation comes into play, along with positive divergences in our indicators.

BOLLINGER BANDS: WHAT THEY ARE, HOW TO READ THEM

Bollinger Bands come to us courtesy of John Bollinger (*www.bollingerbands.com*). They are displayed as an upper and lower band plotted above and below the equity's price pattern, and are calculated at standard deviation levels.

Basically, standard deviation equals a measure of volatility. High standard deviation levels occur when prices change dramatically (think: trend reversal). Low standard deviation values translate into quiet price movement (think: consolidation).

The operative theory behind Bollinger Bands is that the price pattern tends to fluctuate within the upper and lower band. Further, when the price rises (or falls) to touch the boundary of one band, it will then reverse and fall (or rise) to the opposite band.

What you need to know when using Bollinger Bands:

HOT TIP

Say you go to dinner in a New York City diner. Typically, the waitress presents you with a menu as thick as a phone book that lists what appears to be hundreds of entrees. Your taste buds tangle in confusion—you can't make a choice. Similarly, beware of the "paralysis of analysis." If you overlay too many indicators and oscillators on your charts, you may end up with conflicting signals. Please limit your indicators and oscillators to a manageable number.

➤ When the price moves to touch one band, it usually reverses and heads all the way to the other band (good for projecting price targets).

➤ When the bands tighten because volatility lessens, look for a sharp price change to occur. Compare this to a breakout from a consolidation pattern.

➤ When the price penetrates one of the bands and moves beyond it, it implies strength in that direction—or a trend continuation.

Study the following chart, Figure 9-7, to see how Bollinger Bands can be incorporated into a price pattern to give added information.

FIGURE 9-7. OptionsXPress (OXPS) daily Bollinger Bands. RealTick by Townsend Analytics. This daily chart of brokerage house OptionsXPress Holdings, Inc. (OXPS) does a fine job of showing the major operative themes behind Bollinger Bands and how to profit from them. The most common setup we'll typically see is when price action hits a band and reverses to the other band or envelope (all arrows). 1. Here we have a lower band touch (plus hammer and MA support) as the Bollinger Bands contract or tighten. Get ready! 2. The contraction allows for price to continue through or "ride" the upper band for a very nice short-term move. 3. Bearish engulfing marks the end of that Bollinger "trend." 4. It's not a straight ride down to this bullish test of band and MA support, but it was close to a nonstop ride! 5. This is a violent price drop, as the candle completely lies outside the lower envelope. Part of that downward thrust is easily attributed to the preceding and combined force of the Bollinger Bands tightening (contracting) and a price break below all of our key MA supports. Don't say the bulls weren't warned! After the point 5 price "shock" the price action stabilizes to get back inside the lower band. Then it drifts lower for about a week before moving toward the other upper band. 6. Here the bands have tightened considerably as price action tests the prior lows. It's not a setup I'd enter on the long side, with the MA overhead resistance so close by. Nonetheless, OXPS rallies until the bands open up from their contraction phase. 7. We can see that this is actually the first legit touch of the upper band, but those prior two were really close. Ultimately that test did produce the signal for a move to the lower band.

While Bollinger Bands are a useful tool for both long and short entries and exits, I use them most often when selling short. To that end, we'll talk about them again in Chapter 12, when we discuss shorting techniques.

FIBONACCI RETRACEMENTS: WHAT THEY ARE, HOW TO READ THEM

We owe a debt of gratitude to the Italian mathematician Leonardo Pisano (1170–1250). Best known to his friends by his nickname, Fibonacci (he also went by "Bigollo," which may have meant "wandering good-for-nothing"), he wrote the renowned book Liber abaci in 1202.

In this important text, he introduced the Hindu-Arabic place-valued decimal system and Arabic numerals. He also discussed mathematical problems that resulted in what we now call the Fibonacci summation sequence and the ratios derived from it. Here's one of the most important problems Pisano posed, and the result. Although the question sounds lighthearted, the answer produced a unique and important number system.

"If one places a rabbit couple in an enclosed place, how many rabbits would one obtain after a certain time assuming they reproduce once per month, and that those born can reproduce at the age of a month?"

The following infinite progression (now called Fibonacci numbers) results: 1, 1, 2, 3, 5, 8, 13, 21, 34, 55, 89, and 144, after each month.

You'll notice that Fibonacci numbers run in a sequence. Each successive number equals the sum of the two previous numbers: 1, 1, 2, 3, 5, 8, 13, 21, 34, 55, 89, and so forth. The interrelationships between these numbers are intriguing. First, starting with the number 5, any of these numbers equals approximately 1.618 times the preceding number. Second, any number equals approximately 0.618 times the subsequent number.

Remarkably, many objects formed in Fibonacci proportions occur throughout nature, including butterflies, seashells, and spiral galaxies. The pentagram, Christian crucifix, and Pythagorean triangles also contain these proportions, as do the works of art created by Leonardo da Vinci and Michelangelo.

The four popular Fibonacci studies used by traders include arcs, fans, retracements, and time zones. Most basic charting software programs include Fibonacci retracements. Some of the more advanced programs utilize arcs, fans, and time zones. For now, we'll look at retracements.

What you need to know about Fibonacci retracements:

➤ On a scale of 0–100, Fibonacci ratios are calculated at 38.2 percent, 50.0 percent, and 61.8 percent; the ratios are considered to be a leading indicator (predicting possible future price action).

➤ Draw an uptrend (or downtrend) line, connecting a major peak and trough. Then, activate your charting software's Fibonacci retracement option. Start at the bottom of the trendline and drag your cursor to the top of the trend.

(Some charting programs will include a 23.6 percent line.) You'll see five horizontal lines, representing 0.0 percent, then 38.2, 50, 61.8, and 100 percent of the entire move, or trend.

➤ These levels can act as support and resistance areas, depending on whether a stock or index is trading above or below the lines.

Since so many traders use Fibonacci retracement levels for guidance, some support/resistance action may be a self-fulfilling prophecy. Still, it's uncanny how many times a stock in an uptrend will pull back to a Fibonacci level, then bounce. Or, a stock in a downtrend will rebound to a Fibonacci level, and then begin its fall anew.

Some traders use "Fibs" or "Fib lines" as protective stop guidelines. For example, they position their stop points a quarter-point or so (depending on the stock's price volatility) below a stock's 61.8 percent retracement level from the previous high.

Remember, no indicator is bulletproof. No single indicator predicts future price movement with absolute accuracy. Just because your stock happens to be heading for a Fibonacci retracement level is no guarantee it's going to halt there and bounce. It could just as easily slice right through it.

Indicators—no matter how popular—are just that. They indicate. Please don't use them as an excuse to stay in a losing position.

While we're not going to use Fibonacci retracements for our buying criteria, you'll want to use them as a predictive chart tool. I use them primarily to predict future price moves in indexes. Study the weekly chart of Google, Inc. (GOOG) in Figure 9-8 to understand how price patterns use this indicator for support and resistance.

FIGURE 9-8. Google (GOOG) weekly Fibonacci study. RealTick by Townsend Analytics. Here's a solid example of how Fibonacci levels work as both support and resistance using a weekly chart of Google Inc. (GOOG). The retracement levels of 38.2 percent, 50.0 percent, and 61.8 percent are calculated by starting with the Fibonacci Base in the lower left quadrant of the chart and moving up to the trend or Fibonacci Peak. We can see that a few weeks after this cycle, the pullback finds support at the 38.2-percent level. From there a rally of nearly 60 points (Wow! Even though we are talking the mighty roller-coaster Google...) rips to the upside. At that point, a retest of the former highs or a 100-percent retracement from the Fibonacci Peak to the 38.2 percent establishes a top in GOOG. Using the larger Fibonacci cycle, again, we find a small bounce at 38.2 percent, but real support doesn't occur until a deeper test of the 50 percent is formed. Notice too, that this powerful low matches up with the 40-week MA or, if we translated it onto a daily chart, the 200-day MA. (Translation: 40-week MA multiplied by 5 days in a trading week = 200-day MA.)

PRICE GAPS: PLAY THEM WISELY

As you've studied the previous charts, you've noticed vacant spaces in the price patterns. In technical analysis, we call these "gaps." In candlestick terminology, they're called "windows."

Gaps are open spaces in price patterns created by an absence of trading at that price level. They mainly occur when orders placed before the market opens (and/or in after-hours trading) cause specialists and market makers to set the price higher, or lower, than the previous day's close.

Example: Cranky Computers closed yesterday at 35.50. This morning it opens at 35, with no trades exchanging hands between the two prices. That causes a space to form on the chart, and we say the stock "gapped down."

Or, Bossy Bank closed yesterday at 51.85. This morning it opens at 53. Since the stock didn't trade at any price increment between 51.85 and 53, we say it "gapped up."

Many technicians insist that gaps, no matter how small and how far distant in time, always get filled.

Since I maintain that nothing *always* happens in the stock market, and since I happily celebrate getting through a month at a time with my profits, and my sanity intact, I refuse to fret about a two-year-old, three-cent gap until I see the whites of its eyes.

On the flip side, large, nearby price gaps definitely need to be respected and studied.

Gaps form in three basic categories: breakaway, exhaustion, and runaway. A breakaway gap usually occurs after the conclusion of a major price pattern, and presages the start of an important price move. An exhaustion gap takes place at the end of an extended uptrend, or downtrend, and signals the conclusion of that trend. Exhaustion gaps can be filled immediately. A runaway, or continuation, gap usually shows up about midway into a strong uptrend or downtrend. That means the price hops over one or more price levels, then continues in the direction it was headed.

Gaps can add a lot of excitement to your trading life. Of course, excitement arrives in different forms.

Say you're holding 500 shares long of Bargain Biotech, and it closed yesterday at 30. This morning Bargain opens at 33. You quickly bank $1,500 without any effort. That kind of excitement results in self-backslapping and exhortations to your friends about your incredible trading expertise.

On a different morning, you wake up holding 500 shares of Bossy Bank. It closed quietly yesterday at 50. This morning it opens at 48 and dissolves into instant meltdown. You stare slack-jawed at the screen, then frantically grab your mouse and start clicking at the "sell" button. That sort of excitement produces sweaty palms, gulping noises, and graphic comments to your friends that we aren't allowed to print here.

What should you do in either of the previous situations?

1. You own the stock and it gaps up.
   ➤ Swing traders: If the stock has moved up for two to three days in a row, and you have a profit, take some or all of your position off the table

right at the open. Do not wait too long to take action. Most professional day traders will "fade the gap." That means they trade against the prevailing trend. In this case, they will sell short the stock immediately at the open. Result? The stock falls back toward its closing price from the night before. If the stock gapped open the past two mornings, take all money off the table. If you see the market is very strong, and you insist on buying back part of your position, wait until it trades above its first 30-minute high (the 10 A.M. EST price high), then buy limited shares. Place a protective stop immediately, just under the 15-minute candle established by the 30-minute high.

HOT TIP

Monitor gap size in comparison to price per share and trading range. When a "muscle" tech stock that weighs in at $150 per share, and has an average daily trading range of 5–10 points, gaps up $2, that's no big deal. If a stock that trades at $10 per share, and has a range of 2 points per day, gaps up $2, that's a very big deal! Sell that baby immediately and take profits!

➤ Position traders: If you haven't already, tighten your stop to just under the prior pullback or consolidation zone.

2. You own the stock and it gaps down.

➤ Swing traders: Just as the pros fade gaps to the upside by shorting them, they sometimes fade gaps down by buying them. In this situation, wait a few moments (especially in a positive market environment where there's no negative news about your stock or sector) to see if buying comes into your favor. Then, sell if your stock cannot close the gap to yesterday's close in the first half hour, or less, of trading. If no buying comes in, and your stock shows signs of diving to depths unknown—go with the herd and sell. On the chance of a sudden reversal to the upside on favorable conditions, you can always buy your position back.

➤ Position traders: Assess market and sector conditions, along with possible reasons as to your stock's fall. Bad news or a badly tanking market tell you to sell immediately. What if there's no news, and gap down is small and in context with pullback? Watch for signs of recovery with stop-loss firmly in place.

3. You don't own the stock, but you intended to open a position today if it traded over yesterday's high. Now, the stock gapped open above yesterday's high. Is it too late to enter the position?

➤ Swing and position traders: It's not too late if it performs in a certain way. Wait for the stock to trade for thirty minutes after the open. When (or if) it trades 0.25 over its 30-minute high, and market conditions are

favorable, buy. Set your protective stop just
under support at the 30-minute high.

When a big price gap perches
ominously above a stock's current price, know that the stock
may have to struggle to climb
back through it.

Please note: Exhaustion gaps are the exception
to the preceding. If you get caught in one, *sell* your
position. You have a profit—please take it.

What do exhaustion gaps look like? As noted
earlier, they take place at the end of an extended
uptrend or downtrend, and signal the conclusion of
that move.

Look for a stock that's shot straight up in a steep uptrend on a daily chart.
In a typical scenario, these stocks are usually overextended, trading high above
their 20-day MA.

Yesterday would have seen a huge price spike to the upside. Today, the stock
gaps open—either up or down—then tanks. It crashes through yesterday's close,
and then tumbles down toward the center of the earth.

When you see the signs of an exhaustion gap in action with one of your holdings, take profits fast. If you've targeted this stock for an entry to the long side
for a swing or position trade, the entry is negated.

A final word about gaps. Steve Nison (*www.candlecharts.com,*) the candlestick guru, offers this: Gaps, or "windows," offer stock prices support and resistance. If a stock trades above (or below) a rising or falling window—even if that
window remains weeks away—when the stock nears that window price zone, it
may use it for support or resistance.

So, if your stock makes an unexpected U-turn, and you can't figure out why,
check out the gaps, or windows, a few months back. As a wise trader, learn to
check back on your stocks out of habit and note window price zones for this
reason.

We've covered a lot of information in this chapter. If your brain has gapped
closed, rest for a while. Then return to the next two charts (Figures 9-9 and 9-10)
as soon as possible and absorb the information about gaps.

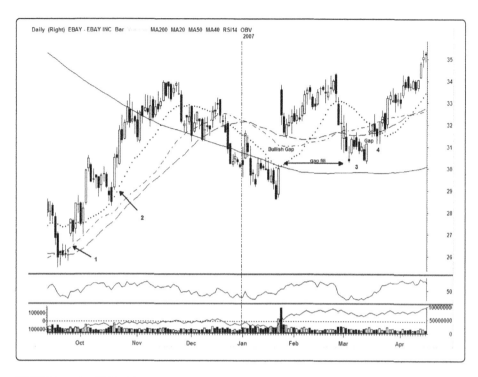

FIGURE 9-9. eBay (EBAY) daily gaps. RealTick by Townsend Analytics. It certainly doesn't move like it used to in the late 1990s, but Internet auctioneer eBay Inc. (EBAY) does a dandy job on this daily chart of demonstrating characteristics that traders anticipate when looking at gap situations. 1. A bullish gap clears key moving averages with the 200-day MA still far enough away as to not be a technical concern for swing traders. A slightly lower close the next day, but more important, the price action finds support around the midpoint of the bullish gap before closing in the upper half of the day's trading range. Testing is also done on lighter volume, a good sign. 2. Here we have what many call a "lap" as the price opens far removed from the prior day's closing price (long, dark candle); however, the next day's open is still within the range of that candle. In this instance we have a bullish lap bar, and what a signal it turns out to be! 3. This is a nice multi-day test of a very large bullish gap set in January 2007. Notice too, how the bullish gap catapulted above all four of our moving averages. Now, that's some power! 4. A second and much smaller bullish gap confirms the aforementioned gap fill test. In wrangling with its three lesser moving averages, this gap is also tested (filled) on an engulfing bullish candle, before the bullish trend resumes.

FIGURE 9-10. Multi Fineline Electronix (MFLX) daily gaps. RealTick by Townsend Analytics. This daily chart of one-time favorite growth stock Multi Fineline Electronix Inc. (MFLX), an electronics products company, is a good example of a handful of gap fills, along with some gaps that have yet to be filled, if ever. Do you think any bulls are still waiting for May's big bearish gap to get filled?

QUIZ
IIIIIIIIIIIIIIIIIIII

1. Define "oscillator."
2. What does "overbought" mean? What does "oversold" mean?
3. What does "RSI" stand for? What does it measure?
4. Say you're swing trading a stock and have been holding the position for five days. The stock price makes a new high but its RSI, which is in the overbought position, hooks down. What action will you consider taking?
5. When you're viewing the Stochastic Oscillator on a chart, readings _____ _____ _____ are considered overbought, and readings _____ _____ are considered oversold.
6. You're using Stochastics as a decision support tool for entry into a long position. At the moment, both lines are below 20 and are hooked to the upside.

The faster %K line just crossed above the slower %D line. What does that tell you?

7. Describe the MACD.

8. How does the MACD-H (histogram) give buy and sell signals?

9. What does the On-Balance Volume (OBV) indicator synthesize?

10. What information does the OBV tell you in an instant?

11. How should the OBV look when indicating a buying signal?

HOT TIP

Stocks often retrace about 50 percent of their last major move up (or down). When the stock you're holding corrects more than 50 percent from its prior high, it may be weaker than you think. Consider taking profits.

12. If a stock's price touches the upper Bollinger Band, and then recedes, where might you predict that price will travel next?

13. Many times, after experiencing a major move up or down, a stock will correct and use Fibonacci retracement levels for _____ and

_____

14. You've been holding a swing trade for three days. You've made 8 points. The stock gapped up yesterday and the day before. Today, it gapped up again. You have the feeling it will rocket forever. What should you do?

15. Yesterday, you bought Bossy Bank before the market closed as a swing trade, buying 300 shares at 48. This morning the bank index tanked, dragging Bossy with it. In fact, Bossy just opened on a gap down at 45. What action do you take?

Answers

1. An oscillator is a technical indicator that tells whether an index or equity currently trades in an "overbought" or "oversold" condition.

2. An overbought stock is trading at the upper extreme of its current price range and may soon pull back or move into a consolidation pattern. A stock that's oversold is trading at the bottom of its current price range and may be due for a bounce.

3. RSI stands for Relative Strength Index. It's an oscillator that measures a stock's current relative strength as compared to its own price history.

4. When your stock makes a higher high, but its RSI diverges from price by hooking down or not making a higher high, you take profits or tighten your protective stop.

5. Readings above 80 are overbought, and readings below 20 are oversold.

6. When Stochastics lines are below 20 and then hook up, and the faster %K line crosses above the slower %D line, it's a "buy" signal.

7. The MACD is a trend-following momentum indicator/oscillator that shows the relationship between the 26-day and 12-day exponential moving averages of a stock's price pattern, in conjunction with a 9-day signal line.

8. The MACD-H (histogram) gives buy and sell signals by crossing over its mid-scale zero line. A buy signal is given when the MACD-H rises above its zero line. A sell signal is given when the MACD-H crosses below the zero line.

9. On-Balance Volume synthesizes, or integrates, volume with price change.

10. The OBV signals whether money's flowing into, or out of, a stock.

11. To give a buy signal, the OBV should hook up or be moving in an uptrend.

12. When a stock rises to the top of its upper band and stays within its boundary, it may then reverse and fall to the lower band.

13. Support and resistance.

14. Will it go up forever? Um, probably not. It's gapped up three days in a row, and you've made 8 points? You know the answer.

15. Quickly assess overall market conditions. If they are bleak (e.g., interest rate hike), and the bank index goes into a free-fall, give your stock a minute or two (not much more) to see if anyone fades (buys) the gap down. On the chance no buying comes in, sell and take the hit. Old trader saying: "Your first loss is your smallest loss."

CENTER POINT: YOU ARE PERFECT RIGHT NOW

"Often people attempt to live their lives backwards; they try to have more things, or more money, in order to do more of what they want, so they will be happier. The way it actually works is the reverse. You must first be who you really are, then do what you need to do, in order to have what you want."

—Margaret Young

We tend to become mired in our hectic lives . . . and it seems one challenge leads into the next. When we struggle and feel overwhelmed with deadlines and formidable tasks, instead of operating from an inner state of happiness and contentment, we start each day from a place of fear. We fear missing opportunities, flubbing deadlines, disappointing those with whom we have relationships. So, we struggle, we push on, we "keep our noses to the grindstone."

How can we change this? How can we free up energy we use to struggle and strain, and rechannel it to flow freely so we can accomplish more with less effort? By rewiring our mental and emotional circuits so that we come from a position of strength, empowerment, and happiness.

Let's start with acceptance. We accept ourselves as perfect, right where we are. We accept what we have, we accept the place from where we're starting. We realize that the present moment is taking place because every thought, feeling, and action we created in our past brought us to this moment. We, ourselves (not someone else), created our personal perspective. Each one of us chose the way we feel about the people, places, and situations in our lives. Knowing this, we can accept our life for what it is, with total objectivity.

Next, we can take responsibility for our life's circumstances and recognize the seeds of opportunity that reside in each. Every event, every person in our lives touches us for a reason. Let's make a game out of tuning into conditions from a caring and nonjudgmental mindset (and heart-set). As your perspective changes, you'll find it astonishing how quickly situations and relationships change. It's even *more* amazing how easily our energy flows, and how our toughest challenges turn into opportunities.

Let's decide that our lives are perfect at this very moment. Once we accept that, we take responsibility for approaching each day with an attitude of caring and happiness. Our energy flows spontaneously and effortlessly, and we live in positive synergy with the world around us.

CHAPTER 10

It's Showtime!

"But my greatest discovery was that a man must study general conditions, to size them so as to be able to anticipate probabilities. In short, I had learned that I had to work for my money."

—Jesse Livermore

As you start this chapter, I'm sure you're muttering something like this: "Hel-looo! I've opened my account and waded through an endless maze of financial Web sites. I've dug into companies and their fundamental rankings. I've studied discipline techniques, candlestick formations, cycles and all the doggoned stages, and how stocks act in each one. I can draw a trendline in my sleep. My brain is stuffed with theories of greed and fear, supply and demand, support and resistance. I know when volume spikes should stick up, and when they should shrink, and I've got indicators and oscillators coming out of my ears. Now, please tell me when I can buy a gol-durned stock. Will it be in my lifetime?"

Just a little more patience, please. And the answer is "yes." Very soon, in fact.

But first you need to learn how to identify basic chart patterns. Did I hear a groan? Trust me, this price action knowledge can make you—and save you—big bucks.

Case in point: In March and April 2000, the NASDAQ indexes (Composite and NASDAQ 100) formed a double top. A double top delivers a lethal warning. If you were holding tech stocks in your portfolio, as most Americans were, and you identified that top, you could have sold and kept your profits intact instead of giving them back—and then some.

Yet another double top reared its ominous head in August and September of that year. The ability to recognize a simple pattern and its prediction would have saved traders and investors from a nasty bear market and the loss of trillions of dollars.

CONTINUATION AND REVERSAL PATTERNS: WHAT THEY ARE

Basically, price patterns on all time frames fall into two categories: continuation and reversal.

Continuation patterns indicate an interlude in a trend where the stock pauses or "rests." In other words, price pulls back, or consolidates, before breaking out and resuming its prior trend. As swing and position traders, we thrive on buying the breakouts that these patterns produce. We scan daily charts searching for stocks exhibiting the price action common to these

As tempting as it is to take an anticipatory jump into a stock that's experiencing a triangle, don't. While they are called "continuation" patterns, there are no absolute guarantees that the trend will continue. Always wait for confirmation.

patterns, and referred to as flags, pennants, and triangles. We'll also look at *Investor's Business Daily* founder William O'Neil's long-term bullish continuation pattern, the cup-with-handle.

Reversal patterns, on the other hand, mean just that: They are price patterns that can forecast an upcoming trend reversal. We'll check out the most prominent of the group: double top, double bottom, head-and-shoulders, and reverse (upside-down) head-and-shoulders.

Continuation Patterns: How to Spot Them in the Making

First, we'll look at the continuation pattern known as the "flag." You already know what it looks like: a tight consolidation pattern in the context of an uptrend (think: parallelogram). Traditionally, a flag lasts three days to three weeks and drifts down against the prevailing trend. When it completes its action, the stock breaks above the flag's consolidation area and resumes its previous trend.

The flag's colleague is the "pennant." The pennant resembles the flag, except that it moves horizontally in the shape of a small, symmetrical triangle. It, too, lasts from a few days to just weeks.

Figure 10-1 gives you an idea of how these patterns look when they appear in uptrends. Naturally, in downtrends they draw similar sideways patterns in the context of price action that's under selling pressure.

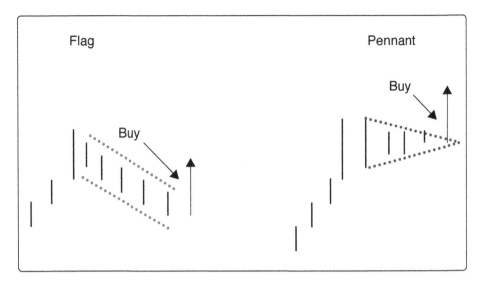

FIGURE 10-1. Continuation patterns: flag and pennant.

Remember the analogy in Chapter 7 that compared consolidation patterns to a pressure cooker? Continuation patterns simply give these consolidation patterns a name. Besides, it makes impressive cocktail party conversation to tell someone you "played the breakout from the pennant."

Another variation on this theme is the continuation pattern known as the "triangle." Triangles come in three basic formations: ascending, descending, and symmetrical.

The ascending triangle consolidates sideways, with the price highs of the pattern forming a horizontal line, and the price lows of the pattern rising.

As you can imagine, especially in an uptrend, the ascending triangle can indicate a bullish price move. Why? Because each consecutive day makes a higher low.

The descending triangle forms the same way, only upside down. The consolidation candles' highs slope down (each consolidation candlestick makes lower highs) while the price lows mostly travel horizontally. This continuation pattern is generally found in downtrends and is regarded as bearish.

As you can guess, the symmetrical triangle formed as a consolidation pattern begins with a wide price range that gets squished from the bottom and the top (equal buying and selling pressure) into a tighter and tighter range. The top of the formation declines, while the lows gradually rise. Although this occurs as a continuation pattern, know that the stock can erupt either way out of this pattern.

Figure 10-2 illustrates these triangles.

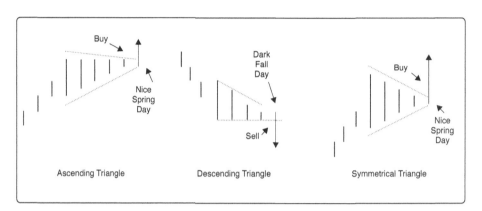

FIGURE 10-2. Additional continuation patterns.

Now, here's important information: Revisit Figures 10-1 and 10-2. Take special note of how the mini-trendlines are drawn right through the arrows. I did that on purpose. Those arrows represent the day (on a daily chart) during which the uptrend (or downtrend) resumes.

Let's assume that all other buying criteria are in place (a list follows soon). In that case, when the stock price (represented in the drawings by an arrow) shoots out of the consolidation pattern and trades three to ten cents above the previous day's high, that's where you buy, or sell short. (To review the 1, 2, 3 buying signals, turn back to Chapter 7.)

In my previous book, *A Beginner's Guide to Day Trading Online, 2nd Edition,* I called the buying day "a nice spring day." Spring has a connotation of release and new growth, and that's exactly what happens when price breaks out of a consolidation pattern—the pressure is released and new growth price shoots upward.

In the descending triangle, which is the bearish pattern used for selling short, I called the breakdown from consolidation a "dark fall day." Obviously, the candlestick that breaks down out of this pattern will be black. (We also associate the fall season with the onset of winter bleakness.)

Yes, these descriptions are a bit picturesque. But when you need a quick mental image of how your target stock should look before you take action, you want these images to come swiftly to mind. The charts in Figures 10-3 through 10-7 show continuation patterns in action.

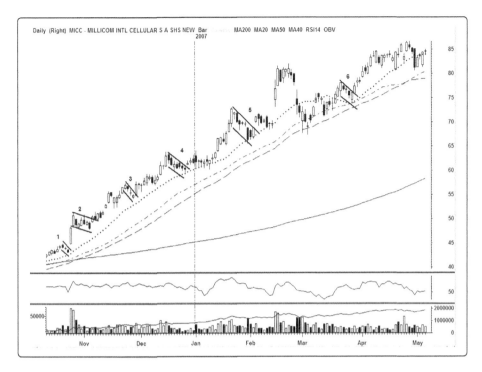

FIGURE 10-3. Millicom Cellular (MICC) daily bull flags. RealTick by Townsend Analytics. On the sturdy uptrend taking place on this daily chart of Millicom International Cellular S.A. (MICC), notice how well this global mobile telecom operator enjoys pulling back into small bull flag formations before resuming its march higher. This price action has provided many low-risk / high-reward continuation entries for traders following the stock.

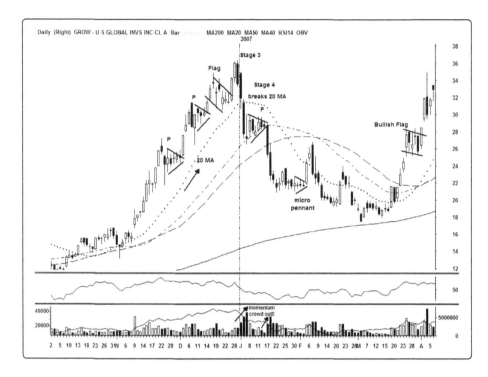

FIGURE 10-4. U.S. Global Investors (GROW) daily flags and pennants. RealTick by Townsend Analytics. Here's a daily view of the volatile U.S. Global Investors (GROW), a high-flying growth stock in the mutual fund management business, which we also illustrated back in Chapter 8. Momentum traders love to ride GROW out of smaller chart patterns like pennants and flags. Look how well the stock breaks higher out of two pennants (denoted "P"), and one flag, before finally reversing in a very quick Stage 3 top bearish engulfing candle. The prices shown here are after the stock split 2:1, so the action shown here, while strong, doesn't quite do justice to how volatile GROW became during its run higher and precipitous slide lower. Notice the nicely formed pennant for right after GROW tumbles below its key 20-day MA. I say "key" because we can see how well that moving average line defined the prior trend as its underlying support in months prior. A small consolidation that I've labeled a micro pennant catapults GROW nearly 5 points, after some very exhaustive selling from the pennant relieves the stock of many bulls. It's not until a test of the 200-day MA is established, though, that the technical picture shapes up again. But when it does, once more, the familiar bull flag is there to help establish profitable positions on quick gains out of the pattern.

FIGURE 10-5. Trina Solar (TSL) daily symmetrical triangle. RealTick by Townsend Analytics. As you might know, initial public offerings, or IPOs, usually provide great returns for the select few that can get their hands on shares before trading actually commences. However, once a hot IPO does make its debut, remember to track it for sturdy continuation patterns as soon as they develop. The reason: Many times we can anticipate extraordinary returns on our swing and position trades from those patterns. Still, they can be risky trades, involving a lot of volatility! Here we have one such IPO, Trina Solar Limited (TSL), a China-based solar power products company that IPO'ed in early 2007. Look how powerful the breakout is from Trina's six-week symmetrical triangle, nearly 25 points in less than two weeks, which does us the courtesy of topping out with a harami. While that's not a bearish signal to go short per se, it is a very good place to take profits. I've drawn a couple more of our now familiar continuation patterns—can you identify their patterns? With gains like those, these formations are definitely worth putting into the memory banks.

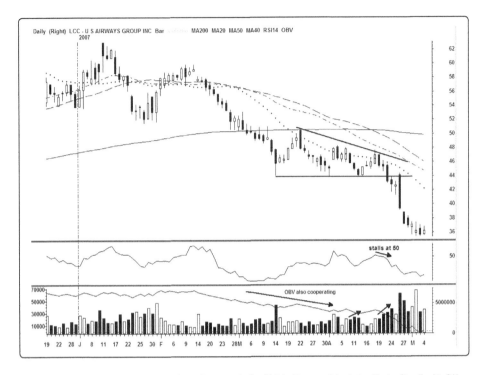

FIGURE 10-6. U.S. Airways (LCC) daily descending triangle. RealTick by Townsend Analytics. Fly the friendly skies? How about "you're cleared to do a nosedive"? There's not much to say about this daily descending triangle in airlines company U.S. Airways Group, Inc. (LCC), except that if you come across a similar situation with moving average resistance, high volume on falling prices, and a bit of secondary RSI stalling, please call me, so I can short it too! After breaking down, the bulls tried to consolidate beneath resistance. By day three, though, our two- to five-day swing trade would have delivered a multiple-point profit.

FIGURE 10-7. Google (GOOG) weekly symmetrical triangle. RealTick by Townsend Analytics. We've shown Google Inc. (GOOG) on more than one occasion. That should be a clue that Google is one of those stocks that's very good to us technicians; that is, it trades well technically. In this instance we're showing a weekly chart that boasts an incredible symmetrical triangle. Notice the positive divergence in the weekly RSI as pattern support is hatched. 1. This denotes the actual breakout accompanied by a nice increase in volume. The next weekly candle, however, is slightly treacherous as higher volume is realized. The candle, however, takes the shape of a near-doji that closes essentially unchanged for the period. A positive confirmation sign is offered the following week, as a lower volume inside bar finds its lows at support. From that point, which is near 420 (this is Google, remember!), Google races higher and continues its uptrend by nearly 100 points before forging a top. Does that move look familiar? It might, as it's from our Fibonacci chart in the last chapter. Now, we've expanded the time shown in order to see what jump-started our Fibonacci cycle, namely the symmetrical triangle.

Cup-with-Handle

As mentioned before, William O'Neil, founder of *Investor's Business Daily*, receives the credit for naming the cup-with-handle long-term continuation pattern. This bullish pattern appears on a chart looking just like it sounds, a coffee cup with a small handle.

Mr. O'Neil advises that properly formed, this pattern takes seven to eight weeks to form. You'll find this pattern on daily and weekly charts. Figure 10-8 illustrates the basic cup-with-handle pattern and the safest long entry.

The cup-with-handle is a wonderfully bullish pattern, and you'll want to monitor high-quality stocks carving this chart formation for an entry setup.

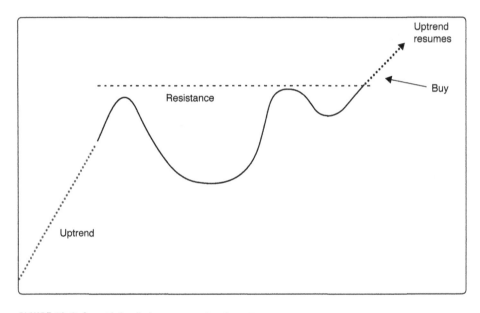

FIGURE 10-8. Cup-with-handle. Long-term continuation pattern.

What You Need to Know about Cup-with-Handle Patterns:

➤ Look for: A stock moving in an uptrend that stops to "rest" by scooping out a cup formation. The cup portion is completed when price rises to previous resistance (top "rim" of cup). Soon, price dips again—flushing out weak hands, or scared sellers—to create the handle, returning once again to resistance (cup and handle top). Within a few days, increased volume and bullish market conditions can ignite an uptrend.

➤ Indication: Bullish.

➤ Completion: When the cup-with-handle forms the handle by rising to the cup's top resistance line, it has reached completion.

➤ What you do: Monitor stock for completion of the pattern, and then enter ten cents to twenty-five cents above the breakout of consolidation, on a "nice spring day."

Figure 10-9 shows a daily chart displaying a cup-with-handle formation.

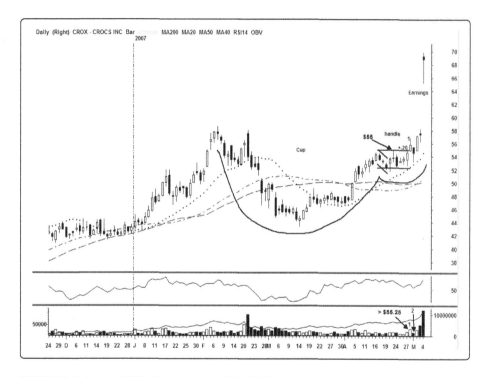

FIGURE 10-9. Crocs Inc. (CROX) daily cup-with-handle. RealTick by Townsend Analytics. This daily chart of the footwear, accessories, and apparel manufacturer shows a cup-with-handle that took just under three months to complete. *Investment Business Daily* and William O'Neil like to see at least seven weeks' duration for the entire formation, with the handle being at least five days in construction before triggering a breakout to the upside. CROX fits those technical tenets nicely. It goes on to do the pattern justice, and you can see why many traders keep it as one of their bread-and-butter formations when the overall market is behaving well. 1. We can see a high-powered breakout occur at this point. An attempt is made in the session prior, but those highs are just twenty cents through the handle high established five days into development. *Investment Business Daily* does use ten cents above resistance, but with this pattern, twenty-five cents to works better overall. The next day, CROX pulls back into the handle. However, look at how much lighter the volume is. That's a classic "shake out the weak hands" sign. Admittedly, if the goal is to be profitable in day one, which we strive for, in this instance price wins, and we'd be out with a small loss. Based on *Investment Business Daily*'s rules (IBD tells investors to establish a 7-percent to 8-percent stop-loss rule), though, the price action is nowhere close to a technical/money stop-loss. Three days later, an earnings-induced blowout (at the time, CROX was high atop *IBD*'s 100 list of growth stocks) made Crocs one for the bulls!

Reversal Patterns: What They Look Like

As mentioned earlier in this chapter, reversal chart patterns indicate that a change or trend reversal is about to occur.

Continuation and reversal patterns show up on charts of all time frames, whether they are monthly, weekly, daily, or intraday.

Remember: You'll see continuation patterns develop on a chart as part of a broader pattern, such as an uptrend or downtrend; continuation patterns form in a few days, or may take up to three weeks. Reversal patterns, however, tend to evolve as important formations in and of themselves.

You've surely heard of the most popular reversal patterns mentioned in trading conversations: double top, double bottom, head-and-shoulders, and reverse (upside-down) head-and-shoulders. As well as forecasting future potential price trend reversals, these patterns act as terrific money-management signals. When you see one in the process of forming, you can take early profits in your established position or start monitoring for a new position entry point.

Here are key points:

Double Top
➤ What to look for: When completed, the double top resembles an "M."
➤ Indication: Bearish.
➤ How it happens: The stock is in an uptrend. It may become overextended at the zenith of the initial top. The price pulls back, and then pivots and resumes its uptrend. When price reaches the resistance established by the first peak, buyers refuse to pay higher prices. The price starts retracing to previous pivot low, or middle of the "M."
➤ Completion: A double top concludes when the price completes the final leg down to the previous middle pivot low of the "M." (Think: An entire "M" is formed.)
➤ Forecast: If the price falls below consolidation support, it will sink lower.
➤ What you do: When you're holding a long position in a stock that's approaching the second peak in an extended uptrend, make sure to monitor the overall market, and the industry group (where your stock resides) for weakness. Get ready to take profits. Also, if the stock is overextended, trading high above its 20-day MA, take profits as soon as you recognize this. To sell short, wait until the stock drops below the support zone formed by the pivot lows, and then enter. This will be a "dark fall day."

Double Bottom:

➤ What to look for: When completed, it looks like a "W."

➤ Indication: Bullish.

➤ How it develops: The stock is basing after experiencing a downtrend. It bounces off previous price support and rallies to establish the middle peak of the "W." It pulls back to the last pivot low (which becomes first pivot of double bottom), and then bounces off that price support. (Buyers recognize a second chance to "bottom-fish." Short-sellers panic as they realize the lows for this trend may be in place.)

➤ Completion: A double bottom is completed when the price makes its final leg by rising to the middle peak of the "W."

➤ Forecast: Price will initiate an uptrend. Typically, though, it will consolidate sideways for days or weeks before that rise. The longer it consolidates, the more powerful the breakout to the upside may be.

➤ What you do: Monitor bases for double bottoms. When you see one forming in a target stock, get ready for buy criteria to be met so you can pounce. (This will be a "nice spring day.")

Figures 10-10 and 10-11 show a double top and double bottom. Study the patterns so you can learn to recognize them instantly on all time frames.

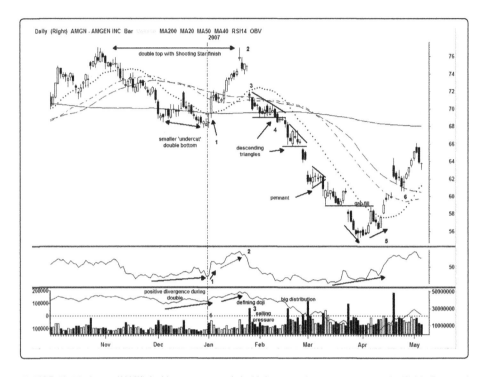

FIGURE 10-10. Amgen (AMGN) double top primary with double bottom and continuation pattern. RealTick by Townsend Analytics. I wanted to use this daily chart of Amgen (AMGN), the biotech behemoth, to illustrate a double-top formation, which it does, but it's also a fantastic chart for demonstrating swing patterns that we've learned in this chapter, from both directions. 1. A double bottom is formed with a small hammer, but with AMGN below the key 50-day and 200-day MAs, it's best to not jump the gun just yet. Three days later, a volume-powered thrust bar may have been considered appropriate with a tight stop beneath pattern lows. The bullish divergences in RSI and OBV are also a great confirmation. This particular double bottom just slices the prior lows. Some call this a "lower low" or "undercut" double bottom. In many instances it's a powerful pattern, as the slight breach of supports flushes out weak hands before the reversal. Still, it's better to watch these patterns for a later entry; wait until price moves above the 20-day MA before taking a position. 2. Here's the largest, or dominant pattern for the chart, a double top. In this case its test of the prior highs matches perfectly and it comes complete with a shooting star top. What could be more perfect? By the way, that's a trick question. The answer is, for existing longs it makes for a great place to take profits and trail a stop. However, in this instance, a still-strong OBV reading and an overbought RSI (remember, overbought can stay overbought) make for a tougher call for shorts and would be considered a more advanced position. 3. A high-volume bearish gap that competes in a near-doji into prior support. Right now, all we know is that a war is about to begin, but the outcome is unclear. 4. Now, the bears are in control. The breakdown from a descending triangle below MA supports on mostly higher selling pressure sure looks qualified for shorts. A couple more continuation patterns with bearish gaps proceed to make good on the bearish trend. 5. We're not calling a bottom here, but the positive divergence, a gap fill, and pullback are shaping up a trade for the bulls and at a minimum, the bears should already have taken some great profits to the bank! 6. A bullish gap above MAs and the prior downtrend, followed by a successful pullback test of MA support.

FIGURE 10-11. SunPower Corp (SPWR) weekly double bottom. RealTick by Townsend Analytics. Here's a weekly chart example of the SunPower Corp. (SPWR) forging a successful double bottom. Since bottoms are notorious for taking time to develop, I thought it was important to emphasize how well the weekly chart lends itself to finding these gems. We see that the solar electric power products provider etches in a very nice "W," as it finds support just above the first low of the double bottom. Notice too how strong the volume characteristics are; the smart money is accumulating, not selling! Further, the RSI also displays a nice piece of secondary confirmation for our pattern. 1. Here's where, without picking the bottom, our "middle" entry begins. We see that SPWR consolidates at its middle peak for a handful of weeks before a solid high-volume breakout occurs. 2. A very nice second "middle" or trend continuation entry sets up. Can you name it? That's right—it's a bull flag, although some traders might refer to this pattern development as a handle, which we talked about earlier in the chapter.

Head-and-Shoulders

The "head-and-shoulders" and "head-and-shoulders reversal" patterns show up less often than double tops and bottoms. Initially, it takes a trained eye to detect them. In a volatile market, recognizing a head-and-shoulders can resemble childhood coloring-book games, where you had to identify several monkeys in a tangled jungle maze of leaves. Still, with a little practice, you'll train your eyes to spot this important reversal pattern.

HOT TIP

Triple tops and bottoms embody the same characteristics as double tops and bottoms, except they have an extra pivot point. Triple tops and bottoms are rarer, and their signals are even more powerful!

The head-and-shoulders formation looks just like its name: It's formed by a left "hump" or shoulder, middle and much higher hump or head, and right hump or shoulder.

Figure 10-12 gives you an idea of the form a price pattern would take when completing a head-and-shoulders. Check out the "neckline," as that represents a very important component of this pattern.

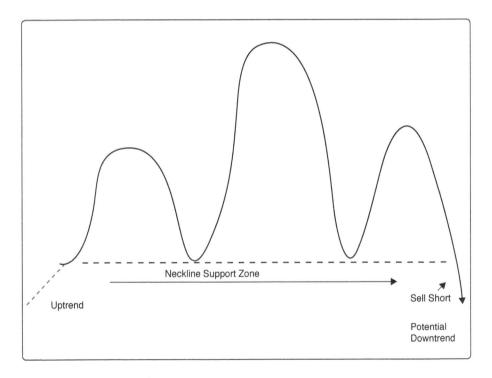

FIGURE 10-12. Head-and-shoulders top reversal pattern.

➤ What to look for: A head-and-shoulders usually forms at the culmination of an uptrend and creates a Stage 3. (On occasion, a shallow head-and-shoulders pattern can show up as a continuation pattern. But we'll only talk about the actual reversal pattern here.)

➤ Indication: Bearish.

➤ How it develops: A stock in an uptrend makes a new high on a daily chart. Then, it rolls over and forms the first shoulder on strong volume, which looks innocent enough. Next it rises to form the head, which at first glance appears as a bullish new high. The caution light blinks when the stock returns to support, provided by the pivot established by the first shoulder, at the soon-to-be "neckline." When the price rises yet again, and rolls over at approximately the same resistance high created by the left shoulder, then falls back to the neckline to complete the right shoulder, the signal is future gloom and doom. The stock is currently too weak to make a higher high, and the uptrend is in danger of breaking.

➤ Completion: A head-and-shoulders is complete when the right shoulder is formed and price falls to rest at the neckline support.

➤ Forecast: If the weak stock slides below support formed by the neckline, it will probably initiate a downtrend. (Many times a stock will gap down at this point.) Strong volume should force the break below the neckline to assure the initiation of a downtrend.

➤ What you do: If you are long this stock, you've sold your position by now (I hope). If you're targeting this stock to sell short, enter the trade when the stock trades three to ten cents below the neckline support zone. This will be a "dark fall day."

Reverse Head-and-Shoulders

➤ What to look for: A mirror image, or "upside down" head-and-shoulders.

➤ Indication: Bullish.

➤ How it develops: Like a double bottom, this pattern occurs in the context of a base. The downtrending stock makes a new low, and then rallies (left shoulder). Price then falls past that low to another new low (head), and then rallies. Price then falls to a low that holds on the support lows of the left shoulder, creating a higher low than formed by the head's low.

➤ Completion: When the price draws the left shoulder, head, and right shoulder, and then rallies to resistance at the neckline, the reverse head-and-shoulders pattern is complete. Typically, the stock will now travel sideways in a consolidation pattern until it breaks out above neckline resistance and initiates an uptrend.

➤ What you do: Monitor target stocks in basing mode for this pattern. When the pattern is complete, watch the subsequent consolidation formation for a breakout above resistance, on strong volume. This will be a "nice spring day."

Figures 10-13 and 10-14 show charts of a head-and-shoulders and reverse head-and-shoulders. Outlines of the forms are drawn into the price pattern to make them more easily recognizable.

HOT TIP

The most reliable head-and-shoulders will form with higher volume on the left shoulder and lower volume on the right shoulder. This indicates that buyers have grown disinterested in the stock and refuse to support higher price levels.

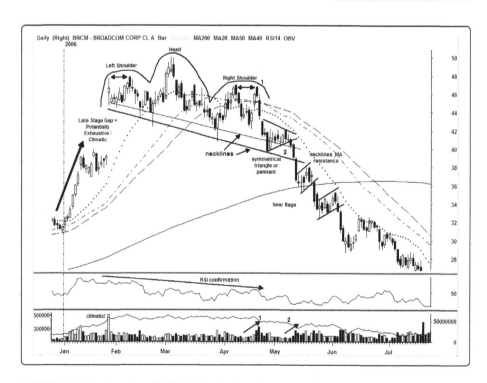

FIGURE 10-13. Broadcom Corp. (BRCM) daily head-and-shoulders top. RealTick by Townsend Analytics. This is a great head-and-shoulders top that formed back in 2006 in the Broadcom Corp. (BRCM). I've drawn in the outline of the formation so you can visualize it better. This particular one is considered a "complex" head-and-shoulders pattern by some technicians, as the left and right shoulders each contain two pivot highs (or small double tops). The key, however, is the shape and height of each component piece. The head forms the highest peak, and the right shoulder is established slightly below the highs of the left shoulder. The shoulders can be equal, but most purists will insist that the right doesn't breach the highs of the other shoulder. More important is the volume characteristic. Once the right top is developed, we need to see higher volume as the

neckline is broken. And if it occurs beforehand, all the better! That gives us a heads up and perhaps an earlier entry if we have enough confirmation in place. 1. In the case of BRCM, with a "double-top" right shoulder and a heavy-volume breakdown of MA supports, this could be a legitimate "early" shorting opportunity for experienced traders with a tight stoporder in place. When the neckline is broken, the real fun begins! 2. BRCM is interesting because, much like any pattern development, "the lines" aren't always perfect. Here, we've drawn in two potential necklines based on the candle bodies and the shadows. The important lesson is to appreciate imperfections and not let a flaw prevent you from seeing the big picture. At this point a small symmetrical triangle or pennant develops with MAs acting as resistance and the necklines as support. However, the high-volume breakdown plummeting price through support and below the necklines confirms the topping pattern is in place. From there, a couple of nice continuation entries are also created for short sellers, as the newly developed downtrend gets under way.

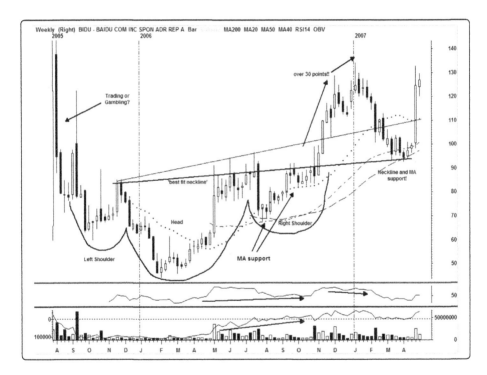

FIGURE 10-14. Baidu.com (BIDU) weekly inverse head-and-shoulders bottom. RealTick by Townsend Analytics. With this weekly chart of Baidu.com, we're returning to the weekly perspective. Bottoming patterns can take time to develop, but for the patient and watchful traders, that means extra opportunity. Here we have Baidu.com (BIDU), a Chinese Internet stock. Look at the left side of the weekly chart—there's plenty of heartache for bulls and bears. No thanks! After several weeks, volatility calms down and the basis for our reversal pattern, the inverse head-and-shoulder pattern, begins. Once more I've drawn in the formation's outline and we see that all three weekly lows conform. Notice too, that aside from the right shoulder forming the strongest low, it has found support off its weekly moving averages. Further, volume picks up throughout this stage of development and is considered a good sign, as it's a bullish phase that sets up the entry through the neckline. Again, this is an instance where we need to appreciate that our lines aren't going to be perfect, but if we can get past that, we'll be all the more profitable for it. In this instance, traders who spotted this breakout on BIDU's weekly chart gained more than 30 points!

TRADING REVERSAL PATTERNS IN NON-TRENDING MARKETS

Generally speaking, position traders need solid uptrends and downtrends to take profits from the market. When the market moves sideways in a languid trading range, position trades are ineffective. Short-term swing trades, well executed, present a lower risk opportunity. (In cases of volatile back-to-back days, when the market rises one day and falls the next, with no follow through, it's a day traders' market. Holding positions overnight during these conditions can be bad for one's wealth.)

With that caveat in mind, if you wish to participate on the long side in a non-trending market, you can enter 2- to 3-day trades as long as you remain aware of the heightened risks involved. Using the reversal patterns you just learned, plan to enter with precision and establish protective stop orders. Once your stock moves up, move your protective stop up and under support areas as a "trailing stop." (The next chapter discusses the placement of protective stop orders in more detail.)

➤ Enter while a stock is still in a narrow base, with high potential to the upside (see "Buy Trigger List" in the next section). When upside momentum is anticipated (the RSI may form a bullish divergence), take a small position as the stock begins to break out of its base on strong volume. Make sure your initial risk/reward ratio is 1:3 (discussed in Chapter 11), and adjust your protective stop order accordingly. As price penetrates and moves above resistance, you may add to the position and tighten your stop order. Check the previous high for the next resistance area; this will translate into your next profit target.

➤ Double bottom. Buy as a stock reverses from second pivot low off support, as it rises over the high of the previous "low day," on strong volume. In other words, as the stock breaks into the final leg of the "W," buy when it trades three to ten cents above the high of the low, or reversal day. Place your protective stop order below the low of the low day (adjust to suit your stock's volatility), adjusting to keep your 1:3 risk/reward ratio. (You may prefer to place your stop under the low of the entry day.) Your initial profit target will probably be the previous high, or midpoint of the "W."

LET'S TAKE IT FROM THE TOP

Are you ready? This is the moment you've been waiting for! Now you can pull your chair up to the playing table, stack your chips into neat piles, cock one eyebrow, and assess the other players with a steely gaze. When conditions emerge that meet your criteria—with rocklike discipline and confidence born of study and planning—you'll deftly slide your money to the center of the table.

Big-Picture Dynamics

When you go to the doctor, she takes your blood pressure and your temperature, and listens to your heart and lungs to determine your overall health before she examines your sore throat. Before a horse race, a jockey walks the track, observes the weather, and inspects his horse to get a sense of how to end up in the winner's circle. The best burglars "case the joint" before they break into a mansion. They learn the entire layout of the estate before they enter the property, in order to eliminate such surprises as snarling Dobermans and noisy alarms. No matter what the situation, evaluating the overall picture before taking action lessens risk and heightens the chance of success.

As astute traders, we always evaluate the overall market before we commit to a trade. It makes no sense at all to enter a long trade—even if your entry price is hit—on a day when the markets feel ornery and perverse. Your stock may hover in positive territory for a while, but overall negative market conditions tend to erode price surges of even the most stalwart stocks. When you enter a trade, you want all possible odds in your corner.

In "trader heaven," the Dow Jones Industrial Average, S&P 500 Index, and NASDAQ Composite move up in concert, drawing spiffy uptrends on daily and intraday charts. Ever-increasing volatility, however, has assigned trader heaven to "special occasion" (think: rare) status.

Therefore, if your target stock is a listed stock, make sure the Dow and/or S&P 500 index is moving up on the day. When you're monitoring a NASDAQ stock, be sure the NASDAQ indexes (100 or Composite) trade in positive territory.

 **HOT TIP**

In summary, here's the first guideline to head the list of your Buy Trigger List: Market conditions, Dow, S&P 500, and/or NASDAQ, are positive.

The S&P 500 stocks reside in ten sectors: Basic Materials, Consumer Staples, Consumer Discretionary, Energy, Financials, Health Care, Industrials, Technology, Telecom, and Utilities. Within each sector, there are several industry groups. You can usually tell by looking at the group name which sector it inhabits.

Choose a Strong Stock in a Strong Industry Group

Say you're the captain of your neighborhood softball team. When you pick players, you select the strongest and most experienced to join your team, not the guy with a clumsy arm, or the girl who runs like a snail.

Just so, when entering the market on the long side, choose a leading stock in a sector or industry group that's a current market leader—not a market laggard.

You can accomplish this in one of two ways. The first is to choose the industry group, and then study the charts and fundamentals of that group's leading stocks. For example, you see the semiconductor industry group currently serves as a technology (sector) leader. Accordingly, you analyze the cream of semiconductor stocks, such as Applied Materials (AMAT), Intel Corp. (INTC), KLA-Tencor Corp. (KLAC), Micron Technology, Inc. (MU), and Varian Semiconductor (VSEA). Conduct a quick once-over of their fundamental ratings (see Chapter 4) to get a sense of each company's internal health. Then, bring up a weekly chart (for a "big picture" view of the stock's health) and daily chart of each of these stocks to determine which one you wish to focus on for an entry.

> **HOT TIP**
>
> When a basing stock dips to the low of its base in a double bottom, reverse head-and-shoulders, or just a simple, plain vanilla sideways formation, weak hands flee and others decide to ignore it. Buyers who come in as (if) the stock turns up and completes the pattern are more likely to hold, so a strong foundation develops.

Build a list of industry groups that interest you. Some of your entries may include the banking industry (BKX), pharmaceutical industry (DRG), biotechnology (BTK), oil and oil services (XOI and OSX), semiconductors (SOX), computer box-makers (BMX), networking index (NWX), retailers (RLX), gold and silver index (XAU), and so forth. For a comprehensive list of industry groups and stock components of each one, go to my Web site, *www.ToniTurner.com,* and click on the "Sectors and Stocks" link located on the ToniTurner.com home page.

Once you've zeroed in on a few focus groups, create a list of prominent stocks in each of these industry groups. If possible, place these stocks in an online focus list that stays updated in real time. Now, when you want to know which stocks are advancing, and which are weak, the information is at your fingertips.

The second way of choosing leading stocks in leading industries is to select those you'd like to target and evaluate their charts. When you narrow down your choice to those with good setups in the offing, make sure they reside in industries currently in favor and poised to lead the market in the present environment. Check the *IBD* proprietary rating, "Industry Group Relative Strength."

For these reasons, the second guideline for your Buy Trigger List is this: Target stock is a strong company in a strong industry group.

Check Out the Fundamentals

Now that you've buttonholed stocks that you're going to monitor for optimal setups, complete your due diligence on their fundamentals. Again, this step was detailed in Chapter 4, where we talked about appraising a company's fundamental rating in *IBD*.

Why do we check a company's fundamentals if the chart looks golden? Because we aren't day traders. Fundamentals aren't mega-important to a trader who intends to hold a stock for only minutes to hours.

Checking a company's fundamental health *does* make sense when the intent is to hold a position from days to weeks. Money is more likely to flow into a stock on a continuing basis—especially by institutions—if that company is blessed with admirable fundamental rankings.

Another reason to appraise fundamentals is because "surprises happen."

Imagine you're an office manager. You place trades before work, during lunch, and on breaks. Today, you place a trade, and then abruptly get called into a meeting before you can set your automatic stop-loss with your online broker. By the time you run out of the meeting and check your new position, it has done a belly flop past today's low. Rats! If you decide to hold it for a bit longer, it may have a better chance of recovery if it has good fundamentals. Translation: If you accidentally get stuck in a crashing stock, make darn sure it's not a fundamental "dog."

Here's an action item that will serve you well: Buy a copy of *IBD*. Then jot down each stock symbol you are interested in trading, its related industry group or sector, and then its *IBD* SmartSelect Composite Rating. Now you've started a watch list of high-quality stocks you can trade, or keep on hold, until the proper setup appears.

Buy Trigger number three is in place when your target company shows an *IBD* Composite Rating of at least 60 to 70, or higher.

The Industry Group or Sector Shows Immediate Strength

Are you going to tell me I've gone addle-brained, because we just discussed this point? Hold on. Let's narrow this point further.

You can target a strong stock in a strong industry group, which is perfect. Still, that industry could be retracing or pulling back on your stock's "nice spring day." If that's the case, and your stock represents a leader in that industry or sector, chances are it will be reined in by the group's weakness.

What you *don't want to do* is to buy a stock that sinks below your entry price on the day you buy it. One of your initial goals is to have a gain, no matter how small, the first day you enter a trade. This gives you a comfortable profit pillow to start with (along with peace of mind). One of the best methods of assuring this is to enter a trade when your stock's industry group or sector is trending up on the day.

To that end, the fourth Buy Trigger: Your target stock's industry group/sector is in an uptrend and positive on the day.

Indicators: All Systems Are Go!

If your final target stock's chart looked good, the next triggers are almost a given.

Still, it's better to be safe and lock this information into place.

➤ Stock has formed a base or is in an uptrend on a daily chart. It's ready to break out of a consolidation price pattern, or a pullback to support.

➤ Strong volume on the break above resistance (resistance = yesterday's high on a bull flag, pennant, or triangle, or tops of consolidation candles on continuation pattern).

➤ Stock is bouncing off of, or is near, the 20-, 40-, or 50-day MA, and it is trading over the 50-day MA.

➤ RSI is below 30 and hooking to the upside, or is drawing an uptrend. (It is not overbought.)

➤ The OBV is rising or is in an uptrend.

The Urge to Fudge

Let's say it's a "nice spring day." Your stock is perched, ready to break out, so the indicators listed should automatically fit into the picture. But what if one of them doesn't match up?

All indicators I listed are important. Still, if I had to choose one that didn't match the Buy Triggers, I'd nominate the RSI, or your momentum oscillator of choice. Caveat: If the RSI or other momentum indicator (for example, slow Stochastics or MACD) showed a definite overbought reading and hooked down into a sell signal, I wouldn't take the trade. But if all other systems were "go," and the RSI (or other momentum indicator) appeared neutral, I might enter the position.

As always, use common sense.

Get Ready to Pull the Trigger: The Buy Setup

Now, zoom in on your stock.

Let's assume that it's midmorning in the trading day. You've been monitoring the market and have checked off the first four triggers on your list. The Dow, S&P 500, and NASDAQ are happy. Your target stock is a leader in a favored industry. Today, the industry is rocketing to the upside. Ah, trader heaven!

If you're planning a swing trade, you're monitoring a stock that's due to break out of its base or due to resume an uptrend from a pullback or consolidation. Today promises to be that "nice spring day." The stock is trading above its opening price and moving up.

Primed and ready, you're waiting for the setup: The stock has to trade three to ten cents above yesterday's high. Then you'll pounce, issuing a buy order, followed by a protective stop order. (You'll learn where to place stop-loss orders in Chapter 11.)

If you're planning a position trade, you also observe your stock moving up, forming a "nice spring day." You wait patiently for it to break out of its base, above resistance. Like the swing trader, when the stock trades three to ten cents over yesterday's high (which should equate with resistance), you issue a buy order. (After you buy, you place your protective stop order.)

When the time is right, remove the safety and squeeze the trigger! Here's number ten on the Buy Trigger List: Target stock is trading above its opening price and moving up on the day. Buy signal: It trades three to ten cents above yesterday's high or consolidation high.

If you think the Buy Trigger List is involved or complicated, or too much to think about, know that as long as you've done your homework, with practice and experience you'll learn to assess current market/industry/stock conditions in just a few seconds.

To review, here's your complete Buy Trigger List. You may want to copy it and print it to keep at your elbow when you trade.

Buy Trigger List
1. Market conditions, Dow, S&P 500, and/or NASDAQ are positive.
2. Target stock is a strong company in a strong industry group.
3. Target stock has *IBD* SmartSelect Composite ranking of at least 60 or higher.
4. Target stock's related industry group is in an uptrend and positive on the day of your entry.
5. Stock has formed a base, or is in the context of an uptrend on a daily chart. It appears ready to break out of a consolidation or pullback to support.
6. Strong volume on the break above resistance (yesterday's high).

7. Stock is bouncing off of, or is near, the 20-, 40-, or 50-day MA, and it is trading above the 50-day MA.
8. RSI (or other momentum indicator of your choice) signals "buy." Indicator is not overbought or signaling a "sell."
9. The OBV is rising, or is in an uptrend.
10. Target stock is trading above its opening price and moving up on the day. Buy signal: Stock trades three to ten cents above yesterday's high, or highs of consolidation pattern or nearby resistance.

Even though you have the necessary information to pull the trigger and enter a long position, you'd be wise to wait until you study Chapter 11 before you jump into a trade. In that chapter, you'll learn money-management techniques that will help you achieve your goal of consistent wins in the stock market.

QUIZ

IIIIIIIIIIIIIIII

1. Name two general categories of price patterns.
2. Give a brief explanation of each of the two categories named in the previous question.
3. Briefly describe an ascending triangle. What category of pattern is it?
4. What is a double top? What does it predict?
5. Describe a double bottom. Where does it mostly occur? How do you play it?
6. Why do you monitor market conditions as a whole, including the Dow, S&P 500 Index, and/or NASDAQ, just to play a single stock?
7. Why is it important that your target stock resides in a strong sector or industry group?
8. True or False? One of your initial goals is to have a gain, no matter how small, the first day you enter a trade.
9. Name three Buy Triggers that describe optimum indicator positioning on a daily chart.
10. Define the final moment you "pull the trigger," meaning issuing a buy order.

Answers

1. Continuation and reversal.

2. Continuation patterns indicate an interlude in a trend where the stock pulls back or consolidates, before breaking out and resuming its prior trend. Reversal patterns forecast a trend reversal.

3 An ascending triangle usually forms in the context of an uptrend. During this period of time, the stock trades in a tight consolidation pattern that can be defined between converging mini-trendlines; the top trendline moves horizontally, and the bottom line rises as the stock makes higher lows. The indication is bullish and the assumption is that the stock will break out of the triangle and resume its uptrend.

4. A double top takes place (usually) after a stock has made an extended uptrend. It reaches a new high, and then pulls back to support, but when it rises to the previous high, buyers refuse to pay more and the stock starts to drop, forming the shape of an "M." When the stock price reaches support of the middle pivot of the "M," the pattern is completed. If it falls below this support, the signal is very bearish, and the stock may fall into a downtrend.

5. Double bottoms, when fully formed, are the mirror image of a double top, and resemble a "W." The form occurs mostly in stocks basing in a Stage 1. You play a double bottom by monitoring it as it completes its pattern, and then moves in a sideways consolidation pattern. When it breaks above resistance of the consolidation pattern, if all other Buy Triggers are in place, you buy.

6. By the end of the day and perhaps sooner, a depressed Dow, S& P 500, and/or NASDAQ will take the majority of stocks down with it. Your goal is to enter on a day when all conditions are positive.

7. It's wise to choose stocks from industry groups that presently lead the market because that gives the stock extra propulsion. A group in disfavor puts a damper on the stocks that reside within it, no matter how strong they are.

8. Positively, absolutely true!

9. Breakout above resistance on strong volume, stock pulling back or consolidating into the 20-, 40-, or 50-day MA, OBV turned up or in a definite uptrend.

10. Issue the buy order when all Buy Triggers are in place, and the stock trades three to ten cents above the previous day's high.

CENTER POINT: FORGIVENESS: KEY TO SUCCESS

"Do not weep; do not wax indignant. Understand."

—Baruch Spinoza

Oftentimes, we establish our vision in our heart and our minds. We declare what we want to feel and define the life we want to live. We may strive for a fulfilling career, loving relationships, vigorous health, spiritual awareness, or all of those goals.

Suddenly, though, we find ourselves "stuck." We sense an invisible roadblock in our path that we can't identify. No matter how we strive to push past it and resume our journey, we remain bogged down. What's holding us back?

Chances are good that if we become quiet and reflect, we'll find a situation or person (including ourselves) in our past that we need to forgive.

It's like we've left a bag of rotten potatoes in our refrigerator. Oh, how sour that bag of moldy potatoes smells! We go to the store and buy a new supply of fresh fruit and vegetables. Arriving home, we open the refrigerator and fill it with the fresh food, but we leave the bag of potatoes on the shelf. Can the newly introduced fresh food overcome the rotting potato smell, or stop the potatoes from molding? No! The potatoes continue to decay, exuding the nasty odor that rapidly seeps into the fresh food.

Just so, we haul grudges and anger from the past into our new lives, and then wonder why we get stuck. Consider this: When we hold resentment in our heart toward someone whom we think wronged us, we actually give our power to that person.

Also consider that the way we feel about a situation is *our choice*. Unfortunately, when we choose to feel anger and betrayal, we end up hurting ourselves!

Could it be that the person who acted badly toward us did it because that was all they could have done, given the conditions of their lives?

Or, could it be that it was easier to blame someone for the situation than to take responsibility for it ourselves? Moreover, did a life lesson permeate the event? Were we so busy judging that we overlooked what could be learned from it?

When we insist on dragging around heavy, moldy "bags of potatoes" filled with past grudges and blame, they weigh us down. The minute we realize how those sacks act as roadblocks and obstacles (think: negative energy) that stop us from reaching our goals, we can toss those sacks away . . . we can forgive.

Forgiveness causes the obstacles in our path to dissolve. We are filled with energizing feelings of lightness and freedom, and we step back on the road to success.

CHAPTER 11

Where the Rubber Meets the Road: Money-Management Techniques

"People who look for easy money invariably pay for the privilege of proving conclusively that it cannot be found on this . . . earth."

—Jesse Livermore

I t's easy to buy a stock . . . a walk in the park. All you need is some cash and a brokerage account. One mouse click, or one phone call, and voilà! You own shares in a company!

What separates the men from the boys and the women from the girls—or more accurately, the winners from the crash-and-burn losers—is the ability to manage a position and the savvy to take consistent profits out of the market.

Many list the three M's that define the stock market experience as mind, method, and market. Know that with or without us, the "market" will always go forward. In order to be successful, it's our responsibility to bring a disciplined mind and method to the table.

A disciplined mind is essential to successful money management. Consider rereading Chapter 3 to review how emotions affect your trading techniques. In fact, I recommend rereading Chapter 3 every month or two. If you are like me and others who participate in the markets day after day, periodic reminders to maintain a disciplined mental approach are helpful.

Remember, your goal is to place trades with the calm confidence that comes with a well-thought-out plan. You also want to make the inner declaration that *the market only hurts you when you allow it to.*

Now, let's proceed with money-management strategies that will give you the edge as a consistently winning trader.

PLAN YOUR TRADE AND TRADE YOUR PLAN

First, let's create a trading spreadsheet and an optional worksheet. I say "optional" because you can enter all the necessary information on one comprehensive log, or split it into two separate forms.

Your trading log will be in spreadsheet form, with headings and columns underneath. Naturally, you'll create the columns to fit your own needs.

Whatever form it takes, just make sure it's in a special place near your computer, where you can see it at all times. Please don't misplace it in a pile of bills or papers—especially if you use mental stop points. On days when the market screeches into an unexpected U-turn and falls like a rock off of a cliff, nothing spells "panic" like realizing you've misplaced your trading log, which lists your protective stops.

A basic trading sheet in Microsoft Excel format includes the headings and columns detailed in Figure 11-1.

	A	B	C	D	E	F	G	H	I	J	K	L	M
1	ENTRY		LONG/	NUMBER	ENTRY	TOTAL	INITIAL	SECOND	EXIT	EXIT	TOTAL	PROFIT/	ACCOUNT
2	DATE	SYMBOL	SHORT	OF SHARES	PRICE	PURCH. PRICE	STOP	STOP	DATE	PRICE	PROCEEDS	LOSS	PROFIT/LOSS
3	May 19	BGBT	Long	500	37.15	18,585.00	36.45	39.80	May 19	41.62	20.800.00	2,215.00	2,215.00
4	May 20	SS	Long	500	29.33	14,175.00	27.90		May 26	27.91	13.945.00	1230.00	1,966.00
5	May 21	TT	Long	400	10.19	4,086.00	9.90	12.73	May 27	13.40	5.350.00	1264.00	3,249.00
6													
7													
8													
9													
10													

FIGURE 11-1. Basic trade sheet.

The sample entry on this Excel spreadsheet details complete trades for fictitious stocks: Bargain Biotech (BGBT), Stealthy Software (SS), and Terrific Trucklines (TT).

The first trade shows 500 shares of Bargain Biotech (BGBT) bought at $37.15 on May 19 for a total purchase price of $18,585 (including commissions). The initial stop was established at $36.45. The stop was later updated and raised to $39.80 (Second Stop column). The trade was closed out five days after it was entered, at the price of $41.62 per share, and we posted a profit of $2,215. Commissions of $10, each way, were factored in. If you plan to scale in and out of positions, remember to leave extra spaces under the initial trade entry to enter the additional shares and prices. The Stealthy Software trade ended with a small loss, and the Terrific Trucklines trade brought in a gain, for a three-trade net positive profit.

Now, let's look at additional information you'll want to keep in front of you when you have an open trade. You can add these numbers in additional columns to the spreadsheet in Figure 11-1, or keep them on a separate worksheet.

Personally, I like to post the following numbers by hand, on yellow legal pads. Do you know why legal pads are yellow? Because the color yellow is known to vitalize and stimulate the brain. (Yes, that's true!)

Let's say you just bought Bargain Biotech, so it's an "open trade." You've calculated your risk/reward ratio, entered the trade, and set your protective stop order.

Now, on your trade sheet or worksheet, jot down major support and resistance areas currently pertinent to your stock, as seen on a daily chart. The prior pivot high on the chart is particularly important, as that price will likely represent your initial profit target for a swing trade. (For a position trade, the strategy is to hold the position as long as the stock is in an uptrend.)

HOT TIP

An event that adds special excitement to anyone's trading day is to get caught holding an open position in a stock that halts trading. That means the company experiences incredible news—nice or nasty—and market officials halt trading in the stock until the news is sorted out or confirmed. This limbo condition can last from minutes to days, and the stock generally opens at a much different price than it closed (halted). What a great reason to diversify holdings in your account!

Next, evaluate weekly charts of your stock and sector, and note important support and resistance areas on them. You will also want to check the daily chart of the related industry group or sector, and note its support and resistance zones. Finally, record important support and resistance levels on the major indexes: the Dow, S&P 500, and NASDAQ 100 or Composite.

PIECE OF THE PIE

Let's rewind to Bargain Biotech. Say that after you buy shares of the whizzy stock, you want to buy even more shares. In fact, it's moving up so strong and fast; why not max out your entire account with this baby?

Not a good idea!

Commit no more than 25 percent, or one-quarter of the capital in your account, to a single equity.

That means if you have $30,000 equity in your account, you would spend no more than $7,500 on Bargain Biotech shares. Calculate this before you take the trade. So, $7,500, divided by the entry price of Bargain Biotech, or $37.15, indicates you can purchase 202 shares of the stock—or 200 shares with commission costs. (Most brokerage houses don't accept orders for odd lots.)

As you have guessed, your goal is to diversify your trading portfolio, so you don't get caught with your entire account maxed out in a diving stock.

RISK/REWARD RATIO: WHAT IT MEANS, HOW TO CALCULATE IT

You're out of beer. It's 7:00 P.M. on a Friday, and you've worked hard all week. You deserve a beer, doggone it, but a quick scan of the refrigerator reveals a definite absence of a cold bottle of golden brewski.

No problem. You'll jump into the car, drive to the store, and grab a six-pack. Because you've done it a thousand times before, and you're familiar with the situation, you don't weigh the risk/reward ratio.

But what if you had to? It might look something like this:

Potential downside risk: Since it's a party night, the store could sell out of beer by the time you arrive. Long lines at the cash register may await you. Friday night means heavy traffic. Your car could get a flat tire, or suffer an unexpected mechanical problem, causing a delay. Or, you could, conceivably, find yourself involved in a fender-bender, which would cause an even greater delay.

Potential reward to the upside: You can easily afford to buy beer. Your car is filled with gas, and you take good care of it with frequent servicing, so mechanical problems rarely crop up. You're a careful driver; you wear your seat belt and have never had an accident. Besides, the store is only a 10-minute drive from home. If your favorite beer is sold out, no problem. More than one brand can wet your whistle. You expect a long line at the cash register, so you'll shrug that off. Besides, you may run into a friend who will want to go out to dinner or the movies over the weekend. Finally, the reward occurs the delicious moment you settle onto the sofa, and sip the icy, golden liquid. Risk? Low. Reward? High.

We routinely—and unconsciously—weigh risk before we initiate *any* action, whether speaking to a stranger, backing out of our driveway, or touching a hot iron.

Learning how to calculate risk/reward ratios when you trade is essential to trading success.

Here's a general rule to implement: *Whenever you plan a trade, please make sure your potential reward is at least two—and preferably three—parts greater than your potential loss, or risk.* That means your risk-to-reward ratio is 1:2 or 1:3.

Figure 11-2 shows a simple example of risk/reward analysis.

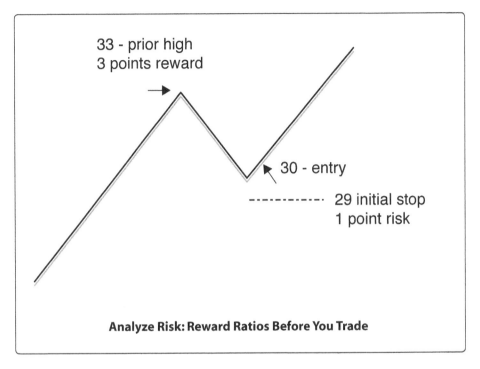

33 - prior high
3 points reward

30 - entry

29 initial stop
1 point risk

Analyze Risk: Reward Ratios Before You Trade

FIGURE 11-2. Risk-to-reward analysis. In this example, our stock's optimal entry was $30. The prior pivot high was $33. That gives the trade approximately 3 points of potential reward. If we put our initial stop 1 point under the entry price, we establish 1 point potential risk. Therefore, our risk-to-reward ratio for the trade is 1:3.

The following represents a high-risk scenario. Learn to recognize the pattern, so you can avoid it. You'll want to refer to Figure 11-3 as we move through the example.

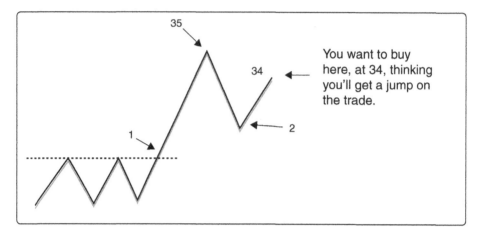

FIGURE 11-3. Daily chart of Bossy Bank and possible trade entries. Is this trade a good choice?

Imagine you follow the 1, 2 portion of the buy setups for a swing/position trade with Bossy Bank: You bought on a breakout from a base (1), and then added to your position on the "nice spring day" (2). Swing traders may have taken profits from the first upswing.

So far, all Buy Triggers have cooperated. Setups 1 and 2 are complete and now your stock, Bossy Bank, is moving up from the first pullback and heading for the previous high established last week. Mother Market is happy, the financial index looks serene, and you're itchy to pull the trigger at 34 and add to your position, before Bossy pokes through 35.

Why is adding shares at 34 a high-risk play? Because when you buy a stock that's trading a point or less than a point away from a recent previous high, you're taking a big chance.

➤ First, where is your stop-loss point? Technically, it could be several points away, which is unacceptable to apply to any shares added here. (We'll discuss stop placement in the next section.)
➤ Second, know that resistance (supply) will cause most stocks to retrace—or at least tread water for a while—when they reach, or almost reach, a prior high. What if Bossy Bank can't climb through 35 and trade above it? In that case, you should be taking quick profits from your 1 and 2 entries—not buying more shares. If Bossy stops short of 35 and drops back, it may form a

double-top pattern. Your added shares' entry at 34 will be history—and you'll get caught in a downdraft. You may have to chase Bossy down to get out of your entry at 34, and instead of taking home tidy profits from your earlier entries, you'll give them back—fast.

HOT TIP

With a smorgasbord of approximately 9,000 equities to choose from, there's no need to chase a stock. If your stock shoots higher without you, there are 8,999 more stocks to choose from, one of which will offer a low-risk / high-reward entry.

The lesson of the story: Don't buy until your stock trades at the proper entry point. Here's another scenario to consider: I will rarely buy a stock that's moving up for the third day in a row. Stocks tend to trade up or down in Fibonacci numbers. That means they may rise for three days, then pull back for two; or, they may rise for five days and retrace for three.

When a stock rockets for three days in a row, it becomes a profit-taking target. As someone said, "Those who buy on the first day up are geniuses. Those who buy on the second day up are late. And those who buy on the third day up are fools."

Whether you're focusing on a double bottom, cup-with-handle, plain vanilla base, or the second swing in an uptrend, you buy the breakout from consolidation or pullback. If you miss the proper entry point, walk away. Don't wander in one or two days late. Wait for the stock to complete the next move up and subsequent retracement. Then enter at the appropriate price, with Buy Triggers in place.

Remember, when you enter a trade early, you're entering on "hope." As discussed in Chapter 3, hope and optimism are gratifying traits to evoke in your everyday life, but keep them out of your trading day. In the financial markets, these two mental qualities are detrimental to your wealth!

WHERE TO PLACE YOUR STOP ORDERS

An ancient saying goes, "Never test the depth of the water with both feet." Stop-losses equal water wings. They keep one foot on the shore, and save your account from drowning!

From this moment on, the very first question you ask yourself *before* you enter a trade is: "Where's my initial stop going to be?" If you find your stop point is too far away from your entry point, or creates a risk (in points) equal to or larger than your profit target, don't enter the trade.

Protective stops can be set with different goals in mind. Determine the method that best suits your trading style—and account balance—and then stick with it. Whether you set a technical stop, a percentage stop, or a dollar-amount stop, set it at an appropriate price *and adhere to it.*

My old commodities coach used to bellow, "Where you set your stop-loss orders simply depends on your tolerance for pain." Let's see if we can refine that and give it a more positive spin: Establish your stops close enough to your entry price that your account doesn't get battered by the potential loss, and far enough away that you give the trade room to work.

The following are options for positioning stop orders:

➤ When you initiate a swing or position trade, place your stop price 0.25 to 0.50 point (twenty-five cents to fifty cents) under the low (of which should be a "nice spring day") you entered the trade. Some traders set it 0.25 under the low of the entry day, or the previous day's low, whichever is lower. Other traders use a percentage of the stock price: They calculate 1 to 2 percent of the stock's per-share price and use that amount as their stop price below the low of the entry day. Of course, you need to use common sense. If you're trading a $100–$400 per share stock, you'll have to adjust your stop accordingly to absorb wider price range volatility. If you are trading the breakout of a consolidation, place your initial stop twenty-five to fifty cents (or 1–2 percent of the stock price) under the lows of the consolidation pattern. As soon as your stock moves up and closes above the consolidation, you can raise your stop to at least the midpoint of the consolidation pattern.

➤ Never put more than 2 percent of your total account equity at risk in any one trade. In other words, say your account total value is $20,000. Two percent of that equals $400. That means if you buy 400 shares of Bossy Bank at $33, you can lose a maximum of 1 point on the trade. You'd set your stop-loss point at $32. If you determined that stop-loss point was too tight, and you wanted to allow Bossy to fall 2 points before you jumped out of the trade (stop-loss set at $31), you could only buy 200 shares. So, no matter what size position you take, you figure your maximum loss at no more than $400.

➤ Some long-term position traders set stop-losses at 7 to 8 percent of the cost of the stock. Say you buy Bossy Bank at $33 per share. Seven percent of $33 is 2.31. So you set your stop-loss at $30.69.

➤ A "trailing stop," as we call it, means that your stop order tags along behind the price rise like a shadow. Position traders use these the most; wise swing traders also apply them. You can keep your trailing stop tight or loose—your preference—but here's one option: Your stock rises in the initial upswing, then pulls back or consolidates. Next, it bounces off price support or moving average support (think: buy setup 2) and starts to move up again. Reset your stop-loss point from twenty-five to fifty cents (or 1 to 2 percent) under the low of the pullback or consolidation. After all, if your stock retests the lows of the pullback or consolidation, then crashes through them, the trend is broken. You don't want that stock any longer!

Once you enter a trade, your next action is to place your stop order. Get into the habit of doing it immediately. If you trade with an online broker, enter the stop as a GTC, which means "good till canceled." On the chance that your stop price is touched, your pending order will turn into a market order, and you'll be filled at the next available price. Many direct access brokers take stop orders, but some orders last only for the current day. These are "day orders," and you have to reset them each morning.

As soon as you enter the order, enter it onto your trade sheet.

If you cannot set an automatic stop order with your broker, or you're in an extremely short-term trade where you don't want to have to cancel it before you sell, you'll have to monitor the stock.

When I set a "mental stop," I not only enter it on my trading worksheet—I circle it. For some reason, the act of circling the stop price declares it law. Is this circle-the-stop ploy a head game? Absolutely. Do I care? Nope. If it prods me to exit a trade when I should, thus saving me money, I'll happily play along.

Why am I rattling on about setting stop orders? Because ignoring these exits, while clinging to "the need to be right," has lost more traders more money than any other mistake I can think of.

Think I'm going overboard? Ask an ex-trader the truth about why he or she crashed and burned. The standard answer is, "I held on to losing positions." In this market, with its ever-increasing volatility, hanging onto losers will blow out your account in a heartbeat.

Truth is, I'm no stranger to this scene. Early in my trading career, I ignored or lowered my stop orders. Sometimes, I didn't even set them. The result? Ugly, ugly losses. Hard experience taught me it takes a lot longer to make the money back than it does to lose it.

So, please raise your right hand. Say the following words out loud and with gusto:

From this day forward, I (your name), do solemnly swear on my mouse to adhere to all stop orders placed. I shall never, ever, lower my stop price. I shall never ignore my stop price. As soon as said stop is touched, I will immediately exit the trade.

If you keep your word, you'll be laps ahead of 99 percent of the traders and investors in this world. And if someone asks you if you're really that tall, you can reply, "No. I'm standing on my wallet!"

NOW THAT YOU'VE GOT IT, WHAT DO YOU DO WITH IT?

Planning your initial profit target before you enter a trade is almost as important as entering your stop order. And, plotting these two components of your trade form a large part of your risk/reward analysis. Think of it this way: If you don't know where you're going, how are you going to get there?

Note that most of the following pertains to swing trading techniques. As you know, in a position, or core trade, you buy the breakout out of the base and stay in the trade until the current trend is broken or until your stop order is touched.

Say you're waiting for Stealthy Software to complete its pullback and to begin the second leg up of its uptrend. Today may be the last day of the pullback. Market conditions improved this afternoon, and the software index gained legs. Tomorrow may well turn into a "nice spring day" for this stock.

On a daily chart, look for Stealthy's most recent high. When was it? What was the price? Write that on your worksheet or log. If Stealthy is breaking out of a base, the most recent high could be weeks or months away. That's a *good* thing. Remember, the further away resistance (in the form of a previous high) lays, the weaker it becomes.

On the other hand, what if the most recent high that preceded the pullback was three days ago? No problem, but if you're swing trading, that may be your initial profit target. (Since position traders stay in a stock for the duration of the trend, nearby highs aren't as important to them.) Check out Figure 11-4 to see what I'm talking about.

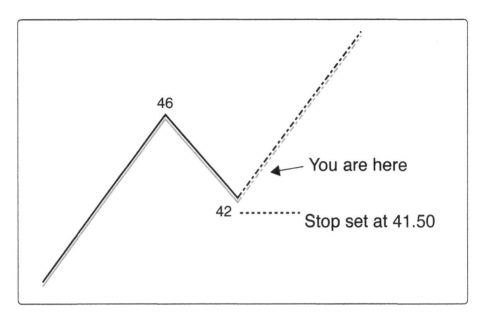

FIGURE 11-4. Daily chart of "Stealthy Software."

You enter this trade on a "nice spring day" as Stealthy shoots out of the pull-back or retracement low of 42. You buy at 42.50. You set your stop-loss at 41.50. Your first possible price target is 46, the most recent high. That's where Stealthy is most likely to run into resistance (supply).

So, the risk equals 1 point; the reward equals 4.5 points (possibly more).

One strategy is to sell one-half of your Stealthy position when it reaches 45.50 to 46. Another, which we've discussed, is to monitor market conditions as the stock approaches 46. If it jets to the upside and trades ten cents over 46, you can add to the position. (It's best to add these additional shares at the end of the trading day, just before the close. You want the stock trading at the high of the day, at or near 46.)

Immediately raise your stop order twenty-five to fifty cents (or 1–2 percent of the stock's price, if you prefer) under your additional shares' purchase price to protect profits. Then look for the next possible resistance area. That's your new price target.

Can you see how to manage a trade as it progresses? Using these methods and sticking to them will raise you to the ranks of the pros and will help you stay a consistent winner.

While we're talking money management, here's a heads up. Just because you have a price target on Stealthy Software of 55 doesn't mean it's going to go there. Sure, it could rocket to 55, zoom right through it, and shoot like a ballistic missile to 75 before you can catch your breath. Stealthy might also crawl up to 44, hiccup, sputter, then sink below 42, past your stop-loss, and finally stop at 20.

A thousand times during the past years I've heard full-of-themselves traders—who ought to know better—make calls that novice traders take as gospel.

Big-Shot trader spouts, "Worldwide Wireless is trading at 60. It'll be 85 by next Friday!"

Novice Trader yells, "Really? Wow, I'm in!" He loads the truck with Worldwide at 60 bucks a share. Then bewildered, he watches it tank to 50. Novice ignored his stop point, because Big-Shot said the stock was going to fly to the moon. *Uh, oh.*

The absolute truth: Nobody on earth knows where the stock market, or a stock, will move to next. Absolutely, positively *nobody.*

Your goal is to plan your trade precisely, with as little emotion as possible. You follow your plan. While you can and should study the methods of market professionals, strive to become proficient in your own right. Make your own decisions based on your own discipline, knowledge, and experience. Take responsibility for those decisions. Then you've arrived at the gates of success.

INTRADAY REVERSAL PERIODS: WHAT THEY ARE, WHAT THEY MEAN TO YOU

In the course of a trading day, market dynamics cause "reversal periods" to occur. If you watch the stock market during trading hours, you've probably observed an ebb and flow, time-wise, that repeats itself each day. While active traders become highly tuned to market rhythms, you—particularly as a swing trader— may want to be aware of them. Then you'll know why certain time slots during the trading day cause stocks to shift in price.

The discussion that follows refers to Eastern time; translate the times to your time zone.

The market opens at 9:30 A.M.

The first reversal period takes place from approximately 9:45 A.M. to 10:10 A.M. This means that if the market has moved up since the open at 9:30, as a whole, it will start to retrace or "come in" at about 9:45–9:50 A.M., and will continue to drift down until about 10:10 to 10:15 A.M. One reason for this reversal period is that market makers and specialists often take the opposite side of your trade. They will "bring the stocks in" to adjust their positions (think: make profits). At 10:10 on a positive day, the market resumes the upswing.

The next reversal takes place at about 10:25 A.M. (yes, just fifteen minutes later), but only lasts five minutes or so. I would call it more of a "shift" than a reversal. You may not notice it.

By 11:30 A.M., the lunchtime moody blues edge in. Traders start taking profits before lunch, and institutional managers leave for a lunch break, so buying subsides. Stocks start to drift down. Conversely, sometimes on a bearish day, stocks will rally at noon. Short-covering may be responsible for some of the pop-up. Whatever the direction on the day, most stocks move sideways during lunchtime.

From 1:30 to 2:30 P.M., fresh action permeates the market. On a positive day, strong stocks may break out.

The next reversal, or shift, begins at 3:00 P.M., when Treasury bonds close. Now, unfettered by its connection with the bonds, the market moves with added lust. At 3:20 P.M., many day traders start closing out positions. At about 3:30 P.M., institutional managers adjust their positions for the following day. Traders who "go home flat" also exit their positions. It's not unusual to see strong stocks fall during this period.

On the heels of the day traders are the short-sellers, covering and closing out their positions. Their short-covering causes stocks to rise. No wonder the last half hour can turn into such a circus!

And remember, just because the market trended up all morning, doesn't mean it automatically resumes that uptrend in the afternoon. It might. It might not. The only absolute in the stock market is change.

ORDER TYPES: MARKET ORDERS, LIMIT ORDERS, AND MORE

The following list describes several order types. Please consult with your broker to make sure you understand each order type offered and how to execute them properly.

Market Orders

When you buy or sell a stock "at the market," you're giving the specialist or market maker carte blanche. That person chooses what price you pay, or receive, for your stock. Yes, you're supposed to receive the inside bid or offer when your order reaches them. But "bad fills" are commonplace when you issue a market order. (This is a form of "slippage," which is discussed in Chapter 2.) If you must buy or sell in a hurry, use a market order. Or, if you are trading a slow-moving stock for which you can enter a market order and easily attain the best price, go for it. When precision is key to a successful trade, enter limit orders. You'll probably have to pay a few dollars more, but limit orders reduce slippage.

Limit Orders

When you place a limit order, you give instructions to buy or sell a specified number of shares of stock, at a specified price. You issue a limit order to buy at a price lower than the posted inside offer. Or, you place a limit order to sell above the posted inside bid. The specialist or market maker will only fill your limit order when the stock's price touches your specified price, or better. Issue a limit order to specify a price when you want to buy a stock at a price between the bid and offer. Say Awesome Airlines is trading at 35 at the bid, 35.25 at the offer. You issue a limit order to buy 300 shares at 35.15. Your order will only be filled if a market maker or specialist decides to sell it to you at that price. If Awesome moves up quickly, and a lot of orders hit the market before yours did, you may not get filled with that limit order. In that case, you must decide if you want to cancel your limit order and raise it (translation: Chase the stock). Of course, you can leave the order in place for the rest of the day (it will cancel automatically at the market's close).

The same procedure takes place with a sell order. If you own a stock and want to sell it at a higher price than is currently posted, issue a limit order to sell your shares at a price above the posted price (example: Sell 300 Awesome at 36). Again, your order may be filled, but if the stock doesn't trade at your specified price, your order may not get filled. Limit orders can be either day orders or GTC ("good till canceled").

AON Orders

Your broker may also give you an order choice designated AON. AON means "all or nothing." If you issue an AON order, you instruct the specialist or market maker to fill the total number of shares you request, or none at all. So, if you put in a limit order for 500 shares at a certain price AON, and they can only give you 350 shares at that price, it tells them to ignore the order.

OCO Orders

Another type of order offered by direct-access brokers is known as OCO, or "order cancels order." This means you can enter a protective stop order with your broker, as well as a limit order to close your position (sell a long position, cover a short position) at your profit target. If one of those orders is executed, it automatically cancels the other order.

Buy-Stop Orders

When you place a buy-stop, it means you specify a number of shares you want to buy at a certain price *above* the stock's posted price. Say Awesome Airlines is trading at $35.50, which is key resistance. If it breaks above $35.50, that's the perfect entry point. You're sure, however, that when (if) Awesome trades over $35.50, every trader in captivity will try to buy Awesome, so the price will rocket. How do you get an edge? You enter a buy stop order for the number of shares you want to execute at $35.60. Then you wait (or go to the beach). If Awesome doesn't trade at $35.60, your order will not be filled.

The drawback is that buy-stops are filled when the stock trades at your specified price, or the next highest price. If you place a buy-stop with your online broker for 300 shares of Awesome at 35.60 before the market opens, then the bell rings and Awesome gaps open 3 points higher than yesterday's close of 35.50, that's where you get filled—at $38.50. Not good!

The lesson: Don't issue buy orders before the market opens. If once the market opens you're unable to watch your stock to see if it reaches the perfect entry, that's good use of a buy-stop order.

Sell-Stop Orders

Sell-stops are many times called stop orders. When you're holding a long position, you can place a sell-stop, or stop order, for the number of shares you own at a price that rests under the stock's current posted price. If the stock touches your stop order price, your stop order reverts into a market order, and your position is liquidated. Because your order reverts to a market order when your designated price is touched, depending how fast the stock moves, you may be filled a fraction of a point or more away from your specified price.

Automatic Trailing Stop Orders

Many online and direct access brokers now offer automatic trailing stop orders. I highly recommend using these types of orders, especially on days where your position is close to reaching your profit target. You may order these orders in a dollar amount, or a percentage amount.

Say you want to issue a trailing stop for fifty cents to your present long position. Once entered with your broker, the stop order will follow the stock's current price higher, staying fifty cents below the rising price. If the price retraces, however, your order will automatically execute when (if) the price falls fifty cents from its high. In other words, the trailing stop will follow your stock higher, but not lower.

If you set the automatic trailing stop for a percentage of your stock price, the same process will take place, only on a percentage basis. For example, 5 percent of a $30 stock would equal $1.50. So if you set a 5 percent stop order, it would trail the price by $1.50.

Of course, if either of these stops is set for a short position, it will follow the price lower, and then execute to cover the position if price moved up to touch the trailing stop order.

IN TIMES OF CRISES

The United States—indeed, the world—struggled to restore a sense of calm in the aftermath of the acts of terrorism directed at the Pentagon and World Trade Center on Tuesday, September 11, 2001. The stock market opening was wisely canceled on that horrific morning, and it remained closed for the following three days.

Many traders and investors waited for the markets to open on the following Monday, September 17, with mixed feelings of relief and trepidation. Would the stock market—which had been weak for months before—gap down with no support and continue down in free-fall? Would entire accounts be wiped out as swiftly as our beloved World Trade Center?

Fortunately, the worst did not materialize. On September 10, the day before the "Attack on America," the Dow Jones Industrial Average closed at 9,605. It opened on September 17 at 9,580, fell to 8,976 during the first hour of trading, and finally closed the day at 8,920. Yes, the fall was dramatic, and even heartbreaking. Still, the day's trading proceeded in an orderly fashion, allowing those who wanted to exit positions to do so. In fact, many e-mails circled among traders on that day, urging people not to sell their positions—and not to give the terrorists the satisfaction of seeing our financial markets in peril.

What we learned from that shocking event: In the event of a crisis, wait a few moments before acting. Don't place a market order to sell right at the opening bell, unless absolutely necessary. Check the next support level on a daily chart, or intraday chart if you prefer, then issue a stop-loss order a fraction of a point beneath that level. On slow-moving stocks, place limit orders to sell at the inside bid price. The most important action you can take is to stay calm and clear-headed. Panicky selling benefits no one.

As well, avoid taking on new positions during periods of extreme volatility. Explosive price swings coupled with overloaded order systems reduce your chances of accurate fills, to say the least. Cut your losses in a composed, professional manner, then step to the sidelines. Remember, in times like these, a single, unexpected news announcement may send the market into excessive fluctuations. Once you've taken your account flat, or to cash, stay in cash until stability returns.

There's a lot of material to absorb in this chapter, but I promise you, if you go slowly and weave these money-management techniques into your trades, you'll keep your losses small and your gains high.

QUIZ
॥॥॥॥॥॥॥॥॥

1. What is the maximum amount of capital in your trading account that you should commit to a single equity?
2. What is the general rule for risk/reward ratio?
3. True or False? As long as the market looks favorable, it's a good idea to get an early start on a swing trade by buying before the stock moves above resistance.
4. What's the most important question to ask immediately before entering a trade?
5. True or False? Buying a stock on the third consecutive day of an upswing is a high-risk play.
6. Describe three possible methods for placing an initial protective stop order.
7. True or False? Once in a while, it's perfectly fine to lower your established stop point because of market rhythms.
8. When you're planning a swing trade, what do you look for to find your initial profit target?
9. Describe a "reversal period." When does the first one occur after the market opens at 9:30 A.M.?
10. Define "limit order."

Answers
1. A commitment to a single equity should be no more than one-quarter of the account equity.
2. The potential profit, or reward, should be at least two times greater than the potential loss, or risk. That means you risk $1 per share to achieve a reward of $2 per share. A 1:3 risk reward ratio is even better! (You risk $1 per share to make $3 per share.)
3. False. While you may get away with this move occasionally, it raises your risk potential. You may end up giving back previously earned profits if the stock suddenly decides it cannot trade over the resistance area.

4. "Where's my stop point?"

5. True. You want to buy a stock that's moving up on the first day from a consolidation or pullback.

6. Three methods for setting initial stop-losses: (1) Place stop order twenty-five to fifty cents below the low of the entry day. (2) Calculate 1–2 percent of the stock's per-share price and use that amount for the stop price below the entry day's low. (3) Calculate 2 percent of your account's total equity and adjust share size and stop-loss amount to fit.

7. False, very false!

8. To find your profit price target, look for the most recent price high on a daily chart. That price can form possible resistance (selling) and so creates your initial profit target.

9. Various market dynamics cause "reversal periods," or shifts in market direction, to occur. When the market is trending up on the day, stocks pull back, or drift down, during reversal periods. On a bearish day, stocks typically move higher during reversal periods. The first reversal period takes place from about 9:45 to 10:10 A.M. eastern time.

10. When you place a limit order, you give instructions to your broker to buy or sell a specified number of shares of stock at a specified price.

CENTER POINT: THE CIRCLE OF GIVING

"In fact, the easiest way to get what you want is to help others get what they want."

—Deepak Chopra

Dynamic energy moves in a constant cycle of giving and receiving. In fact, giving and receiving in some form is a part of our everyday lives.

Because each of us acts as an integral part of this world, it is inherent in our nature to give and receive. When we stop giving, we stop contributing to ourselves and to those around us. Imagine a stream bubbling down a mountainside, nourishing and replenishing life as it flows. If the stream is blocked, the dammed water grows stagnant. The bed below becomes cracked and dried.

Just so, when we stop the flow of positive energy to any area of our lives, it cuts off the natural return of positive energy that would have come back to us. Money is referred to as "currency," which means "to flow." Therefore, if we hoard our money and never share with others, that action blocks and strangles the return of more money to us.

Try maintaining a stern, unsmiling countenance one day. Observe what you receive in return. The next day, offer a generous smile to each person you encounter and notice the difference in the greetings returned.

The law of giving and receiving is clear: Give what you want to receive. Do you want to receive more love in your life? Then give love. Would you like more joy and happiness? Then become a purveyor of authentic joy and serenity. Do you wish for more attention and appreciation? Give your attention and appreciation to those around you. Would you like more prosperity in your life? You can have more by helping others acquire prosperity.

Remember, in order to receive, you must give with sincere intention. Your gifts—whether smiles, hugs, appreciation, or money—must be offered to provide genuine good for others. If you feel that by giving you will have less, the energy behind the giving diminishes the gift and the return.

The life forces that empower giving and receiving are among the most important in our world. The more gifts you give with freedom and joy, the more gifts will circle back and flood your life, multiplied many times over!

CHAPTER 12

Winning Strategies for Selling Short

"As I said before, a man does not have to marry one side of the market till death do them part."

—Jesse Livermore

On any bearish market day, ask a roomful of traders to raise their hands if they sell stocks short. Betcha my duck slippers that only a smattering of hands will shoot up.

Why does selling short earn such a bum rap? For openers, it has to do with the American psyche. We are a land of optimists. We like our glasses half full, not half empty. We like our books and movies to end happily. We won't kick the underdog; in fact, we'll usually cheer him on, even defend him. Our parents raised us to help those less fortunate than ourselves. We've learn that nice people don't benefit from another's sorrow or misfortune. So, it makes sense that we avoid selling stock in a company suffering from financial woes.

Besides, the process of selling short seems downright weird. In "real life," whether stocks, cars, or houses, we buy an item and then sell it. When we sell short, however, we sell a stock we've never owned . . . cross our fingers that it falls like a rock . . . buy it back when it hits the skids . . . then return it to its previous owner. No wonder selling short feels like wandering though a strange jungle with no tour book in hand, and armed only with warnings that the natives are unfriendly.

And if the trade goes against us—unlike a trade to the long side, where the most we can lose is the initial investment—when we short a stock, theoretically, it can go against us to infinity. What a groan!

The first time I sold a stock short, I relived the exact same feelings I experienced while attending competition car racing school.

Picture this: Moroso Race Track, West Palm Beach, Florida. I sat wide-eyed, tightly strapped by gigantic seat belts into the open cockpit of a low-slung, rumbling Formula Ford. I felt like I was driving a rocket with pedals.

My instructor knelt next to me, explaining that when I reached the sharp bend in the track, I was to take the curve's radius *fast—very fast.* My tires should squeal as loud as possible to assure they worked at the outside level of their adhesion.

"Whatever you do," the instructor told me, "*don't* hit the brakes."

Sure. No problem. (Gulp!)

Jaw set, I threw the car into gear and roared down the open stretch toward the bend. As I skidded around the curve, tires screaming, rubber smoking, and pulse pounding in my ears, instincts from thirty years of driving on city streets took over.

I panicked and jammed my foot on the brake.

The car careened off the track and spun like a top. The sky churned, the landscape whirled around me in a blur. Grass and sand funneled high overhead, then rained on my helmet and down the front of my jumpsuit. Finally, the car ground to a stop. The engine sputtered and died into silence. When I divined I was still alive, I exhaled and spit the sand out of my mouth. Good grief. Some days you're the bug, some days you're the windshield.

And, yes . . . I finally learned how to race around a corner at Mach 2 with my hair on fire, pedal to the metal, tires shrieking like banshees. But it took practice and grit to override years of traditional driving habits.

The self-preservation instinct that presses our foot on the brake when we drive around a corner, especially when we hear our tires squeal, insists that selling short is unnatural. Yet, it really isn't. It's merely another skill set we can tuck into our traders' tool kit that will help us glean profits from the market.

And guess what else? Stocks tend to move down three times faster than they rise. Why? Because panic can be three times more powerful than greed! Which leads to this assumption: If you learn to sell short successfully, you can make tidy profits in a hurry.

OVERCOMING MENTAL AND EMOTIONAL
ROADBLOCKS TO SELLING SHORT

Let's drag the mental roadblocks to selling short into the sunlight so we can remove them with logical explanations:

Nice people don't benefit from another's bad luck.

Reply: Trading is not charity work. Besides, when you sell short, you add liquidity to the stock you're trading and help bolster its price when you buy it back.

The market has an upside bias. "It moves up more than it moves down," you continue. "Even taking bear markets into account, the major indexes have risen thousands of points since their inception."

Reply: Absolutely. But even bull markets move down at least one-third of the time.

A stock in a short trade can make a U-turn and go against you ad infinitum. With a short position, it's possible to lose more than your initial investment.

Reply: That's true. But to you, as an astute trader with a plan etched in stone, a large loss is not even a remote consideration. Just as you set a protective stop right after you enter a long trade, you enter an automatic "buy to cover" stop order right after you enter a short position. If your stop is a mental one, you cover the position the moment that price is hit, just like any other trade. If, heaven help you, you allow the trade to get out of control, take your lumps fast, and then reassess whether the trading life is really for you!

Selling short seems like a backward process. It's easy to make mistakes.

Reply: True enough. Humans are creatures of habitual reaction, especially when safety is an issue. It's quite common for new traders to accidentally sell shares when in a panic to exit the trade. Then, instead of closing the trade, they actually double their short position. (Laugh if you like, but as a new trader, I did that!) You can overcome this panic move by paper trading before you sell short. It helps you become accustomed to selling first and buying second.

When you're new to selling short, minimize risk and assure a positive experience by trading small lot sizes, say 50 to 100 shares. Next choose a slow-moving stock—perhaps a NYSE stock—that's highly liquid (high volume). That way, you tame your terror, and lots of doors (sellers) remain in sight, if you decide to beat a hasty retreat.

Before you start selling short, you'll need to understand shorting rules:

➤ Not all stocks are shortable. When you place your order, your broker will advise you whether your stock's shortable or not.
➤ You can only sell short from a margin account.

Here's the Process

Here's a brief description of the shorting process.

Say you enter a limit order with your online broker to sell short 300 shares of Awesome Airlines, at $40. Your broker takes Awesome out of his own inventory or another client's account. If he obtains it from a client's account, he leaves an IOU that guarantees the stock's return on demand. Then he removes $12,000 from your account, plus his commission, and tucks it away as a security deposit so you can return the stock if need be. Next, the broker sells the borrowed 300 shares of Awesome Airlines in the market for $40 per share. He puts the $12,000 away for safekeeping.

During the next two days, Awesome falls to support at $35. You issue an order to buy it back, known as "covering your short." Your broker takes $10,500 out of the safekeeping account, goes to the market, and buys 300 shares of Awesome at $35 per share, the current price. He returns those shares to his inventory, or the other client's account. Next, he cancels the IOU.

Now your broker returns to you the $12,000 security deposit he took from your account, plus the $1,500 left over when he bought the stock back, minus a commission. Your original $12,000 investment yields nearly $1,500 profit. Nice trade!

One or more of the factors in the following list may contribute to a stock's drop in price:

What Makes Your Shorts Fall Down
➤ Overall bearish market conditions.
➤ Anticipation of interest rate hike by FOMC (Federal Open Market Committee).

➤ Industry group labors under institutional disfavor, or is downgraded by analysts.
➤ Weak company fundamentals.
➤ Company announces bad news or earnings. An
"accounting irregularities" announcement almost
always ensures that the stock's price will take a
pounding.
➤ Fear and panic-driven selling.
➤ Disinterested buyers.

When investors sell stocks
to buy bonds, it's sometimes
called "flight to safety." During
those times, the yields paid
on bonds are more attractive
than the potential risk of owning stocks.

FUNDAMENTALS: WHAT TO LOOK FOR

On an overall basis, you choose target stocks to sell short differently in bull markets than you do in bear markets. If you're smack in the middle of a raging bull
market, look for lagging stocks in weak industries to short.

I do not like to sell short weak stocks related to strong industry groups. Even
though the stock may be a real dud, market players might bid it up if the industry
group where it resides is currently in a favorable spotlight.

When you find yourself slogging through the muck and mire of a bear market, industry group leaders can tumble like bricks, as money pours out of them
and into second-tier stocks, bonds, and money market funds.

After assessing market conditions, target stocks to short that have poor fundamentals. Use the same SmartSelect Composite Rating in *IBD* as when you
intend to buy. Now, though, instead of looking for winners, seek out the laggards,
the puny, and the disfavored. That means you'll look for Composite ratings of
50, or less.

When selling short, remember to look at the big picture. Take overall market
conditions into consideration, as well as the industry and stock daily chart. Then
decide if the target stock still looks like a good shorting target.

CHART PATTERNS AND SETUPS: WHAT TO LOOK FOR

Just as you look for stocks experiencing Stage 1 basing patterns for breakouts to
the upside to buy, you monitor stocks moving sideways in a Stage 3 pattern that
may break to the downside to sell short.

As discussed in Chapter 10, look for reversal patterns that include double and
triple top, and head-and-shoulders. Some Stage 3s come in plain vanilla. That is,
they don't draw a fancy reversal pattern. They simply move sideways in a frothy
congestion pattern, alternating highs and lows. At some point, they retest the

bottom of the congestion range, and buyers refuse to support them. As supply floods the market, they plunge into a Stage 4 downtrend.

The position trader will sell short the stock when it begins a Stage 4 downtrend (initiating lower highs and lower lows) and hold it until the stock breaks its downtrend by making a higher high.

The swing trader will short the stock as it falls into a downtrend, and then buy it back to cover, just before it drops the next level of price support on a daily chart. After the stock rebounds to previous resistance (think continuation patterns here, like descending triangle and pennant, or simple consolidation) and finally resumes its fall to the downside, the swing trader enters again.

While position traders essentially make two trades—one to sell short, then one to cover and close the trade—swing traders who sell short successfully must stay nimble. Remember, downtrends are typically more volatile than uptrends.

When selling short, you might want to anticipate a stock's fall early and pull the trigger slightly (slightly being a few cents) faster than you would when trading to the long side. That means you may short a weak, fast-falling stock *as it falls through support*, rather than waiting for it to trade *below* support. To compensate for the added risk, keep initial buy-to-cover stops tight and monitor the price movement until the stock drops into profitable territory.

Also, only pull the trigger early when all odds possible are in your corner. You want bad news on your stock or the industry it resides in. Examples are weak earnings, negative forward-looking guidance, falling sales or rising inventory reports, and stock or industry downgrades.

For example, perhaps your stock is a market leader. Currently Cisco Systems (CSCO) is a NASDAQ benchmark. When the NASDAQ nosedives for several days at a time, technology chieftain CSCO usually falls as well. Similarly, banking giant JP Morgan Chase (JPM) represents a top banking industry nabob. When the bank index (BIX) plummets, count on JPM to dive with it.

Consider this: The biotech index (BTK) is overextended, or rolling over in a Stage 3. Amgen (AMGN) and Genentech (DNA) are biotech leaders. Odds are, if the biotechs fall, AMGN and DNA will tank. Then check their charts for confirming weakness.

Now, review Chapter 10 and the head-and-shoulders pattern. Remember, on a daily chart showing a head-and-shoulders pattern (assuming all other odds are in your corner) you'll sell short a fraction of a point below support, or as the stock sinks through the neckline.

HOT TIP

The steeper a stock's rise in a Stage 2 uptrend, generally speaking, the faster the fall in its Stage 4 downtrend.

The next two charts, Figures 12-1 and 12-2, show stocks experiencing plain vanilla Stage 3 rollovers into Stage 4 downtrends.

SHORTING INDICATORS: UGLY IS GOOD!

When you sell short, you want all indicators showing weakness. In this case, ugly is good! "Ugly" translates into declining moving averages and overbought oscillators. This means they'll be reversed from their earlier readings on long entries.

When you study the charts in this chapter, take a plain sheet of paper and cover up the right side of the chart, up to the entry point. Now you can get a better idea of how the setup looks before you enter.

Volume

Do you recall that when you buy a breakout from consolidation or a pullback, you look for strong volume to assure the move upward?

It follows that when you sell short, it's best to enter on strong volume, as well. Still, stocks *can* fall on low volume. When a stock trades sideways for a long period of time and volume dries up because of disinterest, sellers may have to lower their price to attract buyers.

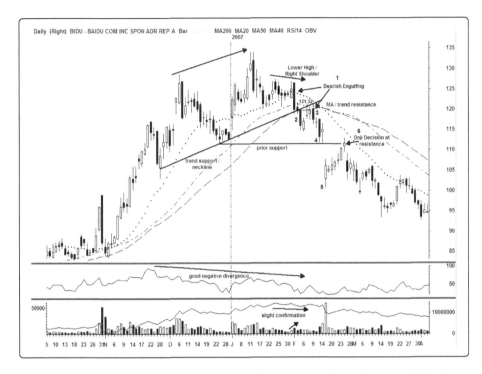

FIGURE 12-1. Baidu.com (BIDU) pattern top daily. RealTick by Townsend Analytics. We used Baidu.com (BIDU) in Chapter 10 to illustrate a weekly inverse head-and-shoulders pattern. In this view, we're looking at the stock's daily chart and a nicely developed head-and-shoulders top. After trying to find support for nearly two weeks off its 20-day MA, BIDU fails to move higher. The result is a lower high. As the price action is also lower than the prior high set back in early December 2006, we can anticipate a head-and-shoulders formation and that the Stage 3 consolidation is moving into a Stage 4 downtrend. At the same time, our RSI indicator is confirming weakness and the OBV has stalled. All told, the pattern is worthy of stalking. 1. The anticipated head-and-shoulders sets up for swing and position traders. Two bearish engulfing candles signal the bears are gaining control. 2. Two days later, after a tight doji consolidation, an entry below MA and neckline support triggered below $199 for a breakdown short entry. 3. The breakdown only proceeds to fall roughly 4.5 points before reversing to establish a countertrend rally into prior supports. This acts as resistance and sets up a number 2 short signal. Traders would likely short slightly below the prior day's closing price of 119.78, as BIDU attempts to move through resistance, but fails. That type of short allows you to enter closer to known resistance and thus place much tighter stops (in this case set above entry day's high of 121.32). 4. A multi-point decliner into potential support far outweighs our initial risk. 5. Earnings-related gap down and a big bonus for any partial short positions still intact. 6. A gap fill results in a doji decision at resistance. However, the aggressive gap lower the next day isn't a move we'd chase.

FIGURE 12-2. Urban Outfitters (URBN) weekly pattern shorting. RealTick by Townsend Analytics. Here's another head-and-shoulders pattern. This time it's shown on a weekly chart of Urban Outfitters, Inc. (URBN), a lifestyle merchandising company. As you can see, shorting opportunities occur on weekly time frames, as well. 1. At our first short entry point, a gravestone harami finds resistance below its moving averages, takes the shape of a right shoulder, and shows continued weakness in our RSI. Several weeks earlier, within the pattern, I've labeled two weeks of back-to-back bullish-looking volume as suspicious. Later, with sufficient time having passed and our other trade criteria taking control of URBN's price development, a solid short opportunity does appear. A bearish gap of nearly fifty cents confirms the trigger, although an ideal entry would be missed. In this instance, we'd likely use a 30-minute low in the stock, as the bulls failed to challenge the gap and moving average resistance. 2. After a multiple point slide into idealized neckline, price support offers a great spot to take profits and trail stops. I say "idealized" because this down-sloping line uses the shadows of the candles. As discussed, the real bodies typically represent more formidable support and resistance. A week later, a doji completes at prior support. A choice to short slightly below that decision candle or through the prior lows and neckline takes place. 3. As it turns out, swing traders selling short at the lower neckline break would have been disappointed. Nearly four weeks of consolidation occurs before a continuation entry appears. 4. URBN's first breakdown entry quickly delivers profits on the stock's largest volume since the initial bearish gap.

Imagine you're selling beaded necklaces on the beach. A woman walks by and you call out, "Want to buy a necklace for only ten dollars?"

No reply.

"I'll lower the price!"

She doesn't look back.

"Hey!" you call to her again, your voice chasing her receding back. "How about half price?"

The woman continues on her way, without a flicker of interest. In other words, *no sale.*

Other passersby show the same indifference. You reduce the price of the necklace with each averted gaze, with each "No, thanks."

HOT TIP

Many long-term traders enter and exit positions based solely on weekly charts. You can do this profitably, using the same general technical strategies you've learned so far. As with any time frame, you must maintain strict risk management.

See what I mean? While a selling frenzy causes a stock to plummet quickly, disinterest and apathy also push a stock downward, albeit with less excitement along the way.

Candle Patterns

Your study of candlestick patterns and those that signal top reversals will serve as a valuable tool to help you spot shorting opportunities. A few of the candle patterns that indicate price weakness include:

➤ Doji at top of—and acting as resistance for—the double-top price pattern
➤ Dark cloud cover
➤ Bearish engulfing
➤ Evening star and evening doji star

Moving Averages

When you look for opportunities to sell short, pinpoint stocks with major moving averages trending down over the stock's price pattern. Just as MAs act as support when a stock pulls back to rest in an uptrend, MAs act as resistance when a stock rebounds in a downtrend. The overhead MA, when trending lower, can act as a ceiling that applies selling pressure to a stock's price pattern.

Also, when a shorter time frame MA crosses down over a longer-term MA, the crossover issues a bearish signal. For example, when the 20-day MA slices through the 50-day MA and continues south, that's a big negative.

Another moving average combination that issues reliable signals for selling short is the 18-day and 40-day simple moving average crossover. We'll show daily charts using this strategy in upcoming pages.

Relative Strength Index (RSI)

When you're looking at a potential short setup, ideally, the RSI should be above 70, signaling an overbought position. A subsequent hook to the downside adds confirmation. An RSI bearish divergence means the stock is moving up or sideways, while the RSI is moving down, optimally from above 70. When you see this divergence, monitor the stock price for signs of weakness.

If you're using an alternative overbought/oversold indicator, such as Stochastics or the MACD, the same signals apply: You want the indicator hooking down in a sell signal that indicates price momentum to the downside, or a bearish divergence issued by the indicator.

On-Balance Volume (OBV)

The OBV should be trending down.

Bollinger Bands

Please turn back to Chapter 9 to review this handy tool. Use the premise that when stocks rise to their upper Bollinger Bands (if they actually pierce the upper band and close above—don't short the stock—that's bullish), they are doomed to eventually drop to their lower band. When all other indicators look weak, apply Bollinger Bands. Keep in mind that they give the most accurate signals on overextended (trading high above their 20-day MA) stocks. Stocks in sharp downtrends tend to stumble down to their lower Bollinger Band, thus emitting a weak signal.

HOW TO PLACE YOUR ORDER

Enter your order to sell short when your target stock breaks five to ten cents below price support. For fast-moving stocks, enter your order as the stock falls through support.

Online Broker

If the target stock is falling slowly, place a limit order one to five cents above the inside bid. If the stock is dropping rapidly, place a limit order to sell short five to fifteen cents below the inside bid.

Level II Order Entry System

If your target stock is drifting down slowly, place your limit order to sell short at the inside offer price. For rapidly sinking stocks, place your limit order one to five cents above the inside bid.

Issue Your Buy-to-Cover Stop Order Immediately

Next, place your automatic buy-to-cover stop order twenty-five cents to fifty cents above the day's high. (Or place a 1–2 percent stop order, as discussed in Chapter 10.)

SHORTING STRATEGY: THE OVEREXTENDED STOCK

We just discussed the most traditional shorting strategy: You initiate a short position when a stock breaks down from a Stage 3 into a Stage 4.

Position traders hold until the stock breaks the downtrend or dramatically slows its descent, at which time they exit.

Swing traders may trade the entire downtrend, selling short each time the stock rebounds to resistance and then continues its fall. Wise traders cover the short and exit the position after no more than two to three days down, and no less than 1 point above the next price support level.

Now, for adrenaline junkies, and those with a bit more experience under their mouse, let's look at overextended stocks as targets for selling short. This is a swing trading strategy and is a high-risk setup! Only traders who can closely monitor their trades and issue automatic buy-to-cover stops with their broker should enter these trades.

Setup

Look for a stock screaming skyward in a Stage 2 uptrend soaring high (several points) above its 20-day MA on a daily chart. (Note: *This is not the same as shorting a stock in the middle of a healthy uptrend.*) The steeper the angle of the uptrend, the better. For confirmation that the stock is overextended, scan the stock's price pattern for the last six months or more. How high, point-wise, can it rise over its 20-day MA before it falls back to the 20-day MA? (Remember, major moving averages act as a magnet.) Is it at least as overextended now, point-wise, as it has been in the past? The more over-extended, the better.

Check out the industry group, or sector, where the stock resides. The best setups take place when the industry/sector is also overextended and beginning to correct.

Now wait for the first sign of weakness. When you see it, get ready to pounce. An ideal setup takes place when yesterday's candlestick developed into a

HOT TIP

Don't hang on to a short position in a falling stock for too long a time period. When you have a multiple-point profit—and hear yourself making oinking noises—take profits!

long, wide-range real body to the upside. Today, the stock gaps down at the open in an exhaustion gap on high volume.

Candlestick alternative: Although stock price rose sharply in the uptrend, yesterday's candlestick results in a doji, indicating indecision, and buyers' reluctance to pay higher prices. Figure 12-3 shows the two basic candlestick patterns just described.

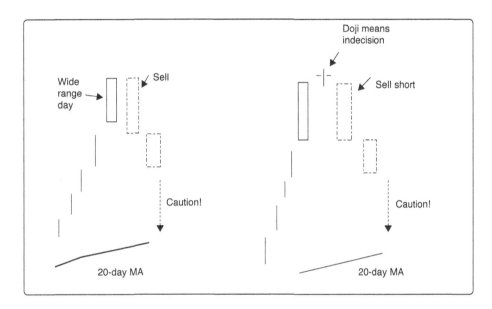

FIGURE 12-3. Two shorting setups for overextended stocks.

To enter, wait for the stock to trade for a few minutes after the market opens, to ensure it won't immediately gain strength and fill the gap. With weakness confirmed, sell short with a limit order. (More details on gap entries follow.)

With this technique, you're probably dealing with a highly volatile stock, so plan to cover this short position quickly. Buy to cover when:

➤ It nears previous support.
➤ It has tumbled for two to three days max.
➤ You have a multiple-point profit. There's nothing wrong—and everything right—with closing a position in a single day if you've made a good profit.

Since you're dealing with an explosive situation, you may take profits early, only to find you left money on the table. My advice? Get over it! Leaving money on the table beats getting caught in a short squeeze.

Indicators

➤ Volume: As previously explained, volume may vary on falling stocks, but in this setup, high volume (panicky selling) squashes the stock faster, giving you a multiple-point profit in a short time period.

Wise strategy: When targeting shorting setups, wait until the price pattern has formed a double top on a 60-minute chart (and all other signals are in place) before entering.

➤ Moving averages: Stock will be trading at nosebleed altitudes above 20-day MA and all other major MAs.

➤ RSI: Oversold—above 70.

➤ OBV: Falling.

➤ Bollinger Bands: Stock touching upper band, but unable to penetrate it.

SHORTING STRATEGY: THE OVEREXTENDED DOUBLE TOP

Shorting the rally to resistance that may develop into a double-top reversal pattern represents virtually the same setup as the overextended stock.

Again, target a stock that's soared in a moon shot uptrend, and has become highly overextended. You may even have spotted the stock when it made its first overextended high. It returns to support, then bounces, forming the middle pivot point. Then it resumes its upward thrust. The previous high acts as resistance (supply), and buyers once again refuse to pay higher prices.

At the first sign of weakness—assuming all other signals flash "go"—sell short and set your buy-to-cover stop-loss as previously discussed. Indicator readings remain the same as for the overextended top setup.

The next three charts, Figures 12-4, 12-5, and 12-6, illustrate the overextended shorting setup and the double-top shorting setup.

Remember, since double tops are reversal patterns, you don't have to endure the high risk associated with selling short the tops or pivots. A safer setup forms for swing/position trades when the final leg down to support (the last leg of the "M") can't hold up, and the stock catapults into a downtrend.

Remember, shorting overextended stocks are *high-risk* trades, as liquidity eventually dries up on the downside of the price action and moves violently to the upside. Result: Getting in and out of positions with precision can be very difficult and severely test your money-management objectives.

Please also keep in mind that our short entry into a highly volatile stock is always on a sign of weakness, such as a move back through the prior close. As an added precaution, trade size should be reduced, and a relatively tight stop should be entered.

Figure 12-4 certainly shows the flipside to overly persistent trends; that is, how brutally fast investor psychology can shift, as greed and demand switch to fear, and supply and opportunities for aggressive short-sellers appear.

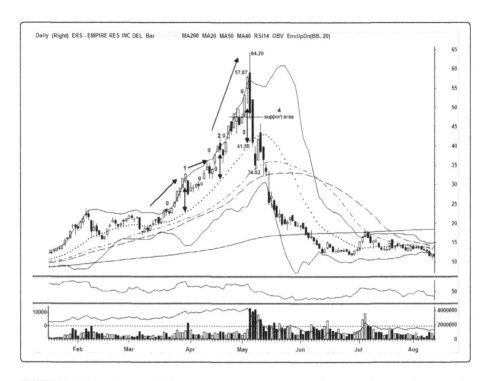

FIGURE 12-4. Empire Resources (ERS) daily: the overextended stock. RealTick by Townsend Analytics. For a short stint in mid-2006 Empire Resources (ERS), the distributor of aluminum semi-finished products, traded in a heavenly uptrend for bulls. Ultimately, though, ERS eventually succumbed to gravity. Looking at ERS's chart, the February to May uptrend shows that demand far exceeds supply, as evidenced by bullish gaps (gaps are labeled "g"). ERS constantly holds well above its 20-day MA and continues to "ride" the upper Bollinger Band. Labels 1 and 2 show two spots within Stage 2 before ERS goes parabolic, but we can see that price action is overextended. Look how high the price travels above the 20-day MA, and how it penetrates through the rising upper band. 3. Two more gaps and back-to-back bullish thrusts push ERS into a close above the Bollinger. This time, though, the price flies an incredible 16 to 17 points above the 20-day MA. The bulls, much to the bear's chagrin, weren't quite done yet. The next day (second black candle from top of move), a slightly higher gap resulted in another almost extraordinary 10 percent (thereabouts) spike in the price of ERS. The subsequent fall presented a short entry. 4. Since the support line is a full 10 points below the initial short entry decision point, it provides an excellent spot to take partial profits, and then move the stop on our balance to breakeven. Price over the next two days drops an additional 13 points and all profits should be taken during that time.

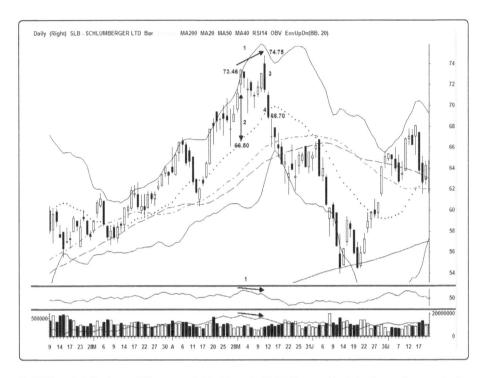

FIGURE 12-5. Schlumberger (SLB) overextended double top. RealTick by Townsend Analytics. Above, a fine example of an overextended double top on a large-cap issue is shown on this daily chart of the oilfields services and equipment company Schlumberger Ltd. (SLB). 1. Here we see that SLB has formed a slightly higher double top. Notice the negative divergence with both RSI and the OBV readings, and how those can act as secondary confirmation. 2. The first peak stretches nearly 7 points from its 20-day MA. If we check the two and one-half months of price history preceding this high, we find that within the uptrend, the stock price typically moves between 3 and 4 points away from that moving average, before pulling back. Therefore, for SLB we have a means of eyeballing a potentially "overextended" situation. 3. The actual trigger for the double top occurs off a bearish engulfing candle. Aggressive traders willing to use the session highs may have shorted before the trade was confirmed by that candle formation. This entry would have been taken by shorting SLB as it reversed back below the prior pivot high of 73.46, or the prior closing price of 73.06. 4. The very next day, at least partial profits in excess of 2:1 could be pocketed. At last, SLB tested the 20-day MA. Trailing stops set on the remainder of the position could have reaped gains in excess of 10 points before all was said and done. Nice trade!

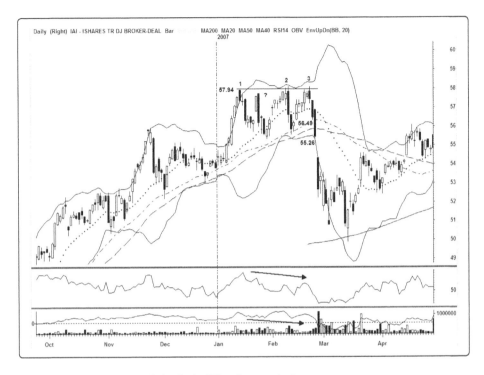

FIGURE 12-6. iShares Trust DJ Broker-Dealer (IAI) triple-to-quadruple top. RealTick by Townsend Analytics. While double tops are quite common, triple and quadruple tops are rare. But as you might imagine, when the extra move up to the highs fails to produce a new higher high, the resulting downside move that creates a third or fourth top can be that much more powerful. Shown here is a daily chart of the iShares Trust DJ Broker-Dealer (IAI), an ETF. This top was shown back in Chapter 9 as well; however, in this instance we're seeing how well RSI and OBV both signaled negative divergence during the triple and perhaps quadruple topping formation. In fact, by the time the engulfing bearish candle at point 3 confirms a low-risk / high-reward entry, the OBV has drawn its own bearish head-and-shoulders formation. In this type of topping pattern, shorts could have looked at both points 2 and 3 for entries. Using the highs of 57.94 from point 1 and stop losses above session highs, or confirmation below each doji or spinning top as each engulfing candle was formed, resulted in great multiple point returns.

HOT TIP

When you're in a profitable short position, remember to peel off part of your position after you gain a point or so profit. That way you reduce your risk and make more consistent profits in the long run.

SHORTING STRATEGY: THE 18 / 40 MOVING AVERAGE CROSSOVER

Many traders use moving average crossovers to the downside as shorting signals. I also favor these signals. One of my favorite moving average combinations for this strategy is when the 18-day (simple) moving average crosses below the 40-day (simple) moving average. At the time of the crossover, the moving averages are riding above the stock's price pattern, acting as resistance.

For the short setup, you'll find a stock moving in a downtrend. Again, the 18- and 40-day lines act as an overhead ceiling to the price pattern. The 18-day crosses below the 40-day. Ideally, the RSI hooks down from an overbought reading, and the OBV trends down.

> **HOT TIP**
>
> Five to ten minutes before the market closes, check the daily charts of all of your positions to observe the candle formation formed that day, and to analyze the movement of the other indicators. You may see a signal—something on the daily chart that tells you it's time to take profits.

Check prior support on the daily chart. This may be your profit target. Calculate your approximate initial protective stop, and then analyze your risk/reward ratio. Just as with long positions, you'll want it to come in at 1:2, or better yet, 1:3.

Setup: Sell short when price breaks five to twenty-five cents below price support. Enter your stop immediately—either above the day's high, or above intraday resistance on a 60-minute chart.

The charts on Figures 12-7, 12-8, and 12-9 show examples of short trades using this 18 / 40 moving average crossover combination. You'll also want to apply the triggers on the Sell Short Trigger List that follows the charts.

FIGURE 12-7. Alliance Data Systems (ADS) daily 18- / 40-day MA crossover. RealTick by Townsend Analytics. They say luck favors those who come prepared, and I wholeheartedly agree. In addition to our other short-selling qualifiers, the 18- / 40-day MA crossover makes for a nice confirmation tool that keeps us looking lucky, when the truth is—we followed a solid trading plan. Here on the daily of Alliance Data Systems (ADS), a marketing services company, we see how useful this technique can be, when used in conjunction with our other tools. 1. Negative divergence with our RSI indicator, while OBV is mostly neutral. Notice too, the Bollinger Band test by ADS is halted in its tracks. 2. Price volatility and some obviously determined longs wanting to get out of Dodge. 3. Our 18- / 40-day MA crossover comes into play. First, ADS puts in a countertrend rally and then consolidates for a handful of sessions below the 18-, 40-, and 50-day MAs. Next, a bearish engulfing candle appears on the seventh day of the rally, which sets up our short trigger. The actual 18 / 40 cross has occurred in the session prior, but up to that time, we didn't have a signal bar with which to confirm positioning. We're out-the-gate the next session, with our trigger just below the low of the reversal bar (62.93), yielding very quick results. With slightly more than 1 point of initial risk at stake, point 4, which represents a 2-to-1 reward-to-risk level, is a great point for reducing position size. Point 5 offers nearly 5.5 points of profit. We're four days into the swing trade and more than a couple of technical reasons for risk reduction (hammer/double bottom and 200-day MA) make for another easy choice in electing to cover the remaining position.

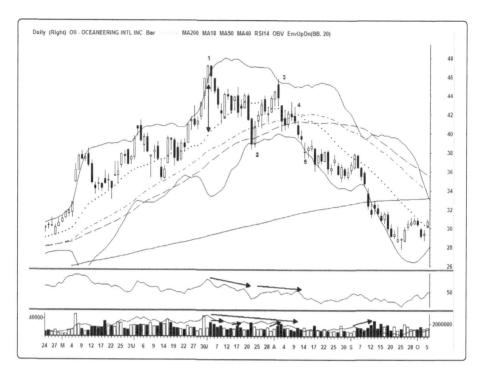

FIGURE 12-8. Oceaneering Intl (OII) daily 18- / 40-day MA crossover. RealTick by Townsend Analytics. Note this 18-/ 40-day MA crossover on the daily chart of Oceaneering International Inc. (OII), a global oilfield services provider focused on deepwater applications. 1. Not much going on at this point, except an overextended stock based on the price penetrating the upper Bollinger Band and the trading high above its 20-day MA. From point 1 to 2 we start to see distribution and/or profit-taking via strong selling volume; that tells us OII may be topping off, here. During the move from point 2 to 3, volume dries up, our RSI and OBV indicators remain neutral to weak, and a test of the upper Bollinger on a higher-volume dark cloud cover candle act as evidence that a lower high/double top is in place. At point 4, the 18 / 40 crossover short entry occurs in conjunction with a bearish black candle. The action finishes off a 3-day pause in the stock. While we might prefer that the consolidation formed below the three moving averages, rather than caught between them, the overwhelming body of technical evidence suggests a solid shorting opportunity. After the stock gapped lower three days in a row, for about 4 points of profit, point 5 closes in a doji. The doji (indecision) is more than enough reason to exit before the close of that day. And, since most of my swing shorts last three days or less, my own risk management criteria would have taken profits without hesitating. Nice trade!

FIGURE 12-9. Walter Industries (WLT) daily 18- / 40-day MA crossover. This daily chart of diversified company Walter Industries Inc. (WLT) is yet another solid illustration of how this moving average crossover can benefit our short positions.

1. Aside from the 18- / 40-day cross, what else is going on here to confirm an entry? First, after four days of consolidating, we have a negative spinning top and price can't break to the upside. We could also look at the head-and-shoulders top being carved out (with the right shoulder being point 1) coupled with a rather neutral OBV, recent selling distribution, and a downtrending RSI. The evidence definitely favors shorts. Also, back in mid-May 2006 the broader market was also going through its own difficult corrective period, which means of course that WLT's downside move was pushed along by the negative environment. Traders could have sold short on the day that gapped down (following the spinning top). Prior support from March, at about 32, was quickly broken, and from then on it was all gravy. The long black candle that finalized the run closed at about 29. If traders hadn't taken profits by then, they should have, as the stock unwound through a consolidation period of seven days. The same principle that applies to overextended stocks to the upside applies to overextended stocks trading far

HOT TIP

When you are in a short trade and your stock is trading above the 200-day moving average, know that buyers usually lurk at that line. I find it best to take profits before my short position falls too close to that moving average.

below their moving averages. That means that stocks, at some point, revert to their mean; as traders, we use moving averages as the mean. And yes, after WLT consolidated, it once again fell in a cliff dive that delivered another multiple-point profit.

Sell Short Trigger List

Here's a Sell Short Trigger List. Some of the points on it may appear redundant. Still, variables abound when you're selling short, so this will act also as a summary. While not every single item on the list may apply when you enter the trade, try to check off as many as possible. Remember, the more odds you corral into your corner before you pull the trigger, the lower your risk and higher the likelihood of fattening your wallet.

Sell Short Trigger List

1. Market conditions, Dow, S&P 500, and/or NASDAQ are negative.
2. Target stock is a lagging company in a depressed industry. (This may not apply in overextended situations.)
3. Poor company fundamentals. (This may not apply in overextended situations.)
4. Stock's related sector/industry group is in a downtrend and negative on entry day.
5. Stock has formed a Stage 3 rollover and is cracking support, or is experiencing a downtrend on a daily chart. Or, it is highly overextended and suffering an exhaustion gap or breakdown.
6. Strong volume on the breakdown is best, but not always absolutely necessary.
7. Stock is trading under major moving averages, and cannot penetrate them. Or, stock is overextended, trading in steep angle, and very high above 20-day MA (swing trade only).
8. RSI is overbought (above 70) and hooking down, or is etching a downtrend. (It is not oversold.)
9. The OBV is moving lower.
10. Target stock is trading below its opening price and moving down on the day. General sell short signal: Stock trades five to twenty-five cents below price support, or yesterday's low.

Selling Short FAQs (Frequently Asked Questions)

What if my target stock gaps down at the market open, taking out my entry price? When a stock you're waiting to short gaps down more than twenty-five to fifty cents at the open, wait at least fifteen to thirty minutes before you sell it short to make sure it won't fill that gap and move higher. Then sell short as (if) it moves below the first 30-minute low. (Please don't chase!)

Can you short the pullbacks of a stock climbing in an orderly uptrend? Yes, but I don't advise it. The odds are not on your side, since the major trend is up, which means buying pressure lurks nearby. Another reason: Shorting pullbacks in uptrends makes you vulnerable to a short squeeze.

HOT TIP

When you hedge a position with a counter position, match the dollar amount of the hedging position to the dollar amount of the position you are protecting.

What is a short squeeze? Say you're short Stealthy Software. The NASDAQ is weak, the computer software sector is weak, and Stealthy falls obligingly. Suddenly, the NASDAQ makes a U-turn and rockets upward. Stealthy also screeches to a halt, finds support, then shoots up. Short-sellers buy frantically, attempting to cover their positions. Now, buyers who were waiting at support are buying. Short-sellers are frantically buying to exit their positions. With little supply on the market and lots of demand, the stock screams straight up. Short-sellers who fail to recognize early warning signs of the stock's reversal give back profits and/or lose money, as they chase the stock up multiple price levels to cover; thus they are "squeezed." Bottom line: Getting squeezed by your honey is fun, but getting caught in a short squeeze is no fun at all. And that's most likely to happen when you short a stock in an uptrend, where the overall bias is to the upside.

Can you hedge (protect profits in current portfolio positions) your account by selling short? Definitely. You can hedge most easily with exchange traded funds, which are the subject of Chapter 13. Or you can hedge (protect) a current position by selling short a weak stock in the same industry group. Basic example of hedging with a stock: Imagine you are long a position trade of 500 shares of Microsoft, Inc. As you know, Mister Softee (Microsoft's nickname) creates and develops computer software. The stock is nowhere near your stop point. Still, the NASDAQ and the software industry group is pulling back and looks like it may continue down for a few days. You can sell shares of a weak software stock the duration of the pullback, then cover the position short at the first signs of recovery. That way, you've reduced your downside risk during the correction, and you may even add to your profits.

I hope you've enjoyed this marathon on techniques and tactics for selling short. In the next chapter, we're going to discuss Wall Street's newest star, the exchange traded fund.

QUIZ
ıllıllıllıllıllı

1. Why do stocks tend to move down three times faster than they rise?
2. When you're new to selling short, what two preventives can help you avoid ulcers?
3. True or False? All stocks traded on major exchanges can be sold short.
4. When you issue an order to sell short, you are selling a stock you don't own. Where do the shares come from?
5. Give one reason a stock might serve as a good candidate to sell short.
6. When targeting a fast-falling stock, how can you raise the odds of getting your order filled quickly and accurately?
7. When scanning for a stock to short for a position trade or swing trade, name one pattern to identify.
8. As a position trader who entered a short trade when the stock initiated a downtrend, where is the most likely place you will cover the short and take profits?
9. When scanning for an overextended stock to sell short, what are some of the first signs to recognize?
10. Assuming all signals for a shorting setup are in place, when do you enter your order to sell short a stock experiencing a double top?
11. Which signal should the RSI issue for the ideal shorting setup?
12. In the best shorting setup, where should the OBV be heading?

Answers
1. Stocks move down faster than they rise because fear and panic are stronger than greed.
2. When new at shorting, trade small lot sizes, such as 100 shares, and only trade slow-moving, high-volume stocks.
3. False.
4. To sell a stock short, you borrow the shares from your broker.
5. The company announces bad news or earnings.
6. You can short a weak, fast-falling stock as it falls through support, rather than waiting for it to trade below support.
7. Look for a stock experiencing a Stage 3 rollover and ready to fall into a Stage 4 downtrend. Neckline (support) break of a head-and-shoulders pattern is ideal.
8. When the stock breaks the downtrend by making a higher low and higher high. (Some traders use the 20-day moving average as a short stop.)

9. Enter your order to sell short when your target falls five to ten cents below support or the prior day's low. For fast-moving stocks, enter your order as the stock falls through support.
10. The best overextended shorting candidates are experiencing a steep uptrend; trading high above their 20-day MAs on a daily chart; correlate with their industry group as being acutely overextended; and have formed a double top on a 60-minute chart.
11. For the best shorting setup, the RSI should read over 70, and/or be hooking down (not in oversold territory, under 30).
12. Down, down, down.

CENTER POINT: LET GO OF FEAR AND LET YOUR LIGHT SHINE

"Our deepest fear is not that we are inadequate. Our deepest fear is that we are powerful beyond measure."

—Marianne Williamson

In Western civilization, we are taught almost from birth to disown our unique talents. Our culture dictates that people who "blow their own horns" are cocky and conceited. They are "egotists" with "big heads."

We take the admonition to heart. Not only do we deny praise when we receive it, we discount and depress our God-given talents, even to ourselves. Over and over, we play the personal mind-tape that reminds us that we're not as good, smart, or attractive as others. No wonder we're so reluctant to put our visions in motion. We constantly come from, dwell in, and paint our perspectives with fear.

A fear-based state of mind stops us from revealing our unique selves. It handcuffs us to our trumped-up limitations and thwarts us from touching, tasting, and learning from all the exciting possibilities available to us.

Our fears are attached to anyone, and anything, outside our comfort zone. We strap on blinders, avoid risk, say "ain't it awful" to anyone who will listen and agree, and set out to prove why the circumstances in our lives detain us—even stop us—from realizing our dreams.

Somewhere along the way, we've forgotten that we create our own canvas. We can paint our lives with brushstrokes full of angst and fear—or joy, love, and fulfillment. Either way, we'll experience what we've chosen.

We can surrender our old fear-based habits of seeing and experiencing ourselves. The moment "I can't do that" escapes our thoughts and/or our lips, try replacing it with, "I *can* do that, and I'm going to have a fantastic experience while I'm doing it!"

Let's banish fear-based thinking, and focus on the truth: We are strong and competent, and highly capable of progressing toward our highest potential. Our talents are our tools that help us reach our goals. Let's use them every day, in every area of our lives!

CHAPTER 13

Exchange Traded Funds: Tools for Sharpening Trading and Hedging Profits

"The people who know what a stock is worth will always buy it when it is selling at bargain prices."

—Jesse Livermore

If ever there was a newcomer on the Street who quickly gained widespread popularity for being attractive, efficient, and versatile, it's the exchange traded fund. Indeed, ETFs have won the hearts—and assets—of nearly everyone on Wall Street, from private traders and investors to professional money managers and institutional hedge funds.

ETFS: WHAT THEY ARE

An exchange traded fund is a basket of stocks, or an investment fund, that tracks an underlying index and trades as a single equity.

The stocks held by the fund focus upon a single theme and are created around every conceivable type of index. That theme might be a market index, such as the Dow Jones Industrials, the S&P 500, the S&P 400 (midcaps), the NADAQ 100, or the Russell 2000 (small caps) Index. Or, the theme could focus on a market sector, such as Basic Materials, Information Technology, or Health Care. Themes also include "style," such as value or growth, or target corporate bonds, Treasury bonds, real estate indexes, and commodity indexes. Specialty ETFs zero in on unique market niches, such as nanotech, water resources, or clean energy.

For those who want to go global, international funds represent the icons of industry in countries that span our globe, from Asia to Austria, and from Europe to emerging markets. Taking the international approach one step further, you can select a sector, such as energy, and purchase a global energy fund. To take the ultimate step, you can purchase or sell short shares in global currency ETFs.

WHERE ETFS STARTED: A BRIEF TIMELINE

In 1993, global money manager State Street Global Advisors partnered with the Amex (American Stock Exchange) to launch the first ETF, the Standard & Poor's 500 Depository Receipt, or the SPYDR; it tracked the S&P 500 (cash) Index. The SPYDR traded under the ticker SPY, and traders nicknamed the stock "the Spider."

The Spiders' success led to the creation and development of the "Middies" or the (MDY), which tracks the mid-cap S&P 400 Index. The Dow Diamonds (DIA), the Dow Jones Industrial Average tracking stock, and the proxy for the NASDAQ 100, the QQQ, or the "Cubes," as we sometimes call them (symbol QQQQ), quickly followed.

In 1996, Barclay's Global Investors launched iShares, a broad brushstroke of ETFs that represent stock indexes, sectors, and countries. Select Sector SPDRS emerged in 1998 and quickly attracted institutional traders. Rydex launched the first currency shares ETF in 2005 (the fund tracks the euro) and has issued more currency funds since that time.

At the present time, ETFs now number more than 660, with more appearing on the market each week. Fund assets grew from $24 billion in 1998 to more than $450 billion in February 2008. Of course, by the time you read this, the number of funds will have increased dramatically, along with their assets.

BENEFITS OF USING ETFS AS TRADING AND INVESTING TOOLS

To make a splash that lasts on Wall Street, a financial product must be cost-efficient, liquid, diverse, and versatile. ETFs have definitely made the cut.

The following are a few of the benefits of trading and investing with ETFs:

➤ ETFs typically involve lower operating costs than traditional mutual funds. Mutual funds charge a cost (expense ratio) ranging between 0.49 percent and 2.00 percent of fund assets. Most ETFs charge 0.20 percent to 0.60 percent. (ETFs paying dividends typically incur higher expense ratios.) The lower cost means a higher total return to you.

➤ ETFs provide diversity within each share. When you buy shares of the PowerShares QQQ (QQQQ), which tracks the NASDAQ 100 Index, for example, you own the top 100 non-financial stocks in the NASDAQ Stock Market. If one of the component stocks wakes up to unsavory news it may jostle the index a bit, but it won't drive the Qs into the dirt. Those who own the individual bad-news stock, though, may be reaching for the Maalox bottle.

➤ Like mutual funds, ETFs earn dividends paid by the underlying stocks. Plus, certain index funds can split; in early 2000, the Qs split 2-for-1.

➤ ETFs are taxed differently than mutual funds. You don't pay taxes on an ETF until you close the position. In a typical open-end mutual fund, however, a flood of redemptions may force the portfolio manager to sell shares in order to cover the obligations. That can trigger capital gains for fund shareholders—gains on which they have to pay taxes. Because ETFs are bought and sold on an exchange, the portfolio manager doesn't have to sell shares or maintain enough cash to meet redemptions.

➤ ETFs undergo continuous pricing. The estimated NAV (net asset value) for an ETF's underlying portfolio is repriced for specialists and market makers every fifteen seconds, or less. Therefore, just as with stocks, you can dispose of them with a single click. Mutual funds are priced at their NAV (net asset value) at the close of each trading day. If you decide to sell your mutual fund shares early in the day (say you own an oil fund, and the price of crude light is falling to new lows), you still have to wait for the fund's end-of-day price to cash out the shares.

➤ Since ETFs represent a basket of stocks, you can minimize the time spent researching fundamentals on individual stocks. As long as you know that a certain index, sector, or industry group is trending up or down, you can target the correlating ETF as a trading candidate.

➤ ETFs can be sold short just as easily as they can be purchased on the long side. This gives traders and investors higher precision entries and improved pricing opportunities for selling short.

WHERE TO FIND ETFS

Currently, the majority of ETFs reside in these fund families: BLDRS, Claymore, HOLDRS, iShares, PowerShares, ProShares, Rydex, Select Sector SPDRS, SSgA Funds, Vanguard VIPERS, and Wisdom Tree. Although the funds in each of these groups fall under the ETF heading, they represent diverse areas of the financial markets and may involve different characteristics.

The American Stock Exchange lists a large portion of the stock index funds, and its Web site (*www.amex.com*) has a great ETF corner. I particularly like the

"Quote Summary," which lists all the ETFs traded on the Amex, their symbols, current price, net change and percent change for the day, and volume.

The NASDAQ has added an ETF Dynamic Heatmap to its Web site. Go to: *http://screening.nasdaq.com/heatmaps/heatmap_ETF.asp.* In addition to the Web sites listed in the descriptions that follow, you can check these Web sites for additional information on ETFs:

➤ *www.etfconnect.com*
➤ *www.etftrends.com*
➤ *www.indexfunds.com*

My Web site, *www.ToniTurner.com*, features an ETF page containing various fund themes, listings of funds under each, and much more information on fund families and ETF trading strategies.

The following gives you the major fund families, their main focus, and Web addresses:

➤ BLDRS. Focus: International Equities funds based on the Bank of New York ADR Index. Managed by the NASDAQ. Visit *www.powershares.com.*
➤ Claymore. Focus: Capitalization, specialty, and unique strategy funds. Managed by Claymore Advisors LLC. Visit *www.claymore.com.*
➤ HOLDRS (Holding Company Depository Receipts). Focus: Sectors and industry groups. Managed by Merrill Lynch. Visit *www.holdrs.com.*
➤ iShares. Focus: Market Cap, Value/Growth, Sector/Industry Groups, International, Real Estate, Fixed Income, and Commodities. Managed by Barclays Global Investors Services. Visit *www.iShares.com.*
➤ PowerShares. Focus: Market Cap, Sectors/Industry Groups, Equity Income, and International. Managed by PowerShares Capital Management LLC. Visit *www.powershares.com.*
➤ ProShares. Focus: Sell short the Dow, S&P 500, NASDAQ 100, S&P Midcap 400, or Russell 2000 by buying these shares. Great for managing risk in IRAs, where short-selling is prohibited. Several index shares also magnify moves in uptrending markets. Managed by ProShares Group. Visit *www.proshares.com.*
➤ Rydex. Focus: Broad Index, Growth/Value, and Sectors. Managed by Rydex Global Advisors. Visit *www.rydexfunds.com.*
➤ SPDRs. Focus: S&P 500 (SPY) and nine Sector SPDRS. Managed by State Street Global Advisors. Visit *www.sectorspdr.com.*

➤ SSgA. Focus: Dow Diamonds (DIA), International, Growth/Value, Sectors/Industry Groups, Market Cap, and Specialty. Managed by State Street Global Advisors. Visit *www.ssgafunds.com.*

➤ Vanguard VIPERS. Focus: Growth/Value, Dividend, Market Cap, Sectors, and International. Managed by the Vanguard Group. Visit *www.vanguard.com.*

➤ Wisdom Tree. Focus: Market Cap, Dividend, International Market Cap, International Dividends, and International Sectors. Managed by Wisdom Tree Investments. Visit *www.wisdomtree.com.*

> **HOT TIP**
>
> Trading Tactic: If you think tech stocks will move into/stay in an uptrend, assign a portion of your account to the QQQQ as a position trade, and then assign another portion to swing trade tech stocks.

Trading with ETFs

You'll find that ETFs make highly valuable trading tools for pure profit plays that target stock indexes and sectors. The funds also work well for diversifying your core account, and for hedging your account against short-term pullbacks in the market.

A note about liquidity. Many ETFs trade with low liquidity (average daily volume). That means low-liquidity ETFs may also move with nominal volatility, trading in narrow price ranges of just a few cents per day. That can limit their attractiveness as candidates for many swing trading plays, because profit potential is minimal.

I recommend swing trading ETFs that trade with an average daily volume of 300,000 shares per day, or more. While that kind of daily volume may not be important to position traders because of the weeks/months duration of the trade, swing traders will be more comfortable (and make more money) with higher volume and expanded daily range vehicles.

I use ETFs to focus on three basic trading strategies:

➤ Index and sector strategies
➤ Diversification
➤ Hedging tactics

INDEX AND SECTOR STRATEGIES USING SWING AND POSITION (CORE) TRADES

As top-down traders, we stay aware of market swings, economic and earnings data, geopolitical events, and national and global news that impacts the financial markets. We stay tuned as to which sectors and industry groups are leading, and which show signs of weakness.

ETFs make excellent tools for taking advantage of major index, sector, and industry group movement. You can chart the major indexes, such as the Dow Industrials, the S&P 500 Index, and the NASDAQ 100 or Composite, and then buy correlating ETFs to profit from the upswings (or sell short to profit from the swings down).

You can also chart the leading sectors and industry groups we've talked about in this book so far, such as the Biotech index (BKX), Retail index (MVR), Bank index (BIX), Semiconductor index (SOX), and Pharmas (DRG), and then buy (or sell short weak groups) correlating ETFs. (For a complete list go to *www.ToniTurner.com* and click on "Sectors & Stocks.")

Look for the same price patterns to enter ETFs as you do stocks: breakouts from bases, breakouts from consolidation patterns and pullbacks in the context of uptrends, and breakdowns from consolidations and rallies in downtrends.

> **HOT TIP**
>
> If you trade a specialty fund, you may want to employ the bottom-up trading style. That means you'll have only news and company earnings to guide you. For example, if you think developed nations will continue to focus on environmental issues, check daily charts of the "green" ETFs.
>
> • • •
>
> While the value of each ETF relates to the value of the stocks in its underlying index, ETFs trade at their own moment-to-moment value according to demand and supply pressure. That means that the actual ETF price can trade at a discount or premium— usually just a few cents—to its NAV (net asset value).

In many ways, swing trading ETFs is easier than trading stocks. Have you ever chosen the *only* stock in a particular industry group that didn't move higher—and watched all the others in the group fly up into the clouds?

That situation doesn't occur as often when you're trading ETFs. As long as there is decisive movement within a certain sector or industry group, the representative ETF will move higher or lower, in tandem.

You will also find that ETFs don't gap up or down at the market open at quite the same rate as individual stocks. And, if they do gap, the ETFs that correlate to the large market indexes usually fill their gaps quickly. One reason is that the stocks representing the ETF open at different values in relation to their closing prices the night before. And, if the ETF does gap up or down at the open, enough of those stocks will fill their own gaps, causing the ETF price to fill its gap, as well.

Figure 13-1 shows a daily chart of the PowerShares QQQ Trust (QQQQ), which has held the record for the most widely traded stock in the U.S. stock market. (As of this date, this proxy for the NASDAQ 100 trades on average more than 110 million shares per day.) As you will see, you could swing trade the Qs with relative ease from mid-March through the first week in May.

FIGURE 13-1. PowerShares QQQ daily. RealTick graphics by Townsend Analytics. From the end of 2006 and through the last week in February 2007, the PowerShares QQQ, which tracks the NASDAQ 100 index and trades under the symbol QQQQ, moved in a horizontal range. These kinds of patterns are frustrating to many traders. Then on February 26, the Qs took a violent tumble, falling from that day's opening price of $45.50 to the March 5 low of 42.06. This was a humbling loss of nearly 10 percent for the highly traded technology vehicle. After carving a quick double-bottom pattern in March, the Qs popped back up to prior resistance in the $44 area, and then rose to make new yearly highs at $47.00. On March 30, the ETF climbed back over the rising 20-day MA, which boded well for the rebound. On April 12, the 20-day MA crossed above the 50-day MA. That day provided traders with a great entry for the following three-week move up.

Figure 13-2 shows a daily chart of the Select Sector SPDR Energy ETF, which trades under the symbol XLE. The run-up in energy prices fueled the move in mid-March to mid-May, and position traders took home dandy profits.

FIGURE 13-2. Select Sector SPDR Energy ETF. RealTick by Townsend Analytics. This daily chart displays the Select Sector SPDR Energy ETF (XLE). As you can imagine, companies in this fund primarily develop and produce crude oil and natural gas, as well as furnishing other energy-related services. While you could have swing traded this ETF, position traders profited without effort by simply buying the XLE on March 20, right as the energy fund popped over its 20-day MA. Or, they could have waited a day or two to enter, when the 20-day MA crossed above the 50-day and confirmed the move higher. Note how the RSI made a bullish divergence to the XLE's price in mid-March, rising higher before the ETF took off. The OBV also rose in tandem with the RSI, with volume confirming price. It doesn't get any better than that!

DIVERSIFYING WITH ETFS

Unless you're a day trader who takes his or her account flat (cash) every day before the closing bell, diversifying your account is always a good idea.

ETFs are the ideal way to accomplish diversification without exposing your account to the risks inherent with holding individual stock.

The concept is simple: You don't keep all of your eggs in one basket. For example, if your account is filled with technology stocks, you could introduce a few shares of the DIA, the large-cap value ETF that represents the Dow Jones Industrial stocks. Or, you might introduce a small-cap fund, a "total market" fund, or a sector fund such as basic materials, financials, or utilities.

To diversify even more, you might purchase shares of a broad-based, multi-country international ETF to your portfolio. Or, say you read an article about a certain country that's thriving; you might decide to add shares of its corresponding country ETF. (The iShares fund family features a nice array of single-country ETFs).

Other methods of diversification might come in the form of adding global energy shares, or adding fixed-income ETFs (bond funds) or REITs (real estate investment trusts) funds. Highly adventurous souls might want to target global currency ETFs—but should do so cautiously.

If you go to the ETFs page on my Web site, you can find a selection of ETFs listed under a variety of headings with which to diversify your portfolio.

Figure 13-3 is a daily chart of the international iShares MSCI EAFE Index ETF that trades under the symbol EFA. (MSCI: Morgan Stanley Capital Investments.) This is a popular fund for traders who want to complement their portfolio of U.S. equities and gain exposure to large companies in the European, Australasian (Australia and Asia), and Far Eastern markets.

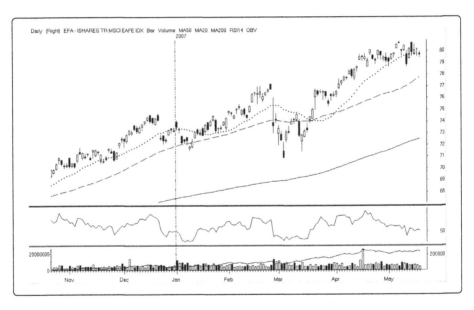

FIGURE 13-3. iShares MSCI EAFE Index ETF daily. RealTick by Townsend Analytics. Traders can diversify their portfolios with international exposure by purchasing shares of ETFs like the iShares EAFE fund. Since this ETF represents companies in the European, Australian, Asian, and Far Eastern markets, it offers diversity to accounts focused on U.S. equities.

Of course, you can also diversify by hedging with specialty ETFs, such as PowerShares' Water Resources (PHO), Clean Energy (PBW), Food and Beverage (PBJ), or even Biotechnology and Genome (PBE).

Just remember that the wisest sages in the financial markets diversify their portfolios with positions that vary from their main focus. If you hold stocks overnight, please consider this strategy. Besides, it's fun to explore the vast array of ETFs on the market and read about the unique focuses they represent.

By the way—what the heck is a *genome*?

HEDGING TACTICS USING ETFS

One of the most valuable benefits of ETFs is their unique ability to act as quick-to-the draw hedging tools.

When you "hedge" positions in your account, you take a counter position to offset losses. Performed properly, hedging, or protecting, the core positions in your account makes for wise risk management.

> **HOT TIP**
>
> Your hedging trade must adhere to the same trading methods you apply to all of your other trades—with entry, stop placement, and exit strategies planned in advance of taking the trade. Please don't hedge hastily, or use it as a "revenge" trade.

The flip side: Those who use hedging tactics as a Band-Aid for losing positions are simply adding additional risk on top of a bad situation.

When you hedge, the basic tactic is that you sell short (or buy, if your current positions are short) shares to equal the same dollar amount you are protecting. Many traders adjust the shares depending on the average daily price range (volatility) of the hedging vehicle.

For example, if your core position fluctuates in an average daily range of $1, and the hedging ETF bounces around in a $2 range, you might want to buy one-half the shares of the hedging ETF to more closely match the original position.

Here's a sample hedge play: Imagine your trading account includes a large core position in the semiconductor stock KLA Tencor Corp. (KLAC). (You may own other semiconductor stocks, as well.) Suddenly, the semiconductor group tops out and begins to sell off.

To hedge, or protect these positions (as long as they don't touch your stops), you can sell short shares of the semiconductor HOLDRS, symbol SMH, and hold it for one to five days, thus averting a sizable drawdown. Make sure to monitor your hedging position, and exit the trade as soon as your core positions show signs of recovering.

Figure 13-4 shows a daily chart of KLA Tencor Corp. (KLAC). You'll note that on the most recent days of the chart, the semiconductor company sold off abruptly. Of course, as you will note on Figure 13-5, which is a daily chart of the Philadelphia Semiconductor Index (SOX), the entire industry group sold off during that time. When you look at this chart, keep in mind that—except for the hint in the chart's caption—you wouldn't have known the stock was going to sell off, until it did.

You could have protected profits already made from KLAC's recent uptrend by selling short the Semiconductor HOLDRS ETF, which trades under the symbol SMH, for a 3- to 4-day period. Figure 13-6 shows a daily chart of the SMH.

If your position in KLAC had held its lows and begun to move higher, you would raise your stop order to a point just below the lows and exit the short SMH position. As it was, however, KLAC was stopped out, as you can see in Figure 13-4. At this point, you can exit the SMH hedge position immediately (with your KLAC profits still intact) *or* at the first signs of improvement in the semiconductor group.

The ProShares fund family offers stock index ETFs called "Ultra." That means if an index or sector moves up or down 1 percent, the ETF moves up or down 2 percent. You can make quick profits with these, but you can also take quick losses. Learn before you burn!

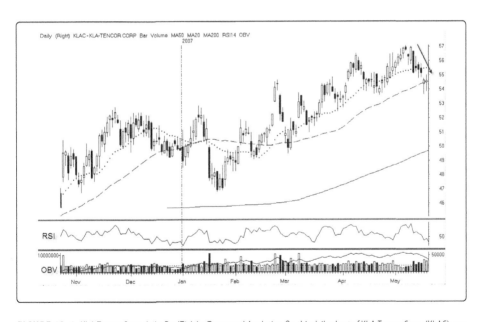

FIGURE 13-4. KLA Tencor Corp. daily. RealTick by Townsend Analytics. On this daily chart of KLA Tencor Corp. (KLAC), you can see how the semiconductor giant moved from its lows in January at about 47 to a high of 57 in the following May. The subsequent pullback looked innocent enough, except for one villain—high volume! That clued traders who are skilled at reading volume that the selloff might be volatile. Still, those who wanted price to confirm the possible pullback could have checked the benchmark Philadelphia Semiconductor Index (SOX) for guidance (Figure 13-5), and then sold short the Semi-conductor HLDR ETF (SMH) to hedge the position. As it turned out, KLAC broke prior support at 53.60 (dotted arrow) and the position was stopped out. Because the position was hedged, however, there was little, if any, loss in the account.

FIGURE 13-5. Philadelphia Semiconductor Index (SOX) daily. RealTick by Townsend Analytics. This daily chart of the Philadelphia Semiconductor Index (SOX) shows the tech index breaking out of a horizontal trend in mid-April at 471, and moving up to a yearly high of 510 on May 9. Note the RSI during the first week of May, and notice its bearish divergence, which said it wasn't impressed with the SOX's new high. Sure enough, the Semiconductor Index rolled over, at least for the time being.

FIGURE 13-6. Semiconductor HOLDRS ETF daily. RealTick by Townsend Analytics. On this daily chart of the Semiconductor HOLDRS, you can see how the fund topped out with the SOX and then rolled over—although not quite with the same volatility. You could have sold short shares of the SMH on May 15, the fourth day from the chart's hard right edge. You would have placed just above the day's high at 38.10. (You would have had a triple top on a 60-minute chart with a failed breakout the day before—a good pattern when you're selling short.) You could have made a fairly easy point. Notice the long shadows on the two candles of May 17 and 18 (last two days at the chart's hard right edge). Long lower shadows on each of those candles indicate buyers. That's evident because although each of those days closed lower than they opened, they each closed above the lows of the days. That's a signal that buyers are lurking on the sidelines. I would close the position with the "bird in the hand" profit—especially since KLAC was stopped out and the reason for the hedge was off the books.

When the entire market moves down, it's a fairly easy play to simply short one of the major stock index ETFs, such as the Dow Diamonds (DIA), the S&P 500 SPDR (SPY), or the PowerShares QQQ (QQQQ).

Please remember, when you hedge by *shorting an ETF that's pulling back within the context of an uptrend*, you do so with the knowledge that this is a short-term play. That means you hold the position for one to five days—*only as long as the hedged position moves lower and the hedging vehicle is profitable*. Keep in mind with your ETF short position, you must analyze its chart pattern and pinpoint where the next area of support lies on a daily chart. Use that as your profit target. It's no fun to get caught in a short squeeze when the hedging ETF's price bounces and the uptrend resumes.

As with all positions, keep a trailing stop in place at all times and remain aware of nearby price support that can act as your signal to close your short position.

IRA Hedging Strategy—Inverse ETFs

Because SEC rules disallow us from selling short in our IRAs, we can hedge long-term positions in those accounts by *buying* shares in one of the ProShares "inverse" stock index ETFs, such as the ProShares Short Dow (DOG), the ProShares Short S&P 500 (SH), or the ProShares Short QQQ (PSQ).

So, when you *buy* shares of the DOG, SH, or PSQ, you are *buying* shares of a fund that is *short* the corresponding long index. For example, if the Dow is headed lower, the DOG will rise higher. When the S&P 500 falls, the SH rises. On days the NASDAQ 100 tumbles lower, the PSQ rises. Just so, if the Dow rises, the DOG falls, and so forth.

The Proshares fund family also sponsors UltraShort stock index ETFs. For every 1 percent the underlying index falls, the UltraShort fund rises 2 percent. The UltraShort Dow trades under the symbol DXD. For every 1 percent the Dow falls, the DXD rises 2 percent. The UltraShort S&P 500 trades under the symbol SDS, and the NASDAQ 100 UltraShort trades under the symbol QID. For every 1 percent the S&P 500 and NASDAQ 100 head lower, the respective UltraShort shares rise 2 percent. Of course, if the indexes reverse and head higher, for every 1 percent they rise, the UltraShort slides south 2 percent.

If you decide to trade the ProShares Short or UltraShort Shares, please do so with caution, as they tend to be volatile. You'll want to paper trade them first, to get used to the feeling that when you're buying index shares, you're actually selling short that index. For more information on Short and UltraShort funds, go to: *www.ProShares.com.*

Versatile, efficient, and flexible, ETFs are indeed the most popular newcomers on Wall Street. They are excellent tools for pure profit plays that can stay in your portfolio for days to months and longer. ETFs also make fantastic diversification tools that lower risk and add balance to existing positions. And, they act as superior hedging vehicles that enhance profits and aid risk management in both short-term and long-term portfolios.

In Chapter 14, we'll move day-by-day through an actual stock trade. See you there!

QUIZ

||||||||||||||||

1. Define the trading and investing instrument known as an exchange traded fund.
2. Each ETF correlates to an underlying index that focuses on a certain theme. Name at least five themes.
3. Describe three benefits of trading and investing with ETFs.
4. What three basic strategies work well using ETFs as the primary tool?
5. What's one benefit of using ETFs for trading stock indexes and sectors?
6. True or False? If you have a core trading account jam-packed full of software stocks, you're best to stick to those stocks and leave the other industry groups alone.
7. When you "hedge" certain positions in your account, what does that mean?
8. If you decide to hedge positions in your account, what is the basic tactic?
9. True or False? It's wise to remember that your hedging trade must adhere to the same trading plan you apply to all of your other trades. Plan entries, stops, and profit targets just as you always do.
10. When you hedge a long stock position by selling short an ETF that's pulling back within the context of an uptrend, do you plan it as a short-term play?

Answers
1. An exchange traded fund is a basket of stocks, or an investment fund, that tracks an underlying index and trades as a single equity.
2. ETF themes: stock index, sector index, international (single country or group of countries) index, style index (growth or value), specialty index, fixed-income index, currency or currencies blend.
3. ETFs are taxed differently than mutual funds, because you don't pay taxes on an ETF until you close the position. ETFs provide diversity within each fund—which in itself minimizes risk. ETFs can be sold short easily and quickly.
4. Index and sector strategies, diversification within core positions, and hedging tactics.
5. When trading individual stocks, we fall prey to choosing the only one within a sector or industry group that doesn't move up with the others. When trading ETFs, however, as long as there is decisive movement within a certain sector or industry group, the representative ETF will move higher or lower, in tandem.

6. Very false! When your account focuses on one market sector or group, you're wise to diversify with ETFs in at least one or two alternative sectors; it's also acceptable to branch into international ETFs, fixed-income, or REIT funds depending on economic conditions. And remember—keeping a portion of your account in cash is always a good idea.

7. When you "hedge" positions in your account, you take a counter position to offset losses. ETFs are a great hedging tool.

8. When you hedge, the basic tactic is that you sell short (or buy—if your current positions are short) shares to equal the same dollar amount you are protecting. Many traders adjust the shares depending on the average daily price range (price volatility) of the hedging vehicle.

9. Absolutely true!

10. Yes. When you hedge a current long position by selling short shares of an ETF that's also in an uptrend, it's imperative to remember to cover your hedge within a short period of time, to avoid getting caught in a short squeeze.

CENTER POINT: BOOST YOUR PERSONAL PRODUCTIVITY

"Whether it's the best of times or the worst of times, it's the only time we've got."

—Art Buchwald, columnist

If you boost your personal productivity during the hours you are working, you can earn more money, and achieve a higher level of success in your chosen field. You will also have more time to spend on yourself, and with your family and friends.

Here are three strategies I use during my workday. These strategies help me minimize stress and ensure I maintain a high level of productivity.

First, I've become a champion list maker. Far from enslaving us, well-thought-out lists actually liberate us. Why? Because it's a proven fact that when we write down a task, whether in a daily planner or on a computer planning calendar, our mind considers the job to be done. That result frees our minds to focus on the task at hand.

Get in the habit of developing a comprehensive daily to-do list, as well as project to-do lists and timelines, and long-term goal lists (long term: six-month, yearly, and five-year goals). You'll find by having those lists at your elbow, you can accomplish more, in less time, and with less stress.

Here's another perk to daily list making: Studies show that busy people who maintain daily planning lists sleep much better than those who dive headfirst into each workday without a written plan.

To create an effective to-do list, record every action item you can think of that you need to accomplish for the coming day. Include telephone calls to friends and replies to important e-mails. If you leave items off of your list, your mind will stray to those unlisted tasks while you are trying to focus on other important projects.

Here's one more tactic I use to manage my time more efficiently: I break my day into hourly segments. Because my natural tendency is to go in ten different directions at once, I have to discipline myself to stick to a project and finish it. Method: I break my working day into single-hour portions, and then assign each hour to a certain action item. Then, for example, I tell myself, "I will work on this project from 10 A.M. to 11 A.M. I will allow no interruptions, not even from myself!"

I also prioritize my tasks by listing each with its ROI. By ROI, I mean "return on investment." If I'm going to invest my time in a job or project, I want a return on that time investment, in the form of mental, emotional, or financial gains. For example, the time I spend on researching a subject yields valuable knowledge. The time I spend having dinner with friends returns enjoyment and the strengthening of relationships. The time I spend studying the stock market can result in profits from a well-placed trade. Review the activities you have planned for today, and spend a few minutes evaluating the possible ROIs on each.

Remember, set aside a few minutes each day to develop a well-thought-out to-do list. Break your day into hourly segments and assign action items to those time slots. Finally, prioritize activity with an ROI value. You will soon discover that you're achieving your goals faster, making more money, and enjoying life more than ever before!

CHAPTER 14

Anatomy of a Trade

"When a man makes his play in a . . . market, he must not permit himself set opinions. He must have an open mind and flexibility."

—Jesse Livermore

When you read a trading book or take a class, it's easy for the instructor, myself included, to point to a chart and say, "If you'd been trading this stock, you would have bought here, at this price, and then sold it here, at this higher price, for a nice profit." Sounds easy, yet many times the actual journey from the entry to exit is filled with bumps and potholes.

From the moment you buy to the moment you sell your stock (or vice versa), its price, its industry group, *and* the market thrash around. You weigh a thousand options in your mind.

"Hey, my stock's going down. So is its industry group. But the market's going up. What should I do?"

Or, "Wow, my stock just flew through resistance! Maybe I'll take half my profits here. Or, maybe I should take them all. If I do, though, I might leave a ton of money on the table." (Quick glance toward the heavens.) "What should I do?"

Or, "Good grief—my stock's tanking! In another half point, it's going to hit my stop point. And I can't find any bad news on the stock—so what's wrong with it? Should I wait for it to hit my stop, or get out now and save a half point?"

By the end of the trade, you either took home a chunky profit, or sustained a small loss. Either way, you probably made a slew of choices on the journey from start to finish.

In this chapter, you're going to experience a swing trading journey. Using actual charts, I'll show you the thoughts and the actions they triggered. You see the actual charts ahead of time. The written journal details each day's thoughts and actions and tells you what I would do in certain situations. Keep in mind that my style—my musings and decisions—will differ from yours, and from many other traders. Use them as guidelines.

FIND AN INDUSTRY GROUP OR SECTOR TO TARGET

Let's start with the assumption that you're aware of the current mood of the market and its major indexes, including the Dow, S&P 500, and NASDAQ 100 and/or Composite. Financial television networks and other information sources will keep you updated on industry groups and sectors in the forefront of the market with statements such as, "Oil stocks and pharmaceuticals have taken center stage lately, while techs lagged."

So, pinpoint the industry group you want to target, and remember to use if/then logic to zero in on it. Then study each group's chart to find one that looks optimal. As mentioned earlier in the book, you'll want to have a list of industry groups and sectors assembled on a "watch list," with five or more leading stocks in each.

One simple way to start your watch list is to go to my Web site, *www.Toni-Turner.com,* and click on "Sectors & Stocks." You will find a roster of sectors/industry groups and stocks that reside in them. This is a complimentary service for my readers.

The Preparation

Now, let's take a specific example of a potential stock trade that we've focused upon.

Our trading time span is from May 16 to May 23 (2007). (Please keep in mind that the actual dates of this trade are unimportant. The important points are price patterns, interaction of the stock and related indexes, and the actions taken to keep losses small and gains high.)

Sector: Telecommunications. The index we'll watch in conjunction with stock movement is the XTC, the Amex North American Telecom Index.
Stock: Sprint Nextel Corp. (S), the giant communications company that provides wireless and wireline products and services to individual and business customers, as well as to government agencies. Sprint's current IBD Composite Rating is 79.

The reason I chose this sector and stock is that the telecom index and Sprint Nextel are both in an uptrend, and telecoms have been strong on the year. The S&P 500 Index, in which most telecom companies reside, has also been climbing in a healthy uptrend for some months.

Acquisitions and mergers in the telecom industry are blazing, worldwide. Earnings have been excellent, and if there is a pullback in the markets, telecom has a defensive edge.

HOT TIP

Remember, individual traders are not in control when the stock market opens (9:30 A.M. EST). The specialists and market makers are. Savvy traders usually wait until the market has been open for at least ten minutes to enter a trade.

The Trade

Wednesday, May 16: I've spotted a great setup on Sprint Nextel (S) on its daily chart: See Figure 14-1. I also like its weekly chart, shown on Figure 14-2. And, no one can argue with the smooth, textbook uptrend recorded on the Amex Telecom Index's (XTC) daily chart in Figure 14-3. The XTC has climbed steadily since the beginning of the year. If market conditions are a go tomorrow, and the setup plays out, I plan to buy 500 shares of S if it moves over today's high of 20.45. Time frame: swing trade.

Triggers

➤ The major indexes are in uptrends. Yesterday, the CPI (Consumer Price Index) economic report and major inflation gauge came out with a more positive number than most analysts expected. (A current monthly Economic Calendar is posted on my home page at *www.ToniTurner.com.*)

➤ The XTC, the Amex Telecommunications Index, is in a firm uptrend.

➤ Sprint is in an uptrend and now moving sideways. Price has retested its prior pullback price of 19.93, and is holding there. Today's candle reversed yesterday's price action, forming a bullish piercing pattern (average volume). It is trading above its 50-day and 200-day MAs and just at its horizontal 20-day MA. If Sprint moves higher tomorrow, it will trade above the 20-day MA (bullish) and should break out of the horizontal move.

➤ RSI is neutral and hooked up (just above 50). OBV neutral to higher.

My usual strategy is to wait until at least ten minutes after the market's open to initiate a position, and many times I wait until I determine a stock's first 30-minute high and low prices. That means I pinpoint a stock's high and low prices recorded in the first thirty minutes of the market's open, from 9:30 A.M. to 10:00 A.M. If a stock breaks its first 30-minute high after 10:00 A.M., that's usually a bullish sign and confirms my entry decision. Those of you who have the luxury of watching intraday 30-minute charts may want to try this tactic for swing trade entries.

FIGURE 14-1. Sprint Nextel Corp. daily chart. RealTick by Townsend Analytics. This daily chart of the Sprint Nextel Corp. (S) shows it trading in an intermediate-term uptrend (above its 50-day MA) since it fell to a major low of 16.93 in January. Since then the telecom giant has recovered nicely. Yesterday, Sprint dropped below its 20-day MA. Today it quickly recovered in a bullish piercing pattern. If it moves higher tomorrow, and above today's high of 20.43, it will present a good opportunity for a swing trade and possibly a position trade.

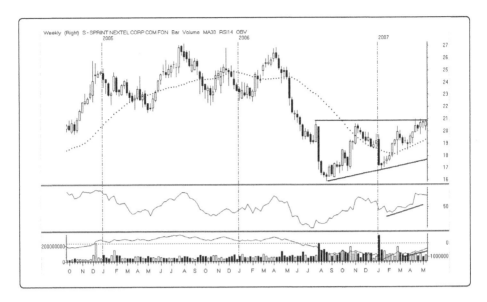

FIGURE 14-2. Sprint Nextel Corp. weekly chart. RealTick by Townsend Analytics. Telecom stocks are in the spotlight now and most are moving higher on good volume. This weekly chart of the Sprint Nextel Corp. (S) shows the communications product and services giant drawing a double bottom on a weekly chart in 2006–2007. The resistance point of the "W" is at about 20.60. If S can climb above that supply point, it may be able to make a run back to the mid-20s. The 30-week moving average is rising under the current price pattern, a bullish sign.

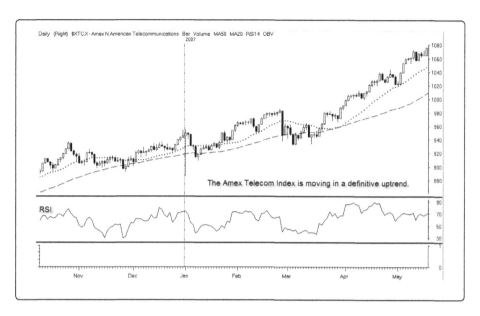

FIGURE 14-3. Amex North American Telecommunications Index daily chart. RealTick by Townsend Analytics. This daily chart displays the Amex North American Telecommunications Index (XTC), which has, for the most part, been trending higher since the first of the year. How long can it continue? Certainly not forever! That's why swing trades come in handy. You can jump in, take "the center out of the Oreo"—the best part out of the current price swing—then jump back out if the market rolls over. We trade what we see, however, not what we think will happen. For the moment, the XTC is in dandy shape.

Thursday, May 17

The stock market (S&P 500) moves down a bit at the open; by 10 A.M., it reverses and drifts higher. The XTC mimics the benchmark's action.

Sprint gaps open thirteen cents to 20.53 on fairly light volume. (Last night's closing price was 20.40.) I wait to see if it will fill the gap, which it does in the next half hour. It falls from the opening price to a 10:00 A.M. low of 20.24, then recovers along with the S&P 500 and telecom index. At 11:00 A.M., it moves back above 20.45 (yesterday's high and our entry price).

➤ Entry: We buy 500 shares of Sprint at 20.48 including $10 commission: $10,250.00.
➤ Initial stop entered at 20.05, twenty cents under current low of day and five cents below yesterday's low. If Sprint falls below that price, it will be a bearish move, and I will exit the position. Assuming Sprint doesn't hit the stop price, the stop order will be raised later in the day to adjust risk/reward.

HOT TIP

Avoid buying stocks at the open that gap higher. Wait for ten minutes to a half hour to see if price fills the gap—or at least part of it, and then returns to the high.

➤ Next minor resistance lies at 21—about 0.50 point away from entry. Once through 21, resistance is at about 23 from February 2006. If the market is bullish, old resistance may not pose much of a problem.

➤ If/when Sprint breaks above 21, I will add 500 shares to the position. The stop order will be moved up and trail position.

➤ Initial profit target: 21.75 to 22.00. (Sprint's average daily range is about forty cents. If we're in the trade for three days, which is the average duration of a swing trade, in the best-case scenario, we can look for 1.20 per share profit. More than that will be gravy.)

➤ Sprint drifts sideways to higher for the remainder of the day, along with the XTC and broader markets. It establishes a midday low at 20.39 at 2:15 P.M., and I raise the stop to 20.20. Now my risk-to-reward ratio is 1:5—which is dandy!

➤ Eye candy for traders: From 2:15 P.M. until the close, increased volume comes into Sprint and the price moves back up to its midday highs at 20.63—and holds into the close. Is someone accumulating? Sprint closes in a spinning top on the daily chart.

Figure 14-4 shows a daily chart of Sprint one day into our trade.

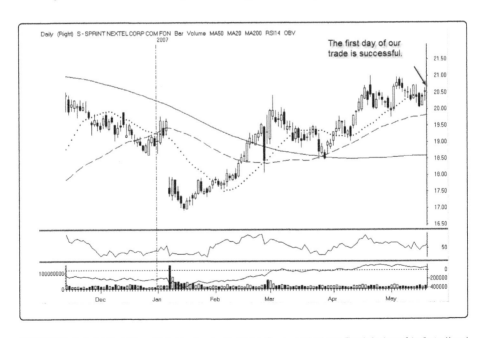

FIGURE 14-4. Sprint Nextel Corp. (S) first trading day. RealTick by Townsend Analytics. This daily chart of the Sprint Nextel Corp. (S) shows the first day of our trade as a success. We bought 500 shares at 20.48, and the stock closed the day at 20.63, on strong volume.

Friday, May 18

The S&P 500 gaps higher at the open, holds the gap, and moves higher for the remainder of the day. The Dow closes at a record high of 13,556. The S&P 500 is within shooting distance of its all-time high of 1,527.46. All sectors closed on a positive note. The XTC drew a smooth uptrend on its intraday chart, with all indicators following suit. Ah, trader heaven!

Sprint opens even with yesterday's close, then trades in a picture-perfect uptrend for the remainder of the day. The stock rose to 20.83 on strong volume by 12:30 P.M. and traded in a very tight range into the close. I raised the protective stop to 20.60, under the afternoon consolidation range. We want to give it room to trade. Now we're better than even on the trade, and the risk (assuming Sprint doesn't expect a violent gap down tomorrow morning) has been removed.

HOT TIP

If you watch your swing trading position on an intraday basis, once you're in the trade, avoid watching the trade's progression on a time frame that's less than a 60-minute chart. If you scrutinize your trade on a 5-minute chart, you're likely to micromanage your trade and limit your profit opportunities. Intraday market action and price "hiccups" often appear much more dramatic on small time frames than they really are.

One reason we've experienced such a quiet week is the lack of economic reports—which can rock the markets. With the indexes at major highs and showing little signs of weakness, company buyouts and stock buybacks at record levels, and global markets accelerating, it's a good time to be in the markets.

If I sound complacent—be assured that I'm not. Experience has taught me—and most other market players—that complacency comes right before a Humpty Dumpty fall.

This market has climbed a wall of worry for most of the last couple of months, with short-sellers and bears out in droves. That's a good thing. When the bears throw up their hands and declare they are beaten and the market's in wonderful shape, we will cash in our long positions and head for the sidelines. Until then, we trade what we see—not what we wish would be, or believe might be just around the corner.

Figure 14-5 shows a daily chart of Sprint, at the end of the day, today. Note that price is nearing resistance at 21. If Sprint moves decisively above 21 on Monday, and holds that price point, on strong volume, we may add more shares.

FIGURE 14-5. Sprint Nextel Corp. (S) second trading day. RealTick by Townsend Analytics. Telecom companies are currently in a favorable spotlight. That's helping to bolster our trade in the telecom sector and our trade in Sprint Nextel (S), as shown in this daily chart.

Monday, May 21

In the nicest gift a trader can receive, Sprint gapped up at this morning's opening bell to exactly twenty-one cents higher than Friday's close at 20.79. The stock gapped up on extremely strong volume, a good sign. A gap up on exceptionally strong volume means the order imbalance at the open was highly weighted with buying pressure. I waited until 10:00 A.M., to see if price would attempt to fill the gap, but the market, the XTC, and Sprint fill all moved higher together.

I think back to the strong volume that came into Sprint last Thursday afternoon (May 17). Evidently some accumulation was going on, and Sprint finally reacted to that pressure by moving up a quick 10 percent.

Important point: Now our trade has broken out of the very short-term resistance area on its daily chart—and more important, the long-term resistance on its weekly chart. This is a wonderfully bullish move.

➤ Fifteen minutes into the open, I move the stop order up to 20.90, which is about midway into the price gap. The price action of the stock, the very strong intraday uptrend of the XTC, and the benchmark S&P 500 tell me that the bulls are in control.

➤ At 10:00 A.M., Sprint is trading at a strong 21.28. Adhering to my trading plan of adding more shares if the stock trades above 21, I add 500 shares more to the position at a price of 21.29. Cost with $10 commission: $10,645.

➤ I add the additional 500 shares to my stop order with my broker. We're not giving these profits back!

By the end of the day, Sprint had moved to a high of 21.67, then backed off slightly to close at 21.40. Volume came in at nearly 51 million shares, more than two and a half times the average daily volume of about 18 million shares. Check the chart in Figure 14-6 to see the closing candle and bullish volume spike.

The XTC closed near the high of the day after a bullish day to the upside.

The S&P 500, which had trended higher until noon, traded in a quiet manner all afternoon and drifted nearly back to its opening price by the time the closing bell rang. With earnings season mostly wrapped up, and no important economic reports to digest, the benchmark is resting on its laurels.

FIGURE 14-6. Sprint Nextel Corp. (S) third day into the trade. RealTick by Townsend Analytics. This daily chart of the Sprint Nextel Corp. (S) shows our trade in bullish mode again today. Sprint closed at 21.40, after moving to a high of 67. Volume came in at nearly 51 million shares, today, nearly triple the usual average (dotted arrow). Both the RSI and OBV are moving higher, although the RSI is not yet registering an overbought signal above 70. (The tiny hook at the top of the RSI is due to S's price not closing at the high of the day.)

Tuesday, May 22

Sprint opened up at 21.47, a seven-cent gap. The S&P 500 Index opens even from yesterday's close and drifts sideways into the lunchtime doldrums. The benchmark index remains within reach of its all-time closing high of 1,527.46, reached in March 2000. With the Dow pushing through new highs, the talking heads on CNBC speculate most of the day as to whether the new highs on these indexes will hold up. The XTC opens even on the day, and sidesteps into the noon hour.

Sprint, the XTC, and the S&P basically move sideways for the remainder of the day. Sprint closes on nice volume. If the stock rises tomorrow morning, I'll raise the stop again.

Wednesday, May 23

Once again I arrive at my computer early in the morning to find the S&P 500 E-mini futures, the mini-sized Dow futures, and the NASDAQ 100 E-mini futures contracts all in the green. (The stock index E-mini futures contracts are a leading indicator for the markets. Most traders use the "mini" contract quotes in place of the standard contract quotes. For more information on these contracts, go to *www.cme.com*.) This positive phenomenon has taken place nearly every day for the last eight weeks. Although it's a pleasant sensation, I—like my other trader friends—have become leery.

We cannot dispute the facts: All of the bullish reasons for the uptrending environment are still in place. Stock buybacks are being announced every day, private equity firms are gobbling up companies by the dozens (reducing the number of available public shares), and inflation reports are mild. To top it off, housing reports (new and existing home sales) are coming out far better than anyone thought possible, considering the subprime lender worries.

Bullish conditions or not, I eye our trade with a raised eyebrow. You have to let your winners run in this business—that's the only way to consistently bring home the bacon. Still, I have no intention of giving back profits on this sweet-so-far trade. I'd rather leave a little money on the table and buy back the position on a pullback, if it seems prudent.

The opening bell rings, and Sprint gaps to the upside about twenty cents to 21.63. It quickly fills the gap and rebounds, moving to 21.90 by noon. The XTC is shooting up like a rocket—obviously experiencing euphoria—and most telecoms are going with it. The S&P 500 is, as well. The trader saying, "Sell when you want to, not when you have to," runs through my mind.

I cancel the prior stop order. Then I enter a trailing stop for 1,000 shares of S at the value of ten cents. Translation: The stop order will follow Sprint's price higher, but not lower. As long as our stock trends higher, or churns sideways, the position stays intact. But if the stock retraces from its highs more than ten cents, the order will go live; the position will be sold at the next available price. These trailing stop orders are now offered by most brokers, both online and direct access. What a great tool for squeezing the last bit of profit out of a position! Plus, they take the emotion (read: greed) out of the trade.

Now, it's 1:30 P.M., and the news commentators on CNBC are sure that the S&P 500 will close at new highs.

Suddenly and without warning, the major stock index futures dive straight down, as if off of a cliff. Down and down they plunge, lower with each second. Of course, stocks follow suit, and my market minder of stocks and indexes turns pure red with downticks.

Sprint traded at a high of 22.16 when the selloff begins. Within seconds, the position is stopped out at 22.05. (The market sold off so fast, by the time the stop market order went live, we lost a penny per share getting filled.)

Finally, we got the word of the selloff catalyst. CNBC announced that former Chairman of the Federal Reserve Board Alan Greenspan commented that the "bubble" in the Chinese stock market was unsustainable and that there would be a dramatic contraction in that economy—and in turn in the Shanghai Composite Index. Of course, our global markets are intimately connected, and a contraction in the market of any developed nation will greatly impact all others, in a domino effect.

Good grief . . . and how about Greenspan? That man always could move markets. And, retired or not, he's doing it again. (Remember his "irrational exuberance" comment? Now *that* made the market grovel in pain—and for quite some time!)

Our trailing stop served us well, though, and our bottom line is a good one: We sold our position (with $10 commission) for a total of $22,050. Our investment: $20,895.

Profit: $1,155. Time duration: five days. Life is good!

Figure 14-7 shows a daily chart of Sprint with the final day, and the two days following. Although Sprint did well for the two days following our exit day, you will note it closed at 22.10 on the final day of this chart. That's only five cents above our exit price. The stock is in overbought territory and closed the current day in a possible hanging man candlestick formation. Since the price is looking toppy, I'm glad we took our center out of the Oreo.

We'll watch Sprint for an orderly consolidation or pullback, and perhaps make a new entry at a reasonable price.

FIGURE 14-7. Sprint Nextel Corp. (S) entire trade duration plus two days. RealTick by Townsend Analytics. In this daily chart of Sprint Nextel Corp. (S), you can see how well our trade acted. Sprint has a recent history of moving up at steep angles, as you can see by looking left on the chart. Still, the current angle is especially sharp. While we were happy to take advantage of the profits it handed to us, we will not assume it will go up forever. Notice the upper shadows on the top of each candle for the most recent three days. That tells us that selling pressure came into the stock each afternoon. Can Sprint go higher after the day we sell? Certainly, and by the looks of the RSI and OBV, it appears poised to do so. When we exited, however, the stock had touched overbought territory on the RSI (70). The sudden selloff created a downdraft in major indexes, and that can easily pull the markets and most industry groups lower during the next few days.

While we're looking at the anatomy of this trade, I've included a 60-minute chart for those who want to see how the trade unwound on that time frame.

Figure 14-8 shows a 60-minute chart of our trade, with each entry, stop order, and the final exit. While it's certainly not necessary to watch your swing trades on an intraday basis—and if you tend to micromanage your trades, it's downright undesirable—still, many traders like to glance at intraday charts a couple of times a day to monitor their trades' progression.

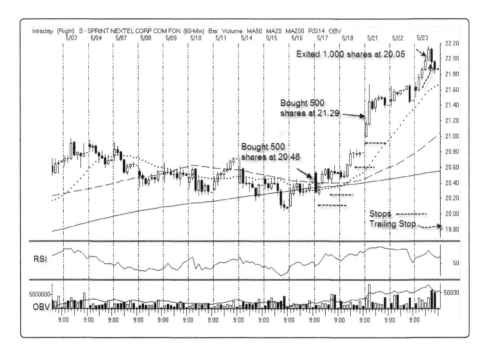

FIGURE 14-8. Sprint Nextel Corp. (S) 60-minute chart. This 60-minute chart shows how our trade unwound on an intraday basis. You can clearly see each entry, stop placement, and final exit.

Figure 14-9 shows a daily chart of the Amex N. American Telecommunications Index. The arrow shows the index's action during the time of our trade. The chart includes an additional after we exited our trade, Thursday, May 24. As you can see, Thursday day was negative for the index, which added another good reason for why we exited the trade.

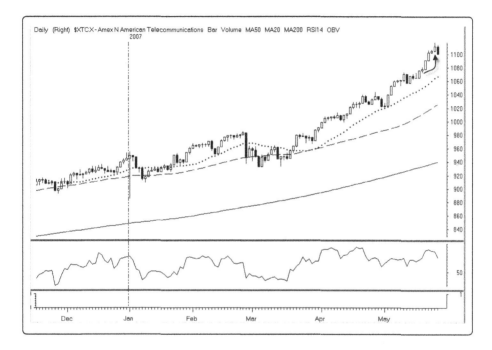

FIGURE 14-9. Amex N. American Telecommunications Index daily chart. RealTick by Townsend Analytics. The arrows ion this daily chart of the Amex N. American Telecommunications Index shows the index's action for the duration of our trade. It's always wise to chart the index of your stock's relevant industry group, or sector. Most components of a group will trade up or down with the movement of the industry group or sector where they reside. If you cannot access your stock's relevant index, find an ETF that represents the industry group or sector related to your stock, and keep an eye on its daily chart. That way you have at least a general idea if your stock's group is in an uptrend, or if it's out of favor (which is good if you're short).

Naturally, you'll want to keep an eye on the major index where your stock resides. If your stock is a Dow component, you'll want to keep an eye on that index. If your stock is listed on the S&P 500, you'll monitor that benchmark index. If you're trading a "four-letter stock" listed on the NASDAQ Stock Market, you'll track the NASDAQ 100 or NASDAQ Composite. Your stock may be a member of the mid-caps, represented by the S&P 400, or a small-cap represented by the Russell 2000 Index. On any given trading day, the mood and manner of these major indexes play an important role in the movement of related stocks.

Figure 14-10 shows a daily chart of the S&P 500, of which Sprint Nextel is a component. That's why we watched this index along with the XTC. The arrow on the chart indicates the correlating days to our Sprint Nextel (S) trade. Check the most current day on the chart at the chart's hard right edge, the black candle. This is the day after we exited our trade, and shows a definite pullback. As traders, these are the days when we want to stand safely on the sidelines.

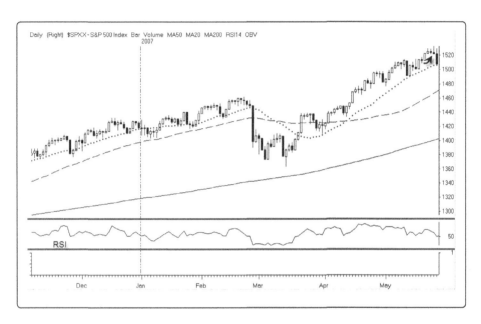

FIGURE 14-10. S&P 500 Index daily chart. RealTick by Townsend Analytics. This daily chart of the S&P 500 Index shows the benchmark index in a dandy uptrend. Sprint Nextel is a component of this index, so we kept an eye on it during our trade. The arrow indicates the days our trade took place.

AT JOURNEY'S END

As you can imagine, there are myriad ways we could have approached this trade. Remember, you can easily play "Monday morning quarterback" and think of all the actions you could have taken if you'd known when you entered the trade how it was going to play out:

➤ We could have bought all 1,000 shares initially, and made a bigger profit. Of course, that would've also increased our risk. Scaling in and out of trades by buying (and sometimes selling) one-half of the intended shares at a time lowers risk. With this method, you don't always take home as much money as you could have, but you lower your risk—which equals a bigger bottom line in the long run.

➤ We could have kept a looser rein on the initial stop orders. I tend to raise my stops more frequently early in the trade to keep losses low. Of course, if you keep them too tight, your trade can get stopped out for no reason. My strategy in this trade was to keep a stop under support areas. There is no "magic stop formula." You have to take into consideration your level of risk tolerance and the stock's price pattern and volatility.

Although this trade was a fairly easy process, in looking back at it I still highly recommend that new swing traders "paper trade" for several trades before they put real cash on the line. Enter trades only when you are comfortable with the setup, the industry group, and the market environment.

Because of the nature of the text in this chapter, there is no quiz to close it out. Before you get too comfortable, though, know that the quiz in the next chapter is a monster!

CENTER POINT: DEVELOP THE ART OF DETACHMENT

"We act as though comfort and luxury were the chief requirements of life, when all that we need to make us really happy is something to be enthusiastic about."

—Charles Kingsley, clergyman

One of the most exciting and rewarding concepts that leads to success in all areas of life remains one of the most challenging to understand: the theory of detachment.

Western civilization teaches us to attach ourselves to everything in our circle of existence. By attaching ourselves to people, places, and things, we supposedly attain an important goal: security. Trouble is, if these things disappear—and they often do—we are left with feelings of emptiness. Our so-called "security" is only smoke and mirrors.

As a consumer-driven, materialistic society, we Americans assign great worth to the attainment of fancy cars, large homes, and impressive financial portfolios. While it may be fun to acquire these symbols of success, the problem arrives when we attach our sense of self-worth to these items. In other words, we identify our self-esteem with how many toys we've accumulated.

We also attach feelings of self-esteem to the outcome of certain situations. In the financial markets, this can be disastrous in that it fosters the "need to be right." In other fields of endeavor, it can lead to noncreative, stagnant mindsets. Surely you've heard someone say, "We can't do it that way. We've never done it that way before." That attitude cancels other options that might result in a more effective course of action.

In practicing detachment, we become free, realizing our security lies within each one of us. As empowered spirits, we know innately how to fulfill every need. We also understand that cars, homes, and portfolios represent the manifestations of our desires.

When we become detached from the outcome of situations, we work with a vision in mind. Yet we stay open to new options and ideas that could produce greater outcomes than we, ourselves, envisioned.

Your real security lies within you. Tune into the exhilaration that occurs when you're secure in your personal inner power. Then you can step easily into a world of infinite choices and possibilities!

CHAPTER 15

You, the Wizard of Odds

"But I can tell you after the market began to go my way I felt for the first time in my life that I had allies—the strongest and truest in the world: underlying conditions."

—Jesse Livermore

In this chapter, we'll talk about big-picture dynamics. You've learned from previous chapters how important it is to take overall market conditions into consideration when you plunk your money on the line. Now we'll define certain circumstances that take place regularly. You'll learn how to use them to your advantage and increase your skills as a successful trader.

BACK UP AND LOOK AT THE BIG PICTURE

When I was new to trading, I took a course from a crusty trader who repeatedly barked, "Back up! Back up and look at the big picture!"

Maybe his delivery lacked charm, but it packed a verbal punch I've never forgotten. He was right on the money! You can find the perfect setup, enter at the perfect point, smile smugly while your stock heads for the stars, and then whap—you get blind-sided. Something happens, like Fed Chairman Ben Bernanke appearing on the financial networks and announcing inflation lurking around the corner. The next thing you hear is the sound of the financial markets crashing like a boulder off a cliff.

I hope that you, as an astute trader, had a trailing stop-loss set on your positions. Perhaps you read or heard that Mr. Bernanke was due to speak. You tightened your stop-losses to guard against any major market reactions to his comments. If so, great—that's big-picture thinking. Here are more ways to align your mindset so you can add percentage points to your profits and earn gains from market dynamics.

THE "IF, THEN" MINDSET

In my previous book, *A Beginner's Guide to Day Trading Online 2nd Edition*, I talked about cultivating an "if, then" mindset pertaining to overall market conditions. That way of thinking is so important to your success as a trader that it bears repeating.

Think: "*If* this happens, *then* that happens." Example: If Uncle Ben comments that "inflation lies around the corner," it means the Federal Open Market Committee (FOMC) may consider raising interest rates at its next meeting to hold inflation in check. Simply put, higher interest rates mean companies pay more to borrow money. That lowers company earnings, which translates into lower stock prices.

Additional "if, then" scenarios follow here, tagged with this caveat: Remember that *nothing* always happens in the stock market. Please consider the following as guidelines:

➤ Gold and the U.S. dollar have an inverse relationship, which means the gold market figures importantly into inflationary environments and many times acts as a leading indicator to inflation. If the stock market tops look toppy and overextended, then gold-mining shares may provide a profitable play.

➤ If the dollar is strong, then American products sold overseas cost more, and some pharmaceutical companies, retailers, and technology companies that export to foreign countries suffer. Conversely, we Americans can buy imported goods cheaper (a strong dollar buys more), so overseas companies that import products to us head north.

➤ The Treasury bond market usually leads the stock market. (When the price of bonds rises, the bonds' yield or accompanying interest rate falls. When bonds fall, interest rates rise.) If bonds rise, then stocks may rise. If bond prices fall, then the stock market may follow along.

➤ Treasury bonds and the CRB (Commodity Research Bureau) Index have an inverse relationship. Falling prices for commodities (for example, soybeans, grains, metals, livestock, oil, cotton, coffee, sugar, and cocoa) can mean higher bond prices. If commodity prices fall, then bond and stock prices may rise.

➤ If bond prices fall and interest rates rise, then money may flow into cyclical stocks. (Companies with cyclical earnings aren't as dependent on interest rates; they include groups such as paper, aluminum, automobiles, some technology, and some retailers.)

➤ If bonds rise and interest rates fall, then interest-sensitive stocks such as financial institutions and homebuilders find it easier to rise. Lower interest rates mean banks pay less to borrow money, so the spread between the money they borrow and the money they lend widens. And, as interest rates fall, people tend to buy new homes and refinance existing residences.

➤ If oil prices rise, then transportation stocks usually fall, and vice versa. Why? Because high oil prices cause companies to pay more to deliver goods; in the case of the airlines, higher fuel prices means it costs more to deliver passengers to their destinations. Higher costs per seat narrows profit margins.

ANALYZE THE BROADER MARKETS

Every day or so, analyze daily and weekly charts of the Dow Jones Industrial Average (DJIA), the S&P 500 (SPX), and the NASDAQ 100 Index (NDX) or Composite (COMP). If your charting source doesn't list these indexes, you can use ETFs, such as the DIA for the Dow, SPY for the S&P 500, and the QQQQ for the NASDAQ 100 Index.

Check out the overall picture of each. How is Mother Market feeling? As the saying goes, "When Mama ain't happy, ain't nobody happy." Conversely, when her exchanges feel perky, she can give generously of her wealth.

Analyze the broad index charts the same way you would a stock chart. Are they in uptrends, downtrends, or moving sideways in a basing Stage 1 or perhaps topping in a Stage 3 mode? Where is support and resistance? Are they overextended? Overbought? Oversold? What does the weekly chart tell you? The monthly chart?

Correlate major market trends with your buy/sell decisions. If you're long a leading NASDAQ technology stock and the NASDAQ 100 just reached into overextended, overbought territory, consider taking profits off the table. If you're long a big bank stock and the Dow also teeters precariously high, grab at least a portion of your gains. Many times, financial stocks lead the Dow higher or lower.

LEARN TO ASSESS THE TRADING ENVIRONMENT

We'll summarize a point here that you may already know: It's important to evaluate the market environment to determine whether it's conducive to your trading style. To trade like a professional, learn which environments offer high-reward / low-risk scenarios, and which should be avoided.

First, let's revisit the old trader saying, "The trend is your friend." While that wise statement advises you to trade with the prevailing trend, it also advocates trading *with a trend in place*. In other words, sideways patterns don't deliver easy profits. When you hold stocks overnight in whippy, choppy, sideways markets, you can get slapped—hard.

As you know, sideways markets exist during Stage 1 and Stage 3. As you remember from your study of top reversal patterns such as head-and-shoulders, Stage 3 can be especially brutal. Breakouts to the upside and downside usually fail. Stocks that act strong and bullish one day gap down and whimper at their lows the next. Result? Holding a stock overnight can prove disastrous.

Who makes money in these choppy sideways zones? Active traders who close out their trades at the end of each trading day may do all right, as long as the intraday action isn't too choppy. Long-term investors, or even position traders who bottom fish in basing stocks can eventually do well, assuming their stocks break out of their bases.

Obviously, when the major exchanges experience a Stage 2 uptrend, traders in all time frames who catch the upswings on the long side make out like rich kids in a candy store.

Short-sellers of all time frames thrive in the downdrafts produced by Stage 4 downtrends.

Important note: It's okay to be in cash. The biggest traders in the world don't trade everyday. Nor do they always hold stock positions in their portfolios. Sometimes, they're in all cash. Remember, "cash" is a position.

If the market is overextended and experiences what appears to be a frothy top, pocket your profits and take a vacation. You'll return refreshed, and Mother Market may have decided which trend she's going to pursue.

THE ADVANCE/DECLINE LINE: MARKET NARRATOR IN A CAPSULE

If you want solid confirmation as to the market's mood and manner, stay updated on the positioning of the Advance/Decline, or A/D Line. If your charting software doesn't include it, you'll find it displayed in financial newspapers or on financial Web sites.

The A/D Line (NYSE, Amex, and NASDAQ) is a line chart that measures the breadth of a stock exchange's advance or decline. Swing traders will want to stay updated on this indicator every few days. Position traders can monitor it weekly.

The A/D works like this: Each day, or week, the number of advancing issues is compared to the number of declining issues on that exchange, or index. When the advancers outnumber decliners, the total is added to the previous, overall total. When decliners outnumber advancers, the difference is subtracted from the total.

On the General Market & Sectors page in *IBD*, you'll see a chart of the NYSE Composite with the correlating A/D Line plotted on it. Typically, when the Composite is trending higher (or lower), the A/D line will head in the same direction.

As the market approaches a market bottom or top, however, they may diverge. For example, if the NYSE Composite is trending higher, but the A/D line is heading lower, it means that declining issues are increasing. That should soon have a negative effect on the NYSE's uptrend. The reverse is true. If the NYSE experiences a downtrend, but you note that the A/D line has diverged from the index and is starting higher, then money is starting to flow into advancing stocks; that should soon have a positive effect on the NYSE.

STAY UPDATED ON ECONOMIC REPORTS

Trading will never rank at the top of the "Comfortable Occupations" list. Just when you think you're safely ensconced in a pillow of profits, and you decide to exhale, economic reports or earnings news pop onto the horizon. Then everything changes. Sigh!

A host of economic indicators come out each month, some quarterly. These reports represent indicators that relate to the overall health of the American economy.

Depending on what sort of economic data holds the most importance to the market at the moment, these reports can deliver a quick belly punch to the market—or propel it much higher. Stocks may sink or soar, depending on the numbers issued.

Most reports are issued at either 8:30 A.M. or 10:00 A.M. eastern time. As mentioned before, you will find a monthly Economic Calendar posted on my home page, so you can stay updated as to when the data will be issued. On the "Tutorials" page at ToniTurner.com, you can study explanations of the most important reports and how they are formulated. Here is a partial list of economic reports and a brief description of each:

➤ Consumer Confidence Index (CCI). A monthly survey that gauges consumer outlook concerning finances, the economy, employment, and plans to purchase expensive items. Since consumer optimism or negative perspective reflects in personal spending, which impacts the economy, this represents a leading indicator. (Economic reports that are regarded as "leading indicators" contain information that may predict future economic growth or contraction. In this case, the consumers' feelings are a precursor for how much money they intend to spend in the future, so the CCI is considered to have the power to lead the markets higher or lower. A "lagging" indicator is calculated using information that has already taken place, so we say the indicator follows or lags the current market.)

➤ Consumer Price Index (CPI). Issued by the Bureau of Labor Statistics, this index indicates the change in prices on the consumer level. The CPI may influence salaries, social security payments, and pensions. Although the CPI is a lagging indicator, it has the power to move the markets.

➤ Durable Goods Orders Report. "Durable goods" are nonperishable goods that last for three years or more. Reported by the U.S. Department of Commerce, this report indicates whether businesses intend to invest capital for future needs. Since a shift in demand influences the need to purchase durable goods to expand capacity, it is regarded as a leading economic indicator.

➤ Gross Domestic Product (GDP). Shows America's total output for a certain time period, taking into consideration all conclusive goods and services. Reported quarterly, the GDP serves as the broadest indicator as to whether America's economy is expanding or contracting. It is a lagging indicator.

➤ Housing Starts and Building Permits. These numbers reflect new homes or units in a building for which a permit is issued. Historically, housing starts fall six months before the remainder of the economy, so this is considered a leading indicator.

➤ ISM: The Institute for Supply Management surveys approximately 400 manufacturers. Information results in a composite report detailing production, new orders, inventories, supplier deliveries, and employment. A reading above 50 percent indicates an expanding factory sector. A reading below 50 percent indicates contracting conditions. The FOMC (Federal Open Market Committee) watches this significant report for signs of inflation.

➤ Index of Leading Indicators. Issued monthly by the U.S. Department of Commerce, this index consists of combined leading indicator statistics. It foretells the direction of the economy three to six months in the future.

➤ Non-Farm Payrolls and Unemployment Rate. The Bureau of Labor Statistics issues this report the first Friday of every month. It shows the number of non-farm jobs created in the United States, subtracting jobs gained through attrition. The unemployment rate indicates the number of unemployed workers who are unsuccessfully seeking jobs. Both Non-farm Payrolls and the

Unemployment Rate influence the American public's confidence in the strength of the economy.

➤ Producer Price Index (PPI). This index measures change in prices on the wholesale manufacturing level. The PPI comes out in the middle of the month, giving the previous month's data. The Bureau of Labor Statistics reports two numbers: the overall PPI, and the core PPI, which excludes volatile food and energy prices. Because the PPI shows advance notice of price changes and thus inflationary pressures, it is a leading indicator.

THE GRANDDADDY OF ALL REPORTS: THE FOMC

The Federal Open Market Committee, headed by the Federal Reserve chairman (currently Ben Bernanke), meets approximately every six weeks and reports its decision to raise or lower interest rates. (FOMC dates are listed on the *www.ToniTurner.com* Economic Calendar.)

As you know, interest is the cost of borrowing money. And the cost of borrowing money is important to everyone—from individuals like you and me, who want the best rates for our mortgages and credit lines, to multi-conglomerates who pay interest on millions of dollars of debt each year.

The main catalyst that causes the FOMC to raise rates is inflation. Inflation is defined as the rise in cost for goods and services.

If inflation rears its ugly head, chances are the Fed will raise rates to cool inflation. When interest rates (the cost of money) are higher, it slows the economy. When interest rates are low, the economy heats up.

The best way to see the Fed announcement is to tune into a financial network on "Fed Day"; the announcement is made at about 2:15 P.M. eastern time.

You can assume that each time the Fed announcement comes out, the market will react. Sometimes it absorbs the news—usually when rates stay the same—with few remonstrations. Other times, particularly when rates are raised or lowered, the reaction is highly volatile. The market may plunge straight down if rates are raised, or fly like a missile when rates are lowered.

Make sure to listen to the statement issued by the Fed that immediately follows the rate announcement. Traders listen closely to the wording of that text, and focus on it for days to come. If, for example, the Fed leaves rates alone, but sees inflation looming in the quarters to come, that can make the markets dive, just on the chance that the Fed is thinking of raising rates in the next meeting.

Also, it's best to keep in mind that fickle Mother Market might not digest rate news in a commonsense way. I've seen the S&P futures crash on news of a rate decrease, taking stocks down with it. Now, we all know lower interest rates mean higher stock prices. So why would the market tank moments after a decrease in interest rates? Choose the reason du jour, depending on current sentiment. Whatever the rationale, you're better to stand on the sidelines and let the bulls and bears duke it out. You can jump back in when the emotional frenzy subsides.

Before we leave this subject, let's talk briefly about inflation. This information gives you more ammunition for your "if, then" scenarios.

Inflation facts:

➤ The top priority of each nation's central bank—ours is the Federal Reserve—is to keep inflation under control. As prices rise in a strong economy, each dollar earned becomes worth less because its power to purchase lessens. Without constant reining in, inflation will strangle an economy.

➤ The central bank controls inflation through monetary policy, meaning interest rates and money supply. Interest rates equate to the cost of borrowing money.

➤ Stocks are vulnerable to inflation because (1) each dollar earned by the underlying company buys less; (2) rising interest rates means the company spends more money to borrow money; that adds higher costs to debt structure and affects future growth; (3) as interest rates rise, bond prices fall, attracting investors who want a safe, secure place to stow their money.

MOTHER MARKET'S CONTRARIAN INDICATORS

As we've just stated, few entities on the face of this earth are more moody and contrarian than the stock market. Seems she's never content with feeling too happy or too sad.

Still, with practice, you can anticipate her moods. All you have to do in times of excessive euphoria or negativity is think backwards!

The next three indicators represent inverse sentiment. Translated, they suggest that excess optimism or excess pessimism in our markets eventually causes the opposite reaction. Keep an eye on them, especially when they shoot to extremes.

Bull/Bear Ratio

Investor's Intelligence in New Rochelle, New York, takes a weekly poll of investment advisers and publishes the Bull/Bear Ratio. CNBC routinely announces the Bull/Bear Ratio during market hours.

The poll scores how advisers feel about the stock market—bullish, bearish, or neutral. The ratio is calculated by dividing the number of bullish advisers by the number of bullish plus bearish advisers. (Neutral advisers don't count.)

Since it's a contrary indicator, the more bullish the advisers feel, the more bearish the indication. For example, if 55–60 percent of the advisers polled feel bullish, then that extreme optimism suggests the market is top-heavy and ready to fall. If the reading slides south to 40 percent showing extreme pessimism, then the Bull/Bear Ratio implies a bullish reversal is in the wind.

CBOE (Chicago Board Options Exchange) Equity Put/Call Ratio

The CBOE Equity Put/Call Ratio tracks investors' trades in the options markets. It's calculated by dividing the volume of put options by the volume of call options. (Puts and calls are options contracts that give participants the right to sell or buy—put or call—the underlying security at a specified price, during a specified time period.) Financial newspapers list the ratios for the CBOE Equity Put/Call Ratio. You'll also hear it mentioned on financial networks. The number may also be listed on your broker's Web site, or even be included as an indicator on your software.

This also serves as a contrary sentiment indicator. The higher the options players' level of pessimism, the more bullish the outlook for the market. The lower the level of pessimism, the more bearish the outlook. For example, a reading in the Put/Call Ratio of 0.80 or higher is considered bullish. Bearish signals flash when the ratio reaches 0.30.

Earnings Season

Companies that issue common stock typically issue their earnings four times a year.

➤ First quarter: January through March
➤ Second quarter: April through June
➤ Third quarter: July through September
➤ Fourth quarter: October through December

This means that the months directly following each quarter, when earnings are announced, can be jittery times for the market.

If you are holding a company overnight that's due to issue its earnings report after the closing bell rings, you may, unless you think the stock will fall in line with Street expectations, want to take profits before the earnings are announced. Earnings surprises can be very positive, or very negative for the stock. Personally, I sleep much better when I exit a stock that could issue a dicey earnings report.

Further, if a giant bellwether is scheduled to announce, and you hold a related stock, you may want to reduce size before the earnings announcement takes place. Why? Because in this age of volatility, when an industry leader so much as breathes funny, all related stocks faint in sympathy. Too many tech stocks depend on each other for integrated equipment and sales. When one gets woozy, they all get woozy. Companies like Cisco Systems (CSCO) and Microsoft (MSFT) can easily take the entire NASDAQ market lower by issuing ho-hum earnings and guidance for the next quarter.

Another onerous market event that stymies new traders: A company reports good earnings. Result? The stock tanks. Rumors of good earnings sometimes leak out before the report becomes public. The stock may soar on the wings of that rumor for a few days leading up to the actual announcement. Since by the time the report comes out the stock's price has already factored in increased earnings, sellers take fast profits and the stock tumbles. Heed the trader saying, "Buy the rumor, sell the news."

Caution: Options Expiration Day

Stock options contracts expire on the third Friday of every month. On the third Friday of every third month (quarterly—March, June, September, and December), options expiration day is called "quadruple-witching day," because contracts expire on stocks, stock indexes, single stock futures, and futures.

On options expirations Friday—and that Wednesday and Thursday, too—avoid entering new trades. You'll be glad you did. During this time period, options players, arbitrageurs, and institutional managers shift their positions, causing erratic and irrational price moves. Breakouts/breakdowns fail, and volatility reigns.

If you have open positions, check your automatic stop orders, and then take a few days off. If you're in cash, you're worry-free.

STAY TUNED TO CHANGING CONDITIONS

One of Steve Nison's favorite Japanese sayings goes, "To learn about the market, ask the market."

It's important to stay updated on market conditions as they relate to world events. Know that a trading style that worked yesterday may not work tomorrow.

That's why many trading systems make profits for a while, then deliver a string of losses. Like our minds, they are programmed to react to a certain stimulus and expect a certain result. When a different result takes place, the system tangles. (So do our brains!)

To succeed in this business, you must alter your trading techniques to fit the changing market. As a smart trader, you'll learn to keep an open mind on a 24/7 basis, and internalize market conditions.

Since global markets are becoming more and more connected to each other, the events that occur in one major economy influence others quickly, and in a domino effect.

Volatile situations cause our financial markets to roil. When a central bank, for example, fights to keep a country afloat, industry groups affected by our ties to that country gyrate wildly, and traders find it difficult to stay on the right side of the market. When supply-side shocks like spikes in the cost of oil or food burst on the scene, it causes the market to make another set of volatile adjustments, which again affects traders. Wars, pandemics, storms (economists call them "exogenous shocks")—all the outside events that we don't expect—can deliver blows to the market environment.

To bring this close to home, here's my personal rule: If I make two trades in a row that immediately go against me, I stop trading and re-evaluate market conditions. Then, I "get small." That's trader talk for reducing lot sizes, setting tight stops, and taking modest profits, to keep "green on the screen." When I feel once again tuned in to market rhythms, I return to my customary lot sizes.

A WORD ABOUT LOSSES

Every trader has losing streaks. The trick is to recognize the symptoms, tie a tourniquet—fast—and then learn from the experience.

Surely you've heard the definition of insanity: repeating the same actions over and over, while expecting different results!

So, again, when two trades in a row hand you losses, my advice is for you to stop trading. Back up and look at overall market conditions. Read a financial newspaper or magazine outside of your usual reference area, to obtain a different viewpoint. Go to cash and take a short vacation. Your goal is to refresh and rejuvenate. When you feel ready to return to the market scene, stay "small" for a while. And make your main goal to keep "green on your screen."

Along the same vein, if you've been on vacation, when you come back to trade, it's best to merely observe the markets without trading. Within a few days, you'll re-internalize current market rhythms, and you can fall back into step.

THE BEST GIFT TO GIVE YOURSELF: A TRADING JOURNAL

One of the best techniques to ensure your success as a trader is to keep a trading journal. A well-kept journal speeds you along the pathway to trading mastery by leaps and bounds.

Either print your charts, or capture them and keep them in an electronic file folder.

Detail each trade in a short paragraph. Start with, "I entered this trade because . . . [glowing stock fundamentals, positive market and sector conditions, stock was oversold but bouncing off of 20-day MA, risk/reward ratio = 1 point risk to 3 points reward, etc.]." Next, jot down the trade events briefly. Include when and at what price you closed the trade, and why. Once a week, read over your journal entries. Does a common thread run through your trades?

Reward yourself for winning trades, no matter how small the profits (little profits add up to big profits). Next, evaluate the trades that went against you. What steps can you take if the same situation pops up? By learning from your mistakes, you turn your losers turn into winners.

And now, it's time for me to congratulate you! By absorbing this book in its entirety, you've come a long way in accomplishing your goal of becoming a consistently winning trader. It takes resilience and persistence to succeed in this field, but you've made it this far, and I know you'll succeed!

Please go slowly. Remember, successful trading is not a destination—it's a journey. For as long as you are a trader, every trade you make should teach you a new lesson. Every trading day should give you fresh insight into the markets and how they change.

I wish you the best of everything. Good luck and keep those trades green. Here's to your good wealth!

QUIZ
IIIIIIIIIIIIIII

1. Traders who use the _____, _____ line of thinking stay ahead of the pack.
2. Gold and the dollar have an _____ relationship.
3. The _____ market usually leads the stock market.
4. When bond prices fall, interest rates _____.
5. When oil prices rise, _____ (industry group) stocks may dive lower.
6. True or False? The best time to load up your account with stocks to hold overnight in swing trades is when the market is moving sideways.
7. The Bull/Bear Ratio and the Put/Call Ratio, when taken as a whole, suggest what theory?
8. Briefly explain the Advance/Decline Line.
9. True or False? The best time to enter a long position is right after the Federal Reserve Board announces a raise in interest rates.
10. The underlying company of the stock you own is due to come out with earnings this evening after the market closes. You: A) Buy up all the shares you can afford, and some for Aunt Bertha and Uncle Fred, as well. Or: B) Take your profits, sit back, and watch with interest.
11. On options expiration day, what is the correct way to trade?
12. Give one reason why stocks are vulnerable to inflation.
13. Why does keeping a journal contribute so greatly to your trading success?

Answers
1. If, then.
2. Inverse.
3. Treasury bond.
4. Fall.
5. Transportation.
6. You didn't say "true," did you?
7. As contrarian indicators, the Bull/Bear Ratio and Put/Call Ratio suggest that when euphoria reigns, it's time to take profits and hide under your desk. When disgust and pessimism rule the day, start looking for buying opportunities.
8. The A/D Line (NYSE, Amex, and NASDAQ) is a line chart that measures the breadth of a stock market's advance or decline between the number of advancing and the number of declining issues.
9. False.

10. B is the correct answer.
11. You don't know the answer, because you have no intentions of placing a trade on options expiration day.
12. Stocks are vulnerable to inflation because rising interest rates means the company spends more money to borrow money, which adds higher costs to debt structure and affects future growth.
13. Keeping a trading journal speeds you on the pathway to success because you can spot winning and not-so-winning behavior quickly, and improve upon it.

CENTER POINT: COME BACK TO CENTER

"Man cannot persist long in a conscious state, he must throw himself back into the unconscious, for his root lives there."

—Johann Wolfgang von Goethe

Recently, I conversed with David, a top trader, about trading psychology.

"You know what's made me so successful?" He stared at me with his intense blue eyes. Then he continued. "There's a cascading fountain outside of my office, in the courtyard. Every morning, I take fifteen minutes to sit and focus on the water. When I feel myself relax, I imagine the trading day. I visualize myself buying and selling trades at the perfect point. I also see trades that go against my plan. I watch as I close the trade with no regret, only satisfaction at taking the right action. It's phenomenal how much these quiet times have increased my trading skills, and my bottom line!"

What a wonderful gift David gave me. He reminded me that for optimal performance, we need to return to our center point. We need to recharge our "energy batteries." Taking some time each day to energize ourselves by quieting our thoughts offers huge returns in physical, mental, and emotional health.

The process can be a simple one. Find a quiet place offering total solitude. Sit comfortably, arms and legs uncrossed. Close your eyes and concentrate on your breathing, letting all the tension flow out of your body.

Now, imagine yourself entering a large, richly paneled elevator. As the doors close, you notice you are on the tenth floor. You push the first-floor button, and then observe each button light up as the elevator descends . . . 9, 8, 7, 6, 5, 4, 3, 2, 1.

The doors open, and you step out into a lush garden. The sun shines warmly, and a breeze caresses your face. Brightly flowering trees and plants surround you. (If you prefer, create a tropical beach or mountain retreat—wherever you feel safe and happy.)

A chaise lounge rests in a corner of the garden. Go to it and lie down, sinking into the cushions. Closing your eyes, invite peace to flow through your body and mind.

Gently visualize yourself going about your day calmly, effectively, purposefully. You give each person you meet a smile, a pat on the back, words of encouragement. Maybe you want to visualize yourself placing trades calmly competently, as David did. When you finish your imaginary day or scene, rise from the lounge, enter the elevator, and push the button for the tenth floor. Watch the buttons glow, from 1 to 10. As the elevator doors slide open, take three deep breaths, smile, and come back to reality.

Try this process and note how your days are happier, less stressful and more productive. When you come from your calm and energized "center point," you can give more to your career, your loved ones, and yourself!

APPENDIX A

Glossary

Accumulation

When a stock is being "accumulated," it may indicate that institutional buyers are acquiring stock. It also means buying pressure is increasing. Accumulation is usually evident by increased volume on a stock's chart.

Advance/Decline Line

The number of declining issues on a stock exchange, subtracted from the number of advancing issues. The net difference is added to a running total if it's positive, or subtracted from a running total if negative. The most commonly noted A/D Line is on the NYSE. When the NYSE Composite A/D Line diverges from the NYSE Index, itself, it gives an early indication of a possible trend change.

Arbitrage

Arbitrageurs (or "arbs", as the Street calls them) typically buy and sell two different but related financial instruments simultaneously. They profit from the spread created by the divergence. This kind of trading is called arbitrage. For example, if the S&P 500 Index rises, and the S&P futures fall, they sell short the cash index and buy the futures. See Program Trading.

Ascending Triangle

An ascending triangle is a consolidation pattern wherein the price range becomes progressively tighter and tighter. The price lows rise, while the price highs stay relatively horizontal. This pattern is usually bullish.

Ask

The price at which a security is offered for sale. Also called "inside ask" or "offer," this is the lowest price for which a broker/dealer (or representative Electronic Communication Network) will sell a stock. It is the lowest price for which the customer can buy it.

Asset Allocation
The process of designating how an investment portfolio will be divided among various classes of assets, including stocks, bonds, and cash. Risk levels of each asset should be deciding factors as to percentages of weighting (i.e., high-quality bonds are less risky than technology stocks).

Basket Trades
Large transactions consisting of a number of different securities.

Bear Market
Generally refers to the overall picture of the stock market when it's in a downtrend, and has fallen 20 percent or more off of its highs. Only short-sellers, and those in cash, experience a bear market without pain.

Beta
A risk/reward measurement of a portfolio's past price fluctuations as compared to the overall market, or index. The market, or appropriate index, has a beta of 1.0. Therefore, a portfolio (mutual fund, etc.) with a beta of 1.20 would be expected to rise or fall 20 percent when the overall market rises or falls by 10 percent.

Bid
The best, or lowest, price at which specialists (market makers) will buy a stock. Therefore, the "inside bid" is the best price the seller will receive for a security sold at the "market" price.

"Big Board"
Refers to the popular nickname given to the New York Stock Exchange.

Block Trades
Large transactions of a specific stock, bought or sold in units of 10,000 shares.

Blow-Off Top
A volcano-like action when a stock explodes to the upside, then suddenly turns and drops back to the downside. May include an exhaustion gap.

Blue Chip Stocks
The Dow Jones Industrial Average Index stocks are often called "blue chips." The name derives from poker, where the blue chip has the highest value. Blue chip companies are commonly referred to as "value" stocks. They typically produce upward growth and dividend payments, and are considered to be icons of American industry.

Bond

A type of loan, or IOU, issued by corporations, organizations, or governments in order to raise capital. The issuer makes regular interest payments and agrees to redeem the face value of the bond at a designated date, called the "maturity date." Bonds can be issued for thirty years or more.

Bracketing

Sometimes used in the same context as a stock trading in a range. Therefore, the stock moves up and down, "bracketed" between a high and low price.

Breakaway Gap

A price gap—to the upside or downside—that takes place subsequent to a significant price pattern. This gap may foretell a meaningful price move.

Broker-Dealer

A securities firm that sells financial instruments to the public, may buy and sell stocks for institutions, and also trades its own accounts.

Buy-and-Hold

A traditional, long-term investment strategy that focuses on the fundamentals of a company and ignores short-term market fluctuations.

Channel Line

A straight line drawn parallel to the correlating trendline. In an uptrend, draw the channel line across the peaks of the highs. In a downtrend, draw the channel line connecting the pivot lows. Prices usually find resistance at the upper channel lines, and support on the lower channel lines.

Confirmation

Confirmation occurs when technical signals agree with one another. For instance, when a breakout takes place together with strong volume, volume confirms the price rise. When signals move in opposite directions, it's called divergence, and the breakout or other assumed price action may fail.

Continuation Pattern

A price pattern on a chart that indicates the prevailing trend is "resting" or consolidating. The most common continuation patterns are flags, pennants, and triangles. When the stock concludes one of these patterns, it typically resumes the prior trend.

Descending Triangle

A consolidation in a price pattern usually considered to be bearish. The price highs decline, while the price lows remains relatively horizontal—forming two sides of a triangle.

Divergence

This takes place on a chart when an indicator moves in the opposite, or different, direction than does the price pattern. For example, the price may make a higher high, while the RSI (Relative Strength Index) or Stochastics hooks to the downside. When a divergence takes place, price reversal may soon occur in the direction of the indicator/oscillator.

Double Top

This reversal pattern forms with two prominent peaks and resembles an "M." The reversal pattern is complete when it forms the final leg down and penetrates the middle pivot point of the "M." The predictive value is bearish. A double bottom is the reverse of the double top and resembles a "W." The indication is bullish.

Dow Theory

One of Wall Street's oldest technical theories, the Dow Theory sends a "buy" signal when the Dow Jones Industrial Average and the Dow Transportation Average close above a prior high. Conversely, a "sell" signal is given when the averages, in tandem, close below a prior low.

Downtrend

A price pattern used in technical analysis in which the stock, index, or market makes a series of lower highs and lower lows. The prevailing downtrend is broken when the price rises above the previous high, making a higher high.

Drawdown

Loss of value in account equity.

Earnings

A company's net revenue after deducting all expenses.

Earnings Growth Rate

A company's average annual rate of earnings during the past five years.

Earnings Per Share

Derived by dividing a company's earnings by the number of shares outstanding.

Efficient Market Theory
This theory states that all known information is taken into consideration by the stock market and reflected in stock prices.

Electronic Communication Network (ECN)
Automated electronic systems that match orders and allow individual traders to present a price better than the current bid or ask (offer).

Elliot Wave Theory
Originally introduced by Ralph Nelson Elliot in 1939. Using Fibonacci numbers, this theory holds that price patterns follow a paradigm of five waves up and three waves down (correction waves), forming a complete cycle of eight waves.

Equity Options
Options traded on shares of a common stock.

Exchange Traded Fund (ETF)
A security that tracks an index, a commodity, currency, or basket of assets, but trades just like a stock on an exchange. ETFs experience continuous pricing throughout the trading day.

Ex-Dividend
The period of time between the announcement and payment of the next dividend. At the time a stock is trading ex-dividend, the buyer is not entitled to the dividend. Newspapers usually list stocks in ex-dividend with an "x."

Exhaustion Gap
A price gap, or rising/falling window (candlestick terminology), that takes place at the conclusion of a trend, indicating that the trend is finished. This often happens in stocks that move up steeply during a short period of time.

Expiration Date
Date on which an option, and the right to exercise it, expires.

Exponential Smoothing
A moving average employing the same data as a simple moving average, but giving greater weight to recent price closes.

Fade
To trade against the prevailing trend. For example, a trader who fades a gap up would short the stock. To fade a gap down, he or she would buy.

Failure Swing
When prices fail to confirm a new low in a downtrend, or a new high in an uptrend.

Federal Open Market Committee (FOMC)
Policy-making arm of the Federal Reserve Board. This committee establishes monetary policy to comply with the Fed's objectives of regulating the money supply and credit. The FOMC's primary actions are the purchase and sale of government securities, which increase or decrease the money supply, respectively. The FOMC also meets every six weeks to regulate key interest rates, such as the discount rate.

Federal Reserve
Also referred to as "the Fed," the Federal Reserve is the U.S. central bank that sets monetary policy. It oversees money supply, interest rates, and credit. Its objective is to maintain stability in the U.S. currency and economy, with emphasis on deterring inflation. Governed by a seven-member board, the system includes twelve regional Federal Reserve Banks, twenty-five branches, and all national and state banks that act as part of the system.

Fibonacci Numbers
Originated by the twelfth-century Italian mathematician Leonardo Pisano, these numbers follow a sequence in which each successive number equals the sum of the previous two numbers. The numbers begin 1, 1, 2, 3, 5, 8, 13, 21, 34, 55, 89, 144, and continue on in this manner. Four popular Fibonacci studies are arcs, fans, retracements, and time zones. The lines created by the studies often act as support and resistance.

Fill
The price at which your order to buy or sell a financial instrument is executed.

Flag
A continuation price pattern that slopes against the prevailing trend. Prices usually break out of this pattern and continue in the direction of the trend.

Fundamental Analysis
The process of evaluating the financial condition of a company that issues common stock, using financial reports, price/earnings ratios, revenues, market share, etc. A large portion of fundamental analysis is based on supply and demand.

Futures (Futures Contract)
An agreement to purchase or sell a given quantity of a commodity (raw materials or metals), financial instrument, or currency at a specified date in the future.

Gap

A space left in a price pattern where no trading occurred. A "gap up" takes place when a market/stock opens and continues to trade at higher price levels than the previous day's high. In candlestick terminology, this is referred to as a "rising window" and is bullish. A "gap down" occurs when a market/stock opens lower than the previous day's low and continues to trade lower, which is bearish. Three types of gaps are breakaway, runaway, and exhaustion.

Gross Domestic Product (GDP)

An economic report showing the value of all goods and services produced in the United States in a given time period.

Growth Stocks

Stocks of companies that have shown brisk growth in sales or earnings. These equities typically offer little or no dividend yields and sell at high prices relative to their book value. Many high-technology stocks fall into this category.

Hard Right Edge

The farthest right side of a price chart.

Head-and-Shoulders Pattern

A reversal price pattern resembling a human head (the highest peak), with a shoulder on each side (lower peaks). If the price penetrates the horizontal neck-line that connects the troughs (support areas), the pattern is complete and suggests the price will plunge lower. When the head-and-shoulders pattern forms upside down, it is called an inverse or reversed head-and-shoulders.

Hedge

A strategy used to limit portfolio losses. Usually, this is a transaction that goes opposite to existing positions. For example, a trader holding positions in tech stocks might sell short the PowerShares QQQ (stock that represents the NAS-DAQ 100), sell short the same stocks in a different account, or buy puts (options) to reduce market risk.

High Bid

When an offer appears on the bid that's higher than the previous bid.

In-the-Money

A call option is in-the-money when the strike price is less than the market price of the underlying security. A put option is in-the-money when the strike price is greater than the market price of the underlying security.

Income
Earnings from interest on bonds or corporate dividends.

Inflation Risk
The possible eventuality that cost-of-living increases will reduce or eradicate investment returns.

Initial Public Offering (IPO)
A company's first, or initial, stock offering to the public.

Inside Day
Easily noted on a chart, an inside day means the price range of one trading day takes place within the previous day's price range.

Inside Market or Inside Price
Represents the lowest bid and highest ask (offer) price for an equity at a given moment.

Insider
An officer/director of a corporation, an individual or family owning at least 10 percent of a company's stock, or anyone with access to nonpublic, "inside" information about that company. Insider transactions are regulated by Securities and Exchange Commission (SEC) Rule 144.

Intraday
This refers to price movement that occurs during the course of a single trading day.

Intrinsic Value
The dollar amount by which an option is in-the-money.

Island Reversal
A price pattern that begins with an exhaustion gap in one direction, and a breakaway gap in the opposite direction. The time frame between gaps is usually brief. The result is a few candlesticks standing alone on a chart, and may indicate a price reversal.

Key Reversal Day
When a stock experiences an uptrend, a key reversal occurs when the price opens at a new high (over the prior day's high), then closes below the prior day's low. If a stock is in a downtrend, the stock price opens at a new low, then closes higher than the prior day's close. In candlestick terminology, these are "engulfing" patterns. The wider the range and the higher the volume, the stronger the chance that a trend reversal will occur.

Large-Capitalization (Large-Cap) Company
A company that has a capitalization (shares outstanding multiplied by current stock price) of more than $5 billion.

Level I Quote
Quote information that shows only the current inside bid and ask (offer) prices for financial instruments. Other data displayed may include last trade price, volume, and intraday high and low prices.

Level II Quote
Level II quote screens show real-time, streaming displays of bids and offers for financial instruments. Typically, a time and sales screen accompanies the quotes, exhibiting current trade execution, lot size, and the time they took place.

Level III Quote
Level III screens are used by market and exchange professionals and allow for "refreshing" inside bid and ask, or offer.

Limit Order
An order to buy or sell stock at a specific price or better. Limit orders may be day orders, or GTC (good-till-canceled).

Liquidity
When used in referencing stocks, good liquidity refers to a stock that trades with high-average daily volume. When used in reference to investments, most stocks are "liquid," meaning you can turn them into cash quickly. A home is considered an illiquid investment.

Listed Stocks
Usually refers to stocks listed on the NYSE and Amex.

Long-Term Capital Gain
A profit, or gain, taken on the sale of a stock or mutual fund that was held for more than one year.

Margin Account
An account provided by a brokerage house that allows the customer to purchase equities by borrowing a portion of the funds from that broker. Regulation T governs the amount of credit advanced by brokers to customers.

Margin Call

When a margined account experiences a drawdown of more than a specified amount, the participating broker may issue a margin call to the customer, demanding that the customer immediately deposit funds to cover the call.

Margin Requirement

The amount of money a trader/investor is required to maintain to cover a margined position. Most accounts are "marked to market" (adjusted to current price) each day, along with margin requirements.

Market Maker

A broker/dealer who applies to the NASD and must agree to make a market in a particular NASDAQ stock. The market maker must hold the stock in his own account and participate on both the buy and sell side simultaneously.

Market Order

An order to buy or sell a financial instrument at the best available price.

Market Value

A company's shares outstanding multiplied by the price per share.

Mark-to-Market

The process of adjusting equity prices held in an account to the present market value.

Moving Average (MA)

A line indicator used in technical analysis that works best when a market/stock is trending. This lagging indicator many times provides support or resistance for a stock's price pattern. A simple 50-day moving average is calculated by taking the sum of a stock's previous 50 closing prices, then dividing it by 50. As each new day is added, the oldest day is dropped from the calculation. Connecting the averages forms the line indicator. When a short averaging period (for example, 20-day) crosses a longer averaging period (50-day) and moves to the upside, the signal is bullish. When a longer average rolls over a shorter average and heads south, the signal is bearish. Technical analysts use simple, weighted, and exponentially smoothed moving averages.

National Association of Securities Dealers (NASD)

An organization of broker/dealers established to regulate and govern the NAS-DAQ Stock Market and to protect the investing public from deceptive acts.

Neckline

This horizontal line connects the troughs, or support zones, on the head-and-shoulders reversal price pattern. When the neckline is penetrated, the head-and-shoulders pattern is complete. The line acts as support or resistance and gives buy and sell signals.

Net Assets

Total liabilities subtracted from total assets.

Odd Lot

Order to buy or sell less than 100 shares of stock.

Offer

Identical to the "ask" price.

Offer Out

The act of offering to sell a specified stock on "the offer," which if executed will give you a higher price than selling "at the market," or the best bid price.

On-Balance Volume (OBV)

A line indicator that shows whether money is flowing into or out of a security by measuring volume. If the stock closes higher than the prior day's close, the total day's volume counts as up-volume. When the stock closes lower than the previous day's close, the day's total volume registers as down-volume.

Open Interest

Measures the number of options or futures contracts that remain open (not liquidated) at the close of a trading day. As open interest rises and falls, it indicates money flow into or out of options or futures contracts, thus showing sentiment and liquidity.

Option

A financial instrument that gives the owner the right to buy or sell shares of stock at a specified price, within a specified period of time.

Oscillator

Technical analysis indicators that identify times when a stock price displays an overbought or oversold condition.

Out-of-the-Money

A call option is out-of-the-money when the strike price is greater than the current market price of the underlying equity. A put option is out-of-the-money when the strike price is less than the current market price of the underlying equity.

Overbought

Condition of a market/stock indicated by an oscillator. When a stock is over-bought, it rises to the oscillator's upper scale and the stock's price may encounter a selloff.

Oversold

Condition of a market/stock indicated by an oscillator. If a stock is oversold, it falls to the oscillator's lower scale zone, and the stock's price may soon be ready to rise in value.

Pattern Analysis

The process used by technical analysts to evaluate price formations displayed on a chart, and to predict possible future trends.

Pennant

A continuation price pattern resembling a flag. A pennant, however, looks like a symmetrical triangle and acts as a price "resting period" before it (usually) resumes its prior trend.

Pivot Point

A price pattern in which a stock reverses direction. Identifying pivot points was a tactic used by early floor traders to determine support and resistance points without having to consult a chart. A stock may pivot when it encounters previous support or resistance.

Point

Term used in stock market jargon that equals $1. If a share of stock rises "3 points," it's increased in value by $3.

Price/Book Ratio

The price per share of a stock divided by its assigned book value per share.

Price/Earnings Ratio

Ratio of an equity's present price to its per-share earnings during the past year. A stock's P/E indicates market expectations for a company's future growth. There-fore, equities referred to as "growth stocks" typically have higher P/E ratios than do value stocks.

Program Trading

Program trading usually defines the trading tactic used by arbitrageurs who trade index futures contracts against the cash indexes when a divergence takes place. See Arbitrage. Program trading also refers to automated orders that execute large transactions and sell baskets of stocks when the market becomes over-bought, or buys baskets of stocks when the market becomes oversold.

Protective Stop or Stop-Loss

A tactic to limit losses. A trader places a "stop," or "stop-loss," below (or above) his or her entry point in a stock. When that stop-loss is touched, the stock is sold (bought) at the next available price (as a market order).

Put

An option contract that gives the holder the right to sell an underlying stock at a specified price during a specified period of time.

Put/Call Ratio

Ratio of volume in put options divided by the volume in call options. This is used as a contrary indicator. When the Put/Call Ratio is high, the market is regarded as oversold, which is bullish. When the Put/Call Ratio is low, the market is considered overbought, which has bearish implications.

Rally Top or Rally High

Pivot point that forms when a rising price pattern meets with supply and sells off.

Retracement

When a stock experiences a strong price move to the upside or downside, the price will correct, or retrace, some part of that move before continuing the original trend. The 50 percent retracement is most commonly known. Technical analysts also use Elliot waves and Fibonacci retracements of 38, 50, and 62 percent.

Reversal Gap

Price formation on a chart that takes place when the current day's low is above the prior day's high, and the current day's close is above the open.

Reversal Pattern

Formations on a chart used by technical analysts that predict that a trend reversal, or change, may soon occur. Common reversal patterns are double and triple tops, and head-and-shoulders.

Risk/Reward Ratio

The process of measuring potential risk, or loss of capital, against potential reward, or gains.

Round Lot
A unit or lot size usually consisting of 100 shares.

Rounding Bottom or Saucer
Chart price pattern in which the stock gradually halts a downtrend, curves into a sideways movement (on low volume), then climbs back to higher prices—a bullish move. This formation can be seen in the cup portion of cup-with-handle patterns and reversed head-and-shoulders, as well as by itself.

Runaway Gap
A price gap typically occurring midway in an uptrend or downtrend. Also called a "measuring gap."

Securities and Exchange Commission (SEC)
The government agency that regulates the U.S. stock and bond markets, registered investment advisers, broker/dealers, and mutual fund companies.

Sentiment Indicator
A psychological indicator that measures the degree of bullishness or bearishness in the stock market. Sentiment indicators act as contrary signals and work best in extreme overbought or oversold markets.

Share
A unit of ownership issued to shareholders by a corporation.

Short Interest
Shares of a financial instrument that have been sold short and not currently repurchased.

Short Sale
The process of borrowing shares of stock from your broker, then selling them in the market with the intent of buying them back at a later time for a lower price. The spread between the price at which you sell the shares and the price at which you buy them back is your profit.

Short-Term Capital Gain
The realized profit on the proceeds from the sale of stock or a mutual fund held for one year or less.

Simple Moving Average
A moving average giving equal weight to each day's data (closing price).

Small-Capitalization (Small-Cap) Company

A company that has a market value less than $500 million. Small-cap companies typically use profits for additional development and expansion projects in lieu of paying dividends.

Specialist

Assigned to a certain stock or stocks on the floors of NYSE and Amex, the specialist must ensure a fair and orderly market and fill orders out of his or her own account when no matching order exists.

Spread

The difference between the bid and ask (offer) price.

Stock Index Futures

Futures contracts traded based on the underlying stock index.

Stop Order (Buy-Stop or Sell-Stop)

Order placed to buy a stock at or above, or sell at or below, the current market price. When the stop order is touched, it turns into a market order.

Support

A price area where buyers support the stock sufficiently to hold the price up.

Symmetrical Triangle

A consolidating price pattern that occurs between two trendlines sloping toward each other. The buying and selling pressure is even, but becomes more and more compacted. When the price breaks out, it usually resumes the prior trend and can be quite volatile.

Technical Analysis

The study of market/stock action that utilizes charts displaying price patterns and volume. These charts and the indicators applied offer predictive price movements and trends.

Tick

A minimum upward or downward movement in the price of a financial instrument. For stocks, one tick is a penny. An "uptick" takes place when the stock trades higher than the previous trade. A "downtick" occurs when a stock trades lower than the prior trade. A "zero-plus tick" means the stock makes an uptick on the prior trade, and then the current trade is executed at the same price.

TICK Index
A short-term indicator that subtracts the number of stocks currently ticking down from the number of stocks ticking up. A reading above zero indicates bullishness, and a reading below zero indicates bearishness. Each exchange has its own TICK indicator.

Ticker Symbol
Capital letters that identify a security listed on the exchanges.

Time and Sales
A ticker that usually runs in a column adjacent to a Level II screen and displays current trades by time, price, and lot size.

Trailing Stop
Now automated by brokers, a trailing stop refers to a risk control method in which you move your stop-loss up as your stock advances in price. If you've sold short, you move your trailing stop down as your stock falls in price.

Trend
A price pattern revealing a strong move to the upside, or downside. An uptrend forms from a series of higher lows and higher highs. A downtrend forms from lower highs and lower lows.

Trendline
A straight line connecting at least two pivot lows in an uptrend, or two highs in a downtrend. The more points connected, the stronger the trendline. When the price "breaks" a trendline, that trend is considered broken; a change in direction may soon take place.

Triangle
Continuation pattern in which prices form the outlines of triangles. Three types of triangles are ascending, descending, and symmetrical.

TRIN
Originally developed by Richard Arms and sometimes called the Arms Index, the TRIN is an acronym for Traders Index. A short-term indicator often used in conjunction with the TICK, the TRIN is calculated by dividing the number of advancing issues/declining issues by advancing volume/declining volume.

Triple Top
Price pattern featuring three highs in approximately the same price zone. When the pattern is completed, the indication is bearish. The "triple bottom" is the same pattern, upside down, and is considered bullish.

Volatility

The measure of price ranges in a financial market or instrument. The wider the price range, the more volatile the market.

Volume

Equals the number of shares traded for a specified time period. Volume is usually displayed as a histogram at the bottom of a chart. It gives important information to the technical analyst in interpreting price patterns.

Weighted Moving Average

A moving average utilizing a specific time period, but giving greater weight to recent price data (closing prices).

Whipsaw

When a trader enters both sides of a stock's price movement—both buying and selling short—and loses money on each trade.

APPENDIX B

Recommended Reading

Beyond Candlesticks: New Japanese Charting Techniques Revealed, by Steve Nison. New York: John Wiley & Sons, 1994.

Candlestick and Pivot Point Trading Triggers, by John L. Person. Hoboken, NJ: John Wiley, 2007.

High Probability Trading, by Marcel Link. New York: McGraw-Hill, 2003.

How I Made $2,000,000 in the Stock Market, by Nicolas Darvas. Lyle Stuart, 1986.

Japanese Candlestick Charting Techniques, 2nd Edition, by Steve Nison. Paramus, NJ: NY Institute of Finance, 2001.

Mastering the Trade, by John Carter. New York: McGraw-Hill, 2006.

New Stock Market Wizards, by Jack D. Schwager. HarperBusiness, January 2001.

Reminiscences of a Stock Operator, by Edwin Lefevre. New York: John Wiley & Sons, 1994.

Secrets for Profiting in Bull and Bear Markets, by Stan Weinstein. New York: McGraw-Hill, 1988.

SFO Personal Investor Series: Online Trading. Cedar Falls, IA: Wasendorf & Associates, Inc., 2007.

Short-Term Trading in the New Stock Market, by Toni Turner. New York: St. Martin's Press, 2005.

Technical Analysis from A to Z, 2nd Edition, by Steven B. Achelis. New York: McGraw-Hill, 2001.

The Richest Man in Babylon, by George S. Clason. New American Library, reissue 1997.

Trading in the Zone, by Mark Douglas. New York: New York Institute of Finance, 2001.

Understanding Options, by Michael Sincere. New York: McGraw-Hill, 2007.

Index